*Women clerks in Wilhelmine Germany*

# Women clerks in Wilhelmine Germany

*Issues of class and gender*

## CAROLE ELIZABETH ADAMS

*Lecturer in History*
*University of Sydney*

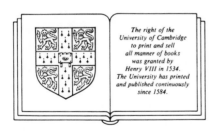

The right of the
University of Cambridge
to print and sell
all manner of books
was granted by
Henry VIII in 1534.
The University has printed
and published continuously
since 1584.

Cambridge University Press

Cambridge

New York   New Rochelle   Melbourne   Sydney

Published by the Press Syndicate of the University of Cambridge
The Pitt Building, Trumpington Street, Cambridge CB2 1RP
32 East 57th Street, New York, NY 10022, USA
10 Stamford Road, Oakleigh, Melbourne 3166, Australia

First published 1988

Printed in Great Britain at The Bath Press, Avon

*British Library cataloguing in publication data*
Adams, Carole Elizabeth
Women clerks in Wilhelmian Germany:
issues of class and gender.
1. Germany. Women clerical personnel,
1888–1918
I. Title
331.4'8165137'0943

*Library of Congress cataloguing in publication data*
Adams, Carole Elizabeth.
Women clerks in Wilhelmian Germany: issues of class and gender
Carole Elizabeth Adams.
   p.   cm.
Bibliography.
Includes index.
ISBN 0-521-32634-6
1. Women clerks – Germany – History. I. Title.
HD6073.M392G42   1988
305.4'3651 – dc19   88-2368

ISBN 0 521 32634 6

*For my parents*

# Contents

## Acknowledgments

There are people on three continents to whom I owe thanks. In Germany Professor Jürgen Kocka, Ursula Nienhaus, Ute Frevert, Heidrun Homburg and Michael Prinz took time to discuss my project and share information with me. Herb Levine offered helpful comments on an early chapter. I also benefited from the help of archivists who volunteered their professional assistance to my search for documents, including Professor Dr. O. Dascher of the Stiftung Westfälisches Wirtschaftsarchiv, the staff of the Hamburg Staatsarchiv and archivists at other centers. The cordiality and generosity of Frau Rasch of the Berlin office of the Verband der weiblichen Angestellten greatly facilitated my work there. In England I would like to thank the editiorial staff of Cambridge University Press, especially Ann O'Quigley, whose thoughtful suggestions aided my clarity of presentation. I am grateful as well for the suggestions offered by Leonore Davidoff and a second, anonymous, reader for Cambridge University Press. Their thoughtful advice aided me greatly in the task of revision.

I also owe a debt of gratitude to friends and colleagues in Australia, who criticized and commented on my ideas and drafts. In Adelaide I benefited from the help and intellectual stimulation offered by fellow members of the Working Group in Social History, the Feminist Theory Collective, and the Collective in Educational History and Theory. In Sydney, research assistants Gail Reekie and Martin Braach-Maksuytis helped me to obtain much valuable information. Peter Cochrane's careful reading of the opening chapters improved both argument and presentation. Barbara Caine generously undertook a thorough critique of the study, which helped me greatly to clarify both my meaning and my prose style.

A number of people also aided my work in the United States. Paul

Weissman and Kate Scott gave helpful criticism of an early draft. At Harvard, Charles S. Maier supervised the doctoral dissertation that provided the basis of this study, proffering invaluable advice and criticism, while David S. Landes kindly offered pertinent and informative suggestions for expanding the work for publication.

I have profited enormously from the efforts of colleagues, friends, and family, whose fellowship and support make research and writing such a pleasure. In the final stages, Ben Tipton and Rhona Ovedoff helped greatly with the index, and Pat Lacey and Janet Adams provided careful assistance in proofreading. Finally, I owe a debt of gratitude to my children, Justin and Elise, who experienced their mother's work on three continents and remained confident that "Mommy's book" would some day be finished.

*Sources of illustrations*

The photographs between pages 18 and 19 are from the Bildarchiv Preussischer Kulturbesitz, Berlin; the Archiv für Kunst und Geschichte, Berlin; and the Ullstein Verlag, Berlin.

*Newspapers and journals*

| | |
|---|---|
| *AfF* | *Archiv für Frauenarbeit* |
| *AGS* | *Archiv für soziale Gesetzgebung und Statistik* |
| *ASS* | *Archiv für Sozialwissenschaft und Sozialpolitik* |
| *BT* | *Berliner Tageblatt* |
| *BV* | *Berliner Volkszeitung* |
| *CEH* | *Central European History* |
| *EHR* | *Economic History Review* |
| *FB* | *Hamburger Fremdenblatt* |
| *Frau* | *Die Frau: Monatsschrift für das gesamte Frauenleben unserer Zeit* |
| *GA* | *Hamburger General Anzeiger* |
| *GG* | *Geschichte und Gesellschaft* |
| *HB* | *Handlungsgehilfen-Blatt* |
| *HC* | *Hamburger Correspondent* |
| *HG* | *Die Handlungsgehilfin* |
| *HKZ* | *Die Hamburger Kontoristinnen Zeitung* |
| *HN* | *Hamburger Nachrichten* |
| *HZ* | *Handlungsgehilfen-Zeitung* |
| *IRSH* | *International Review of Social History* |
| *JfF* | *Jahrbuch für Frauenarbeit* |
| *JGVV* | *Jahrbuch für Gesetzgebung, Verwaltung und Volkswirtschaft* |
| *JSH* | *Journal of Social History* |
| *KB* | *Korrespondenzblatt für den Verband katholischer kaufmännischer Gehilfinnen Deutschlands* |
| *MKV* | *Mitteilungen der kaufmännischen Vereine weiblicher Angestellter* |

| | |
|---|---|
| *MWA* | *Mitteilungen für weibliche Angestellte* |
| *NHZ* | *Neue Hamburgische Zeitung* |
| *S. Praxis* | *Soziale Praxis. Zentralblatt für Sozialpolitik* |
| *Stat. d. dt. Reichs* | *Statistik des deutschen Reichs* |
| *VVKU* | *Veröffentlichungen des deutschen Verbands für das kaufmännische Unterrichtswesen* |
| *ZGKU* | *Zeitschrift für das gesamte kaufmännische Unterrichtswesen* |
| *ZWH* | *Zeitschrift für weibliche Handlungsgehilfen* |

*Archival abbreviations*

| | |
|---|---|
| AHKD | Akten des Handelskammer Duisberg |
| BA | Bundesarchiv Coblenz |
| BB I | Berufschulbehörde I |
| Hamb.St.A. | Hamburg Staatsarchiv |
| HKB | Handelskammer Bochum |
| HKBf | Handelskammer zu Bielefeld |
| NL | *Nachlass* |
| PDM | Polizei Direktion München |
| PP | Politische Polizei |
| RWWA | Rheinisch-westfälishes Wirtschaftsarchiv |
| St.A.Mu. | Staatsarchiv Munich |
| SWWA | Stiftung Westfälisches Wirtschaftsarchiv |

*Organizations*

| | |
|---|---|
| ADF | *Allgemeiner Deutscher Frauenverein*: General German Women's Association |
| BDF | *Bund Deutscher Frauenvereine*: German Women's Federation |
| DHV | *Deutschnationaler Handlungsgehilfen-Verband*: German-Nationalist Commercial Assistants' Alliance |

Given the cumbersome titles of clerks' associations in Wilhelmian Germany, I have chosen to refer to each by an abbreviated English translation. Below are the abbreviated and the full titles of the major organizations in English, along with the full German titles and a brief description.

*Berlin Clerks' Aid Association*
Aid Association for Female Salaried Employees in Commerce and Trade: *Kaufmännischer Hilfsverein für weibliche Angestellte in Handel und Gewerbe.* Became the:

*Berlin Commercial Alliance*
Commercial Alliance for Female Salaried Employees: *Kaufmännischer Verband für weibliche Angestellte.* Began as the Aid Association and headed by Minna Cauer; later led by Josef Silbermann and Agnes Herrmann. The largest female clerks' organization, it came to emphasize the interests of all white-collar workers, male and female.

*Catholic Alliance*
Collective Alliance of Female Catholic Commercial Assistants of Germany: *Gesamtverband katholischer kaufmännischer Gehilfinnen Deutschlands.* The rather conservative organization headed by clerics and prominent Catholic women.

*Central Alliance*
Central Alliance of Male and Female Commercial Assistants of Germany: *Zentralverband der Handlungsgehilfen und Gehilfinnen Deutschlands.* Allied with the Free Unions and the Social Democratic Party, this union attempted to address women's issues. Headed by Max Josephsohn of Hamburg.

xiii

*Confederation*

Confederation of Associations of Female Salaried Employees: *Verbün-dete Vereine weiblicher Angestellter*. A loose national organization that attempted to place gender above occupational grouping.

# Introduction

A visitor to Hamburg or any other large German commercial center at the turn of the century would have noticed a sight unfamiliar twenty years earlier. For each morning hundreds of neatly dressed young women appeared in the city center and entered offices, department stores, shops. They were "commercial assistants" – office and sales clerks – hired when the service sector of the economy expanded in the late nineteenth century. The "working girls" seem a visible sign of the new independence and assertiveness of women. But further investigation reveals that the women worked long hours in uncomfortable surroundings, that they were paid less than their male colleagues, that they had few opportunities for adequate job training or vocational education, and fewer opportunities for upward employment mobility. Although they demanded "equal pay for equal work," the general public was convinced that they worked only for pin money and that their employment was not meant to be a career but only a way-station to marriage.

Perhaps this sounds familiar. The phrases, the conditions, the attitudes may still remind one of the present-day circumstances of female sales and office staff. To be sure, there are some differences. Work conditions have improved since 1900; hours are shorter. The German women at the turn of the century were mostly single, while today throughout the West, larger numbers of married women work. Then, women were a minority of clerks; today, they predominate. These are conditions we associate with slow progress. But in one respect there seems to be a reverse development. In contrast to the lack of interest in organization found today, professional associations of female clerks were strong and respected in Germany before World War I. Their leaders sought to improve women's work and pay conditions, to expand their educational opportunities, and to institute legislative reforms. At the same time, they worked to give women a "career consciousness," to foster in them an independent spirit and to politicize them; for, in addition to their function as professional groups, they had explicit feminist goals. Yet they failed. The reforms they sought did not eventuate: women did not gain employment equality, nor did they greatly increase their dedication to a career.

To explain why women in clerking were unable to establish professional equality with men despite their relative organizational strength requires an inquiry incorporating issues of both class and gender. We must examine women within the employment milieu of clerking, that is, within lower-level white-collar sales and office work. This demands an analysis of women's position as workers who faced working conditions and a labor-market situation different from men's and to whom many male clerks were hostile. Further, we must investigate the situation of women as a group of employees who differed from their male colleagues because of their particular role in the home. Both gender and class affected women's consciousness and activities. But at the same time, the interests of gender could run contrary to those of class, so that one major source of tension faced by leaders in clerks' associations with female members was the continual conflict between feminist goals and those of clerks in general.

This book contributes to discussions of the emergence of white-collar work and to the scholarly debate concerning the motivations for organization and the political attitudes of German clerks and other white-collar workers. In addition, it explores issues concerning women's work and labor-market situations, women's class positions, and their political mobilization. It has sometimes been argued that women are uninterested in their employment and that their class location should therefore be defined by their home situation. This can imply that women are incapable of organizing to represent their employment interests (which of course follows logically if women have been defined as a group having none). Yet Germany's women clerks were relatively well organized, and middle-class female clerks' associations expected that their efforts would raise women to equality with their male colleagues. The analysis of this study suggests that the problem lies not in female employment behavior but in the dual responsibilities of women in the public and private spheres. It is not that women's paid employment is not relevant to their class location and class consciousness, but that one must take account of gender as well.

The study begins by examining the situation of clerks before World War I, discussing the emergence of routinized low-level white-collar work, or clerking, as a particular occupation, and describing the work environment and social profile of clerks. Women's participation in clerking occurred within the context of their great commitment to the domestic sphere, both to their families of birth and to expectations of future marriage. Chapter 2 therefore explains the home and family circumstances of women clerks.

For the historian looking back at clerks in 1900, the changing nature of the clerk's work situation is striking, as is the creation of a dual labor market. For as clerking developed, a segmented labor market developed as well, creating a primary labor market that offered responsibility, career mobility, material benefits, and status, while the secondary labor sector offered routine or menial work with no promotion opportunities, low pay, and limited status. Women were largely confined to the latter. These interacting processes of the proletarianization and feminization of clerking make class categorization difficult. Nevertheless, this study argues that by World War I, clerking had become largely a working-class occupation distinct from the evolving service class of bureaucrats, managers, and professionals who comprised the middle classes along with entrepreneurs and members of the "old middle estate" of peasants, shopkeepers, and master craftsmen.

That is not to say that clerks' own sense of location within an employment hierarchy and a social system should be ignored. As Chapter 3 indicates, clerks in the nineteenth century were preoccupied with figuring out social location, for they emerged as a new group that older categories failed to describe. More importantly, in their efforts to prevent deskilling, many leaders of clerks' organizations distinguished between blue-collar and white-collar work, according higher status and social position to the latter. Their agonized attempts to define themselves, and their divergent allegiances to older social groupings both indicate the complexity of the development of group consciousness in a period of transition.

As female clerks began to organize, they relied in part on male models and male perceptions. However, as the middle chapters of the study show, women in clerking owed much more to the bourgeois and socialist feminist movements arising in the Wilhelmine era than they did to male clerks. Women leaders in the middle-class women's movement offered female clerks leadership and allies. Socialists also offered a model, and indeed both movements provided theories of female employment and sets of feminist goals.

"Feminism" is a term requiring further elaboration. This book defines as feminist those persons who worked actively for full female equality with men in their society. Feminism must not be conflated with other social or political movements; a feminist need not insist that all adults in a society be granted suffrage, for instance, or that capitalism be overthrown. Feminists in Wilhelmine society need not have been democrats, much less social democrats; they did need a commitment to end discrimination against women as women, and they had to do more than just object to discrimination in a particular area.

After tracing the attention paid by German feminists to the issue of female employment and recounting the bourgeois and socialist feminist theories of women's work, the book describes the early years of female clerks' associations when leaders worked in alliance with the bourgeois women's movement. Both bourgeois and socialist feminist theory stressed female equality in the public sphere – in civil and political society – while ignoring any possible transformation of the private sphere, of women's domestic and family lives. Socialist theory predicted that the private sphere would disappear as domestic tasks were mechanized and rationalized. Bourgeois feminist theory, on the other hand, accepted the notion that women had innate nurturing abilities that required the constant attention of mothers to the home. While socialists expected individual domestic life to disappear, therefore, bourgeois feminists felt that it would inevitably continue unchanged, while women structured their employment lives around this fact.

The book then examines the tensions created in clerks' organizations by the reluctance of bourgeois feminists to challenge the notion of women's "natural profession" as homemaker and by the inability of socialist feminists to perceive of the private sphere as a site of inequality. As a result, neither bourgeois nor socialist feminists recognized the interrelationship of women's home and work roles, behaviors, and attitudes. The socialist Central Alliance ignored the question, while the bourgeois all-female clerks' associations presented members with a contradictory message: women were to be assertive and career-minded, but nurturant and domesticated at the same time.

In addition to conflicts arising from women's dual roles in the public and private spheres, others resulted from the organizations' attempts to combine a politics of gender with one of class. It was here in particular that the model of the male organizations was brought to bear – and found wanting. The bourgeois all-female clerks' associations attempted to press for female equality at the same time that they excluded some women on the basis of class, for their chief strategy was based on occupational control, particularly over entry. Clerking was to remain a profession of the "middle estate" (*Mittelstand*), and only those women found within its boundaries deserved equality. The socialist Central Alliance, on the other hand, a union with female and male clerk members, insisted that class was of greater importance than sex, and failed sufficiently to address the needs of its female members or to provide female equality within the organization.

The concluding chapters detail two case studies that examine in depth the conflicts of class and gender. The campaigns for educational reform and for white-collar insurance testify to the narrow limits within which feminist professional organizations worked. The all-female clerks' associations joined with male clerks' groups and with business interests to press for reforms that actually benefited the men at the cost of their female allies. When one female association, the Confederation, attempted to press for a feminist reform, it became isolated and its ideas were ignored. The socialist Central Alliance remained marginal.

The existence of strong associations of women clerks testifies to the fact that women are not incapable of organizing to press for economic or political goals. But the difficulties that they encountered reinforce the conclusion of many historians that only by joining an analysis of gender to one of class can we adequately explain their experience.

# 1

# Clerks and clerking

## The emergence of clerking in Germany

In Germany in the middle of the nineteenth century neither the secondary nor the tertiary sector of the economy was fully developed, and most entrepreneurs engaged in commerce rather than industry. Firms were small and patterned on traditional guilds: young men began their business experience with three-year apprenticeships and then became "commercial assistants" (*Handlungsgehilfen*) much as artisan apprentices became journeymen. They expected to become independent merchants after this, just as journeymen artisans theoretically all became masters.[1] Life-long employment as a clerk was rare.

Commercial assistants at that time were responsible for a variety of operations that depended upon skills in writing and arithmetic. They had to maintain correspondence and records and, especially in smaller businesses, to ship goods and engage in some sales work. There was some division of labor in larger firms – one man might be trained as a bookkeeper, for instance – but often an assistant worked his way up a clerking ladder, from messenger boy to copyist or salesman and then to a more responsible job that might involve specialized tasks. Being cultivated young men with a secondary education in a period when many adults had not completed elementary school, clerks were assured a respectable salary.

The relationship between the commercial assistant and his employer or principal was paternal in the mid-nineteenth century. Assistants often boarded with their employers, ate at the family table, and were subjected to close supervision in their personal lives. "Volunteers" in the workplace reinforced this. Usually the sons of businessmen, these young men "volunteered" their labor for the experience they gained as assistants. Some volunteers were truly family members, for many entrepreneurs selected relatives or future sons-in-law for assistantships. In this milieu, any specific description of a paid category of clerking could emerge only with difficulty, for one would find no set wage scales, no particular work hierarchy, and little division of labor.[2] For these people, being an employee was indeed a mere stage preceding independence.

This German picture mirrors the situation in Great Britain and the United States. In all countries there was a preponderance of small paternalistic firms with small, predominantly male, staffs that included apprentices. Clerks' middle-class status and salaries were tied to their high educational level. In all three countries, clerking was seen as a mere step to independence. Only in Germany, however, was clerking viewed as predominantly commercial, as training for independence as a merchant. Perhaps this is one reason why both office and sales clerks in Germany kept the label "commercial assistant" and joined the same clerks' associations, giving them a strength unknown elsewhere.[3]

By the late nineteenth century, although many German clerks still believed in their future independence, industrialization had made that expectation largely unrealistic. As firms grew larger, business management became more complex. The administrative structure of firms changed as the expansion of communications, transport, and business all spawned much more paperwork. In addition, in both industrial and commercial enterprises, authority came to be delegated to a greater extent, and a hierarchy of authority was constructed,[4] expanding the range and number of white-collar positions. The greatest growth occurred in the lower and lower-middle levels of the hierarchy, so that it was clerking that expanded most rapidly.

Administrative rationalization also involved specialization of tasks, so that one person became less likely to carry out a variety of operations or to have an overall view of the business. Specialization sometimes involved new technological devices such as the typewriter, but often simply separated and routinized non-mechanized operations. In this process, office work became detached from sales. Future independence became less likely for clerks, for they lacked overall knowledge of business practices, although they could work at their specialized tasks in a variety of firms. They had become replaceable parts in a more complex industrialized economy.

In the larger firms that had developed a hierarchical office structure, clerking was considered to range from responsible mid-level management positions down to those workers carrying out simple routinized tasks. The accepted fiction was that one began at the bottom of this hierarchy and worked up it. In reality, by the late nineteenth century there was a separation between upper-, middle-, and lower-level positions that was very difficult to bridge, both because of the different educational requirements imposed and owing to the limited training received on the job by employees at lower levels.[5] This fact was obscured not only by the past reality of upward mobility, but also by the employers' practice of deliberately complicating their employees' rankings. Contracts were often secret, with clauses that forbade any divulging of information to colleagues. Salaries were individual and secret and employees were rewarded with privileges on an individual basis. Formality entered the workplace, and employees were now often physically separated from the employer. Impersonal rules applying to all employees replaced personal decisions taking the individual into account.

This picture, however, focuses perhaps too much upon the large modern firm. Even in the period 1890 to 1910, most businesses were relatively small, without a great deal of labor-saving office equipment or large numbers of employees.[6] Business practices were slowly rationalized in large firms like Siemens, but many clerks remained apart from these trends; this was no doubt another reason why many continued to believe in their own future independence. What had changed nevertheless, although the firms remained small, was the nature of the work done by the commercial assistant. More extensive transport and communications, and the example of larger firms, meant that office workers even in small, poorly organized offices were faced with increased paperwork and expanded correspondence and book-keeping, so that some division of labor was instituted and workers were hired solely for routinized tasks. Mobility into the ranks of the "independent merchant" was blocked.

Sales clerking underwent the same sort of changes as office work. A majority of sales clerks worked in the retail branch, which was expanding and rationalizing just like industrial and commercial firms, although small outlets continued to predominate. Larger "branch shops" began to sell all the goods within a particular manufacturing branch, followed in the 1890s by department stores offering even greater diversity. By 1907, there were approximately two hundred department stores in Germany.[7] Once department stores had become accepted, the cooperative movement established similar retail outlets for their consumers' societies. By the beginning of the twentieth century, most large German cities had at least one cooperative store, whose clientele was drawn largely from the working class.[8]

With the growth of the retail sector came increases in the number of sales personnel. Just as the office worker was no longer doing the same tasks as the one-time commercial assistant, neither was the salesperson. In smaller shops a clerk might help with the stock and carry out other menial jobs besides waiting on customers, but fewer assistants ever learned the details of the business or performed office as well as sales procedures. In department stores, a salesperson served customers in a single department and often would not have the opportunity to learn about goods in another branch, let alone gain an understanding of the entire retail operation. Tasks were subdivided[9] and deskilled while hierarchies increased.

These developments changed the nature of white-collar work. The chasm that separated the small number of responsible managerial occupations at the top and middle levels from the growing number of routinized, deskilled, and subordinate clerking positions at the bottom grew constantly wider. By 1914, owing to this split, the composition of the middle classes in Germany was changing. A new service class was in the process of formation, comprising managerial white-collar positions in both business and the civil service, joined by the increasing number of trained professionals, especially lawyers and teachers. At the same time, clerking positions were becoming proletarianized as the work process in the field was deskilled. It is not that clerking no longer required a number of skills, but that specialization and job hierarchies limited the skills required for any one position and robbed employees of the opportunity to integrate skills, to perform autonomously, or to take responsibility for complex operations. If a small number of managerial positions composed the core of the new service class, clerking generally was coming to be located within the working class.[10]

The turn of the century was also a period of transition in labor relations, and interactions between employers or supervisors and clerks were often fraught with tension. Germany's industrial revolution had changed the structure of work and administration, but many paternal attitudes remained. This was partly owing to the continued existence of small firms and shops. But the chief reason for the survival of the old values was employers' manipulation of paternal authority as a tool to maintain their staffs' loyalty and obedience.

Employers carried family discipline, including physical punishment, over into the work sphere. In smaller firms, employees were often treated like personal dependents, subject to correction and even abuse. Commercial courts heard case after case in which clerks resigned and demanded a month's pay after principals had screamed abuse at them in public. In one instance, an entire office staff quit when the employer shouted at them, "You pack of pigs!"[11] A Berlin civil court supported a saleswoman who had been struck by her employer because he did not feel that she had closed the door leading into the store quickly enough.[12] In large firms supervisors rather than principals insulted employees. A Berlin warehouse chief slapped a young saleswoman who had left stock disordered in the cellar. The employer, when he saw her crying, merely commented that "she probably deserved it."[13]

Firms of all sizes maintained strict rules of behavior, controlling the personal as well as the work lives of their employees. Siemens' work regulations prohibited private telephone conversations during work hours and demanded that no employee take a second job (even a volunteer activity) without its permission. Nor could an employee marry or change address without prior notification.[14] The large department store chain of Tietz insisted upon contracts in which saleswomen agreed not to go out in public after work.[15] At work, regulations were often niggling and seemed designed only to reinforce authority. Tardiness, even being only one minute late to work, was fined. Conversation on the job, especially for sales personnel, was punished. Employers sometimes refused to accept the excuse of illness without a letter from the firm's own approved physician.[16]

The "competition clause" (*Konkurrenzklausel*) in the contract also enforced patriarchal authority. Coming from the pre-industrial era, it stipulated that an employee could not open a rival business or work for a rival firm for a set number of years. The clause had made some sense in an age where commercial assistants learned all aspects of a business and had valuable information to divulge to a rival or to use in a business venture, but it had little validity when clerks merely fulfilled routine segmented tasks. By agreeing not to work in stores or offices in the same city in the same field (e.g., chemicals, clothing),[17] clerks restricted their ability to find a new position and the employer strengthened his control.

The principal's ability to bestow individual reward served to reinforce employee deference as well. Employees were often rewarded for loyalty and service with such perquisites as salary increases, Christmas bonuses, or paid vacations. Inadequate performance, or behavior deemed inappropriate by the employer, meant that the benefits were withheld. One Munich principal, dissatisfied when his sales personnel demanded better pay and work conditions, gave them a Christmas bonus of cookies instead of the traditional and expected gift of money.[18]

These examples were not merely isolated incidents, but reflect the incomplete nature of the transformation of business before World War I. This must be borne in mind, for one tends to think that the creation of a white-collar work-force followed in the wake of rationalization. In reality, the two occurred together, and the values and attitudes of both employers and employees reflected a past of incipient industrialization rather than the modern economy of corporate industrial capitalism that was taking shape. Because the changes affecting white-collar work occurred slowly, the consciousness of male clerks did not reflect the reality of a segmented labor market and a deskilled field of clerking. Rather, they defined themselves in terms of the recent past when clerks were budding entrepreneurs and had little in common with the working class.

From 1882 clerking expanded rapidly; but there are many difficulties facing the historian who attempts to calculate numbers. Some authors have simply taken the Imperial census category of "employees" rather than distinguishing among technical, overseeing, and commercial employees in administration or office work. In addition, sales personnel are difficult to calculate because they were grouped with skilled blue-collar workers, so that most commentators have therefore simply ignored them. Taking only the white-collar categories that refer to clerks, we find there were over 1.4 million clerks by the time of the 1907 census, almost a doubling in numbers in twelve years.[19] This represented a jump from 3.3 percent to 5.2 percent of the German work-force.[20]

The changes affecting clerking cannot be understood without reference to the simultaneous feminization of the clerking field. While changes in the work process were transforming the class position of clerks, the changes in the labor market were transforming the gender composition of the clerking work-force. As industrial capitalism developed, the increasing division of tasks and the deskilling of many of them was paralleled by the evolution of a segmented labor market.[21] Within white-collar work, workers in the primary segment of the labor market increasingly filled positions that were managerial and responsible, paid well, provided job security, and offered career ladders. The holders of these jobs were male. Clerking was increasingly left to the secondary sector, where positions did not pay well or offer job security or career ladders; job-holders were not expected to remain long. More and more women filled these positions.

## Women enter clerking

During much of the nineteenth century in Europe, as the middle class increased its wealth, power, and prestige, paid employment for middle-class women was taboo. These women were expected to care for the home and children, supervise servants, and reflect their husbands' financial and social position. Paid employment was considered degrading unless it fit certain genteel categories, but genteel work was sorely lacking. Only towards the end of the century, with state expansion of welfare, health, and educational facilities, did a group of acceptable professions emerge. Some middle-class women, however, did not possess the qualifications or inclination for teaching, social work, or nursing. For them, industrialization and economic expansion had created another option: white-collar work as an office or sales clerk.

These occupations suited middle-class women, and were considered suitable, for a number of reasons. They fitted in with women's gender role of nurturance, for they were caring occupations that allowed women to serve others. Unlike industrial work, the occupations allowed women to maintain ladylike dress and behavior. Finally, middle-class women could fill the new positions with little additional training. This benefited women, to whom higher education was closed until the twentieth century and who often could not afford it in any case. It also suited employers, who gained access to a labor pool that was competent but, being new to paid employment and having no employment tradition or elders to counsel them, would work for lower pay and with greater docility than their male counterparts.

However, clerking did not appeal only to middle-class women. Unlike nursing, teaching, and social work, clerking did not require any advanced education; indeed, some positions were filled by applicants who had but minimal schooling. Working-class daughters therefore entered the field in ever larger numbers.

Female employment in clerking expanded rapidly in the closing decades of the nineteenth century. Saleswomen had been employed as early as 1848. In that year a group of male commercial assistants in Prussia petitioned the Ministry of State for protection against "store demoiselles."[22] Women made significant gains from the 1880s, when there were but a few thousand female clerks, to World War I, when they had become about 25 percent of the clerking work-force. By the 1907 census, women comprised about 22 percent of office workers, but their greatest gains occurred in retail sales, where almost 80 percent of staff was female.[23]

However, women did not enter the same labor market as male clerks, nor did they compete for the same positions, for they were welcomed only in the deskilled field of clerking, not in the managerial occupations that were becoming the basis of the new service class. Within clerking, women held positions of lower status, less responsibility, lower pay, and fewer chances of upward career mobility than did men. Female clerks predominated in routine clerical work, retail sales, and warehouse staffing. Very few women ascended the occupational ladder in clerking, failing to become wholesale sellers, travelers, or buyers in the sales field, or head clerks, supervisors, or section chiefs in the office. They rarely moved into managerial or technical positions.[24] Women were also more likely to experience unemployment than their male colleagues, and the length of that unemployment lasted longer.[25] Older women were especially likely to be unemployed; with the increase in clerking positions in the early 1900s, older women, even those with considerable work experience, seem to have experienced increased discrimination.

Women were hired as clerks in Germany for the same reasons that they were hired elsewhere in industrial societies; their employment suited the development of a degraded work situation and a segmented labor market. As a new group of employees, women were unfamiliar with the traditions of clerking, and did not expect to have non-routine work assignments that taught them all aspects of their profession and that were the key to upward mobility and to the dream of independence. Since few women worked in clerking after marriage, they did not expect to move up into more responsible slots. Without a career consciousness, women were less likely to organize and were therefore more likely than men to put up with poor conditions and unfair practices. Women worked for less pay and were willing to undertake the ever-expanding number of routine, mechanical, and repetitive tasks.

Women were employed in different areas of clerking than men. Office work was held in higher regard than sales or warehouse work, and office positions comprised about two-thirds of all those in clerking, yet the 1907 census reported that only 30 percent of all women clerks worked in the office, while approximately 22 percent of office staff were female. Women were also more likely than men to be employed in the offices of small- or medium-sized firms than in the largest firms. The greatest expansion of male white-collar work occurred in the cities, while women experienced an increase in employment in both cities and towns, where firms were small and less modern.[26] Small businesses were less likely to pay good salaries and offered fewer opportunities for training and advancement; in these circumstances a greater number of women were hired.

Certain branches of the economy were more receptive to female office workers than others. Women were more frequently employed in traditional "women's" fields, such as firms producing or marketing clothing, cleaning supplies, instruments, or books. Among large firms, those in light industry or new and rapidly expanding branches such as chemicals were more likely to hire women, indicating that women were hired whether the area was "suitable" or not when much hiring was to be done.[27]

Women were unwelcome in prestigious office positions. Although they comprised almost 27 percent of routine office staff in 1907, women held only 18.5 percent of the more skilled and responsible jobs, such as bookkeeper or correspondent, and about 4 percent of supervisory positions. They failed to gain access to the financial world, to banking, stockbroking, or insurance, holding only 5.5 percent of the clerical positions in financial institutions and 8 percent of those in insurance.[28] Since women were not eligible for bank apprenticeship programs until 1922, they were not trained in banking procedures as were their male peers. So few were their professional skills that less than half of the 2,408 women employed in German banks were entrusted with "technical" (i.e. banking) work. The majority carried out routine clerical tasks.[29]

Sales work was an especially promising field for young women in the late nineteenth century, for it was rapidly expanding and required little or no advance training and only an elementary education. In the decade from 1895 to 1907 the number of salespersons doubled to over half a million, with women becoming over 35 percent of all sales personnel. However, the more prestigious sales fields, in which commercial assistants were sometimes groomed for an entrepreneurial or managerial role, were almost entirely limited to men. While men moved into industrial and wholesale selling, women entered the retail field, selling light consumer goods both in small shops and in the large department stores that had been instrumental in the advance of women into saleswork. By 1907 women made up three-quarters of retail sales personnel, but less than 2 percent of traveling salespersons. Yet even within retailing, women remained at the lowest levels, for only about 4 percent of supervisors or buyers were female.[30]

Although a high percentage of branch managers (*Filialleiter*) of chain stores were women, their job entailed simple sales work, with few managerial responsibilities. When men held the position, the shop was often large and the manager supervised a number of employees. When women were employed, they usually worked alone, keeping a small one-room branch shop in a residential area that was open from morning until well into the night. They often worked without adequate heating or light and could not even interrupt work to eat a meal. Pay was extremely low and sometimes included sleeping quarters, which was an inducement to older single or widowed women. The fact that the branches catered to neighborhood customers and were located in residential areas also made them attractive to married women, who could bring their small children to the shop.[31]

Not only did women fill different positions than men in clerking, however; they also received different training. Men's clerking careers began with uniform two- to three-year apprenticeship programs, which not only provided training and experience and a rung on a career ladder, but was in addition a means of limiting numbers in the field. As befitted their secondary position in the work-force, few women received apprenticeships; the 1907 census shows that 90.1

percent of the white-collar apprenticeship positions in industry were held by boys; in commerce, 77.7 percent.[32] In some fields, especially prestigious ones, women were completely barred from apprenticeships on the grounds that they did not have a secondary school-leaving certificate, which was only granted by examination after attending an academic high school, impossible for a girl until the beginning of the twentieth century.

Girls were not only excluded from apprenticeships, but usually received relatively brief training, often less than one year, and they were more likely than boys to encounter "apprenticeships" offering no training, for they were more likely to be hired by small retail shops, which expected new personnel to undertake the variety of menial jobs that had to be accomplished daily, such as sweeping the walk, dusting, or arranging stock. Some young women complained that they were expected to cook dinner or mind their employers' children.[33]

Women in the office had fewer opportunities for apprenticeship than saleswomen. It was commercial schooling, rather than apprenticeships, that provided the typical road to office work for women. Yet although this was the case, women were less likely to receive a commercial education than men. Commercial courses and school programs had become increasingly popular as office work expanded in the course of the nineteenth century, when tasks became specialized and the number of employees with modest educational backgrounds increased. Four basic types of commercial programs existed: colleges, day schools, continuation schools, and part-time courses. Each of the four could be found with public and with private funding, and on both non-profit and profit-making bases.

Over half the young women clerks in one poll who attended commercial schools only completed short private courses.[34] Over half received less than one year of training of any sort. Only a third had been trained at commercial secondary schools, which were those most likely to provide the breadth of knowledge and depth of skills-training necessary for upward mobility. Not a single woman had attended a commercial college. Women were not expected to have business careers: they were to be lowly clerks in routine jobs and nothing else. But even in this capacity, they faced prejudice and hostility. As Agnes Herrmann, leader of the largest female clerks' association, recalled concerning her own early working days:

And the so-called social position of the female clerk? It was so low, so little respected, that I – even as an independent correspondent in a large factory firm – was not addressed politely by my male colleagues, since "a lady who takes to trade is *de facto* no lady."[35]

*The conditions of clerking in Germany*

In the decades before World War I, although standards improved, clerks faced physical surroundings that were a far cry from the brightly lit offices and stores of today. The best conditions for clerks tended to be those found in large cities, in large firms, and in the office rather than on the sales floor. Wherever the workplace, however, clerks often found a depressing environment. Clerks' organizations complained of unheated offices and shops, inadequate safety and sanitary facilities, and poor lighting. Clerks were required to endure long periods of standing. Small-town employers frequently included room and board as part of the contract, which meant longer working hours, less pay, and a work-load that included a variety of menial tasks not mentioned in job descriptions.[36]

Hours were long for both office and sales clerks. Just as the work environment was better in the office, so too were work hours, with more than 85 percent of office employees working a week of forty-eight hours or less. Although Saturday was a full workday, Sunday work was not common,[37] and office workers usually received fifteen-minute breaks in the morning and afternoon. Since Germans took their main meal at midday, office employees often received a two-hour lunch break, but because they commonly returned home to eat, the time did not provide much leisure. Breaks were often staggered, as well, so that some employees might only be relieved after two o'clock.

Hours in the office were often irregular. During busy seasons, employees might be expected to work until midnight or later, and periods of stock-taking often found clerks working round the clock.[38] The pace of work often varied over the course of the day as well. Dull stretches in the office would be superseded by sudden pressure to accomplish much in a short time; immediately after a postal delivery had been made, for instance, or before the deadline for postal pick-up. Since a postal delivery was made in most cities at six o'clock in the evening, the last work hours of the day were often hectic and extended beyond the official closing time. That this disorganized routine was fairly common attests once again to the incomplete nature of rationalization at the turn of the century.

Hours were longer for sales personnel, especially in the early 1890s when some shops regularly stayed open until midnight, with the rest following suit during Christmas season and at other sales peaks. Even after legislation prevented shops from remaining open after nine, retail sales personnel commonly worked fourteen hours a day, seven days a week.[39] As in busy offices, stores might require employees to work through the entire night during inventory. There were no shifts, and the work period extended beyond opening hours, for there was stock to arrange, tidying to do, bookkeeping to be figured, and even furnaces to be stoked. There was a long midday break, but again employees usually traveled home and might be sent at times earlier or later than meal time. Some salespersons were required to eat on the premises, interrupting meals to serve customers.[40]

Salaries for clerks varied greatly, and levels dropped as white-collar work expanded, giving most clerks a salary little better than the wages of a skilled manual worker.[41] Clerks received a monthly salary rather than an hourly wage, a distinction they took to be symbolic of their greater commitment to work and their broad-based knowledge and responsibilities. However, the salary also meant that white-collar workers were often paid no overtime. In all cases, women were paid less than men for the same or equivalent work.

The average 1913 clerks' salary was 1,941 M for males and 997 M for females.[42] Comparable figures showed an average male blue-collar wage of 925 M a year in 1907 and 939 M in 1908,[43] while one scholar estimated 1,500–2,400 M as the average annual wage of a male skilled manual worker in 1910 and 1,200–1,500 M as the earnings of a semiskilled worker.[44] Salespersons were always paid less than office staff. In 1898 the average salary of a saleswoman was about 690 M a year, and that of a salesman 1,200 M,[45] testifying to the lower status of sales personnel and indicating the poor circumstances in which they lived.

Paternal values were reflected in some salaries, for a number of firms paid their employees on the basis of need. Young people living at home might receive lower pay than those living independently and unmarried men receive less than married men.[46] Women's lower salaries were justified on the supposition that they were dependents within the family and were only working for pin money. Female salary levels were also linked to factors such as education, years on the job, and the type of position held, which placed women at a disadvantage because they had breaks in their employment histories and predominated in saleswork. Saleswomen who had worked more than six years did receive higher pay, being more likely to earn over 100 M a month. However, experiential factors alone cannot explain women's lower salaries, for about 10 percent of saleswomen who had seven or more years' experience still earned under 70 M a month, an amount earned by only 3 percent of all male white-collar workers, including new entrants to the labor force.[47]

## A social profile of clerks in Wilhelmine Germany

As the field of clerking changed and expanded in the decades before World War I, the social profile of male clerks changed along with the occupation. As women entered clerking, their social circumstances were distinct from the men's. The age, marital status, class background, and educational level of German clerks must be understood in order to weigh the impact of the changes that had come to clerking and to analyze the issues, demands, and political views of clerks' associations.

The young men and women who became clerks in the Wilhelmine period came predominantly from the middle classes, although the proportion was decreasing so that by World War I, about one-third of clerks came from working-class families.[48] This was especially true in sales, where personnel was more likely to have come from the working class and to have received only an elementary school education. Both male and female office workers tended to have some education beyond elementary school and to have fathers who were not manual workers. The changing patterns of class and educational background and the increasing differentiation between the work-force in the office and on the sales floor both reflect the deskilling and segmentation of clerking.

The changes also reflect the gender differentiation of clerking, however, for women were more likely to have come from working-class backgrounds than were men. In 1897 less than 10 percent of women office staff had working-class fathers and about one-quarter of saleswomen. By 1910, however, studies estimated that up to a third of female office staff and two-thirds of female sales personnel came from working-class backgrounds. At that time, about 20 percent of men in clerking had fathers who were manual workers.

Clerks of both sexes were younger than was the labor force as a whole, for the average age of all German workers was over thirty in 1907. Female office workers had a mean age of 21.8 years and males 26.9 years. The average age of saleswomen in 1907 was 23.5 years and of salesmen 26.6 years. Although both men and women were young, however, their life patterns were different, as the younger female mean reflects. Women left clerking to marry and end paid employment, while the men who left changed occupations or moved up into more responsible positions.

As would be expected of young clerks, the majority were unmarried. However, although only about two-thirds of the male clerks were single in 1907, about 95 percent of the women were. Even younger men in clerking were more likely to be married than women, testimony to the fact that married women were not expected to work, especially middle-class women holding white-collar jobs. In 1895, 62.8 percent of the general female work-force was single, and 64 percent in 1907. Among female clerks, over 90 percent were single in 1895 and an even greater percentage in 1907.

*Clerk in a general store, about 1870.*

*Saleswomen with their male supervisor in a Hamburg stationery store, about 1900.*

*Saleswomen in a grocery store, 1913.*

*Saleswomen or shop manager of a small neighborhood grocery store in basement of apartment building, about 1910.*

*Shop manager of neighborhood fruit store with her son, about 1900. Women valued the opportunity to have employment near home or where children could be present.*

*Saleswoman and shop manager at a dairy goods branch in a better neighborhood, 1913.*

*Saleswomen at a bakery, about 1900.*

*Saleswomen at a medium-sized dry goods store, about 1910. Such stores were often the basis from which department stores arose.*

*Saleswomen and butchers at a butcher's shop, 1912. They were grouped in the same category by the census, making calculations difficult.*

"In a Modern Berlin Department Store," engraving by Eduard Cucuel. Note the saleswoman, dressed in black.

"Berlin Department Store Saleswomen on Their Way to Work," by Heinrich Kley, 1912.

Ein Blick
in die
Confection.

*"In the Department Store: A Look at the Clothing Department," engraving
by Ewald Thiel, about 1900.*

Publisher's office. Note the small work space and inadequate office furnishings. About 1910.

Offices within AEG Berlin. Note the inner room for section chiefs or middle management, with glass windows to observe the section. Note the single woman clerk, a typist, 1906.

*Kracht's Commercial School. The sign advertises typing. One of the "presses" that female clerks' associations opposed. About 1914.*

*Switchboard operators at a publishing house, about 1910.*

*Woman office worker, about 1910.*

*Advertisement showing woman using a typewriter at home, 1898.*

*Young ladies at home. Some young women from bourgeois backgrounds entered clerking, especially office work. About 1912.*

*Cellar apartment of a working-class family. More and more young women from such backgrounds entered clerking, especially sales work. 1906.*

*Cellar apartment; room in which six people slept. 1905.*

Women who succeeded in attaining managerial positions are the most interesting exception to the general picture of a youthful and unmarried female clerking labor force. These women had a median age in 1907 of 35.5 years, and 62.9 percent were unmarried (of male directors, only 27.5 percent were), indicating that most women in the early twentieth century who took their careers seriously found it difficult to combine work and marriage.

# 2

## Women clerks at home and work

The generation of young women who entered German offices and salesrooms after 1890 were breaking with tradition, for during much of the nineteenth century in Europe, their sphere was the family. Married women were expected to care for the home and children, for their "natural profession" was to be wife and mother. Unmarried daughters, too, were expected to attend to domestic duties. This was not only the prevailing ideology, but the reality as well. The working class accepted that economic necessity forced some women to enter paid employment, but, within the middle class, even women in straitened circumstances were expected to rely on their kin for assistance.[1] So strong was their feeling of degradation that many impoverished middle-class women made and sold handicrafts secretly, and their poverty was so extreme that in 1888 a women's philanthropic organization, the Lette Association, opened its "Victoria-Bazaar" as a place where women could sell their handiwork.[2]

The consensus that the female sphere was domestic ranged across the political spectrum and was based on the belief that women and men were essentially different by nature. After 1890, however, a new acceptance of a public role for women emerged. A shift in popular opinion can be noted in novels and periodic literature, in records of public discussion and in the press, where the "Woman's Page" was now as likely to contain reports of feminist affairs as it was household tips.[3] The prevailing sentiment was changing, however, only for unmarried women. It was still accepted that a woman's "natural profession" was to be a wife and mother; but commentators within and without the women's movement now agreed that technological change had reduced her burden of housework, so that daughters could be freed from their earlier obligation to contribute. At the same time they agreed that an individual's need for self-expression and self-fulfillment demanded that middle-class girls before marriage should not remain isolated in the home, but should be permitted to travel, to study, or to work. Some went so far as to assert that this experience would improve their performance as wives and mothers by making them better partners to their husbands and educators to their children.[4]

The women who entered clerking, then, were not exactly like their male counterparts, who knew that men of their fathers' generation had held similar positions and that by concentrating on their careers they were acting in accord with the values of their culture. For the women, older female models were non-existent, and cultural values defined the home as the dominant factor in their lives. To understand women in clerking, we must therefore also understand their lives within the family. Germany's women clerks came from working-class and middle-class families with structures similar to those of their English and American peers. Their work lives were typically structured by their roles as mothers, wives, and daughters and by attitudes emphasizing the importance of home and family. Far from representing a cultural ideal, women's work in clerking had to be justified, and it only became acceptable by linking it to the domestic sphere, to its benefits to others in the woman's family of birth or marriage.

## Female clerks in the bosom of the family

For both the middle and the working classes in Germany at the end of the nineteenth century, the family was a cooperative unit whose members fulfilled different roles. Although the nuclear family – i.e. the two generations of parents and their children – was the core of the household, sometimes family members would be missing, and others were often resident as well. A grandparent might share the home, for instance, making three generations under one roof, or aunts or uncles might extend the two generations. In addition, servants, lodgers, or foster children brought non-relatives into the household.

However, the nuclear family was modified in different ways in working-class and in middle-class households. Working-class families had no servants, but were far more likely than middle-class families to include lodgers and foster children. Grandparents in working-class families were more likely to share homes, while in middle-class families elderly parents were only present in great numbers in the households of adult working women who were single or heads of families. Unmarried sisters might extend middle-class nuclear families, however, since women who did not expect to work before marriage had to be accommodated by kin.[5]

The father was the family head and breadwinner. As head, his authority included overall responsibility for the children and even decision-making in the home. Foreign visitors were struck by the degree to which German bourgeois husbands not only controlled the household purse but also insisted on making household decisions that they felt were largely left to women in England or America.[6] Fathers usually participated in or controlled their children's choice of schools, occupation, and spouse. Employers expected fathers to accompany young adults at job interviews.[7]

The mother's sphere was domestic; she kept the home running and looked after the physical and emotional needs of children. Yet while it was accepted that women were mothers by nature, they held sway only over the daily activities of childrearing, for their husbands had ultimate parental authority, as they had in other domestic matters.

In working-class families, it was acceptable for a mother to supplement the budget by earning money, although the ideal of the home-centered woman was so strong that wives contributed to the family income only in the most poverty-stricken working-class households.[8] For some mothers this meant full-time or part-time paid employment outside the home. However, since families were often large, outside employment meant that working-class mothers had to make child-care arrangements, a difficult undertaking when few child-care centers existed. Even in the 1920s, one study of women clerks found that half the working mothers had to rely on relatives to look after children, while one-eighth left their children at home unattended.[9] Such problems led many mothers to seek part-time or home-based employment, taking in domestic piecework, laundry, or sewing, caring for children or lodgers, or becoming independent businesswomen running neighborhood shops or lunchrooms.[10] Grandmothers could be important members of workers' families because they helped with household tasks and child care. Mothers also received help from other relatives and from neighbors, indicating that among workers the family did not exist in an isolated nuclear form but was a collective that reached out to kin and to the community. Even with the working-class family drawing on every available resource, however, survival was often difficult. One researcher found that many of the salesgirls she interviewed showed signs of malnutrition, which, she suspected, dated from infancy.[11]

In middle-class families a mother earned money only if absolutely necessary for the welfare of the family, although providing for the children's education and career training was often considered a necessity.[12] Her work in the home, including child care, was often a full-time job, particularly since many families who considered themselves part of the "middle estate" kept no servants.[13] Even with the help of "a serving girl," many onerous household tasks remained, especially given a wife's obligation to foster her husband's career by entertaining and maintaining the household at a standard appropriate to the family's status, often on minimal funds. Just as foreign observers were sometimes amazed at the husband's decision-making in the household sphere, so were they confounded at the weight of housework undertaken by the wife.[14]

Children too in both workers' and middle-class families had extensive obligations, and their needs came second to those of adults. Children owed obedience to their parents, especially to their fathers, even as young adults. Thus a delegate to a Free Union clerks' conference could demand that parents prevent their children from joining a rival political organization.[15] Children were also obliged to help their parents and other kin in hard times once they were old enough to do so.

In families of both classes, a greater level of obedience and obligation was considered appropriate for daughters than for sons.[16] Daughters were more likely than sons to leave school early in order to take up paid employment; for working-class girls this might happen at age twelve, while in the middle class it could mean the end of schooling after junior high.[17] Older women were far more likely than their brothers to continue to aid family members. Finally, working women who lived at home also had to help with the housework, which was not expected of their brothers.[18] Indeed, sometimes the oldest female child left school not to enter employment but to take up tasks in the home, to look after smaller siblings, for instance.

At the same time, more effort was made to help sons get on in life by supporting their apprenticeships or their secondary and tertiary education.[19] Parents anticipated that their daughter would marry, so less educational and professional help was usually given her. Indeed, she could even be asked to contribute financially to aid her brother's education or career. The oldest daughter especially was expected to sacrifice herself for parents, brothers, and even younger sisters.[20] On the other hand, once sons had their own families, they were no longer expected to care for their parents if a sister was available.[21]

## Women clerks in their daily lives

The majority of women clerks in Germany before World War I were young women working before marriage and usually living at home. A much smaller group comprised older women clerks working from economic necessity whether they were single, married, divorced, or widowed. It is here that we find those "career women" who defined their work as primary and saw it as a satisfactory alternative to marriage.[22]

Younger clerks were part of a familial community and participated in a family budget, handing over their wages and receiving pocket money. They viewed their clerking employment as temporary and expected their lives to change with marriage. Older women clerks were more likely to have created their own life patterns and to be economically self-supporting, although a majority of them continued to acknowledge family obligations and to make financial contributions to kin. Women clerks of whatever age were far more likely than men to view their work lives as intertwined with their home and family.

For most young female clerks, the salient factor once they became old enough to help was the family's need. This need could be pressing; of the young saleswomen studied by Mende who lived at home, over 20 percent had lost their fathers.[23] Studies have shown that many female clerks gave their entire pay to their parents.[24] When their pay increased, therefore, so did their contribution to the family. Sons, on the other hand, paid their families a fixed amount, so that when their pay increased, they had increased spending money. Similarly, boys received more pocket money than girls. Overall, therefore, almost all daughters made a greater relative contribution to the family than did sons.[25] Working-class families experienced the greatest financial need, but middle-class girls also entered employment to help their families. Here, however, another motive came to bear, for daughters in better situated families sought to develop their interests, to go beyond the home sphere before marriage, and worked for personal reasons as well as financial necessity. They were often allowed to spend their own earnings as they wished or to save them.[26]

The young female clerk's obligations to her family were reinforced by the communal living arrangements and lack of privacy evident even in modest middle-class homes. Homes varied greatly, depending on the class background of the family, its income, and the number of persons in the household. Working-class families had more children, but were also more likely to send them elsewhere to live (to relatives, an institution, or an apprenticeship with board), so that both working-class and middle-class families tended to have the same total numbers. Mende found that a majority of the young sales clerks she studied lived in households with five to seven members, living in small apartments of one to three rooms, making an average of 2.1 persons per room. For middle-class households in her sample, she found an average of 1.5 persons per room. In working-class households, several persons commonly slept in one bed, and few families had a non-sleeping room besides the kitchen in which to relax. In addition, lodgers would sometimes be present, or a flat would be shared with a second family.[27] In middle-class families, bedrooms would typically be shared, although privacy could sometimes be found in the family's living rooms.[28]

Since women's family obligations were lifelong, older women clerks, especially if unmarried, often had to maintain parents and other kin. An overwhelming majority of adult women clerks helped to support relatives, while only about 10 percent of their male colleagues regularly contributed to relatives' maintenance.[29] The situation of widowed and divorced women was particularly hard, for they often had to support two generations, their children and their parents.[30] The majority of older women clerks lived with relatives in addition to supporting them financially. Usually, they made homes with their parents or mother, but sometimes with fathers, siblings, or more distant relations. Even in the 1920s, only about 15 percent of female clerks lived completely on their own. This contrasts with the situation of the male clerks, for only about 30 percent of single men lived with relatives.[31] Whether they lived at home, with relatives, or on their own, women calculated that half to two-thirds of their salary went toward food and housing.[32] Budget analyses of the period showed the unfairness of characterizing women who lived at home as needing less money, for they paid the same amount for room and board as their independent colleagues.

Women were socialized within the family towards a goal of service to its other members and towards a lack of perception that they themselves had rights and needs; that is, toward that *Bedürfnislosigkeit* against which feminists railed. Their sense of subordination was reinforced by the financial drain upon them by their families. Yet, in addition to their substantial contributions to kin, most female clerks faced other heavy costs. Because of the importance of outward appearance in office and sales work, women had to pay substantial amounts for new clothes or clothing material and for clothing maintenance. They also had to spend money on hair and personal care. Their male colleagues also faced clothing expenses, but women's items cost more and they had to pay a far higher percentage of their salaries toward these personal costs. Where married male salaried employees paid 10 to 12 percent of their salaries to maintain their appearance, women paid an average of between 25 percent and 40 percent. Respondents to a Weimar poll explained that they often went without food in order to pay for clothing.[33]

The main difference between female clerks with family ties and those on their own came in their daily living environment. Women who were completely on their own had greater overall expenses than had women who shared the costs of rent or had another person to help keep down food and clothing costs by preparing them at home. Women in lodgings often had no facilities to cook or wash clothes in their rooms, while women who lived alone in a flat found that housekeeping took hours each day.[34] Women on their own could feel isolated and lonely; testimony to this are the recurring plans among leaders and members of female clerks' organizations to build homes for single women.[35]

## The public world of women clerks

It was not only within the family that women received the message of their secondary status. Stepping out into the public sphere, women were clearly confronted with their subordination as well. By word and deed they learned that unless accompanied by men they were unwelcome interlopers in the greater world beyond the home. Even finding a home could be difficult, for women seeking lodgings were often told "we don't rent to ladies."[36] Restaurant patrons and managers looked askance at unchaperoned women diners, which led women clerks to prefer eating in a family setting – with friends or at their landlady's – which was often not easy to arrange.

Leisure time could be hard to fill, as one clerk noted, for "concerts and theaters may be attended by the single woman today without male protection, but that ends the list of entertainment possibilities."[37] Women also found it harder to make personal contacts than did single men. In addition to their greater freedom of movement, male employees might be invited home by their employers, while female clerks rarely were. Middle-class women, even those working from economic necessity, found that their old friends no longer acknowledged them, and it could be difficult to find new friends who were social peers.[38]

Merely appearing in public, out of the shelter of home and the protection of male relatives, could provoke sexual harassment. One female clerk complained that "nowhere is a lady totally secure from serious badgering. In the street, on the electric tram, everywhere, she is exposed to it . . ."[39] Women who were not members of any organization might well find that they had nowhere to relax or invite friends. This in part explains the appeal of female clerks' associations to their members. A report by one group in Königsberg showed the importance of comfortable leisure and sociability to women clerks:

Every Wednesday evening, members gather in the two extremely comfortable front rooms of the office (which are opened out to make one) for completely spontaneous goings-on: here some chat or read at a table while others play piano or sing. In short, each passes a few hours as she wishes in pleasant rooms and pleasant company. The third room, usually our employment office, is used as a kitchen. Members take turns preparing coffee, tea, chocolate, as they wish.[40]

Given low pay and long work hours, as well as constraints on their movement, it is amazing that female clerks were as sociable and energetic as they were. Class background rather than available funds determined the choices. Girls from working-class families tended not to seek cultural or educational activities, even those that were free, while girls with middle-class backgrounds took courses, attended concerts or the theater, visited museums. The most highly valued free-time activity for both classes lay in trips and excursions, with reading an additional favorite.[41] By favoring group activities as they did, women clerks were able somewhat to overcome the hostility they encountered in public.

Working women not only confronted a public realm in which they were unwelcome, but they were also required to adopt a new set of behavioral forms. The home-centered mores of the time demanded that gentlewomen keep their distance from men, that they be shy and obsequious. But this behavior ran counter to the demands of the job and could not be accommodated by the physical space of the office and sales floor.[42] The situation of the new working woman was uneasy: she had taken on a role outside the bounds of that which contemporaries saw as appropriate for her sex, yet she otherwise remained within her assigned feminine role.

Employed women did not just face individual hostility, but also public campaigns against women working and agitation by groups hostile to any activities by women deemed contrary to their particular domestic nature.[43] But female clerks also faced concerted attacks by male clerks' associations that emphasized the unsuitability of women in clerking. The arguments were often couched in terms of the negative effects of employment on women themselves or on the wider community; that is, they claimed to have an altruistic purpose. There were two types of arguments, often intertwined, the practical and the moral.

Practical arguments against women's employment in clerking asserted that women could not do equal work – they were not as intelligent, their characters were not suited to the demands and stress of employment, their short employment careers meant that they wasted work-related education and training and were less accomplished on the job. A second set of practical grounds emphasized effects on male clerks, claiming that female employment drove down pay and took jobs from men, who then could not afford to marry.[44]

The arguments based on morality were couched in strong emotive language. Critics in male clerks' associations asserted that women's work outside the home was unsuited to women's nature: "The profession of service is the particular profession of the female; her activities should be domestic . . ."[45] Through paid employment, they argued, women undermined the German family and weakened the fiber of the nation. They became susceptible to disease and were the competitors of men rather than their companions and helpmeets. Leaving the home also exposed women to grave moral danger, which for many led to lives of "shame and disgrace." Children found themselves on their own, receiving no moral guidance or discipline, and girls did not learn how to manage the house.

Women clerks even had to face libelous assaults on their character. Rumor campaigns spread through Germany at various times claiming that female clerks had engaged in prostitution or set up prostitution rings. The most sensational rumor, which spread nationwide and persisted (with changes of locale) over a period of years, asserted that a dead baby had been found in a department store washroom – here prostitution and unwed motherhood joined with murder to show the degradation that occurred when women worked.[46]

Women's subordination was enshrined in law. Before 1900, family law was covered in the codes of the individual states, whose statutes were often based on the Prussian General Code (*Allgemeines Landrecht* or ALR). The Prussian Code set the man as head of the family and the legal guardian of his wife, who did not exist as a legal person and could not sign a contract. Since all property therefore devolved on the husband in marriage, any money earned by the wife belonged to him. A father had full control over his children – indeed, he determined how long his wife would breast-feed their children. Until a daughter married, he represented her legally and controlled her property, while a son could gain independence by setting up his own household. A wife could only gain authority over her children if her husband was obviously unfit.[47]

In the late 1890s a new Civil Code (*Bürgerliches Gesetzbuch* or BGB) was drafted. Although feminists had agitated for this, few of their demands were included. The Civil Code made women legal persons and gave both spouses rights and duties within the "marital community," so that each was obliged to maintain the other. But the two partners were not equal, for "the husband takes the decisions in all matters affecting married life." The Code insisted upon a division of labor within marriage in which a wife's outside employment had to remain secondary and dependent upon her husband's consent. Divorce became more difficult.

Although married women were now legally in control of their earnings, they lost control of any property they brought to the marriage. When a wife helped her husband in his business, profits were his alone. All marital goods (furniture etc.) were considered the husband's, making it difficult for women to get credit. A wife had no right in law to receive even a minimum sum for maintenance, nor even the right to know the details of the family's economic situation.

The new Code made both parents responsible for their children. However, many important parental duties were explicitly granted to the father and his decisions were preferred to the mother's, for "the father's predominance is founded upon the nature of things." This held even after divorce in which the man was the guilty partner. Upon the father's death the mother became responsible for the children only if no other guardian was named in the father's will or by court order. One positive reform was that under the new Code children of both sexes became independent upon reaching their majority.

Schools also emphasized the distinct female role and female subordination. All German children under twelve were required to attend elementary schools. In addition to receiving a message of loyalty and duty to the state and to one's betters, children learned gender-oriented values.[48] All children attended single-sex schools, but separate education was not equal, for girls in many states attended home economics courses as part of their elementary education. After the first five years of elementary school, middle-class children often attended junior high school and then high school. But fewer girls than boys had that opportunity, and girls received a different and lesser education. Most girls' schools were private and varied greatly in quality. Few offered girls the classical education or technical and scientific study that was necessary for tertiary education. At the tertiary level, girls were excluded from universities far longer than in other industrializing lands. Only in the 1890s were they admitted to some universities as guests, and then only with permission from the lecturer. Most states denied women the right to sit for certain examinations or to gain degrees until after 1900.[49]

Finally, the German political system reinforced female subordination. Despite universal male suffrage for national elections, women were excluded from voting rights except in some communal elections that tied suffrage to a high property qualification, so that loss of property, as upon marriage, meant loss of the vote. Many of the approximately 2,000 women who had communal suffrage were only permitted to vote through a male proxy, who could disregard the woman's orders if he felt that she did not completely understand the issues. His vote stood even if the woman protested.[50] Finally, most states had laws of association that barred women from participating in political organizations, which denied them not only party membership, but even the right to attend public meetings where political matters would be discussed.

Women clerks experienced a great sense of disjunction in their lives. The new ethos of the age directed them into employment before marriage, and employers welcomed them into the new deskilled field of clerking. Yet the rules of the public realm still dictated that women needed protection, that they were dependent, and that their primary allegiance was to home and family. Female clerks' associations were aware of this "dualism" in women's lives and attempted to deal with it in their programs and proposals for reform. However, that issue was treated as secondary. More important for most of the leaders of female clerks' groups was the question of the class and status position of clerks in the expanded world of white-collar work, and this agenda they took from their male colleagues.

# 3

# An ambivalent estate: the ideologies and organizations of male clerks

The white-collar work-force in Germany arose at a time of transition in capitalism. A localized economy of small businesses was developing into a national economy in which large industrial and commercial enterprises played an increasingly important role. A political transition was also underway. To govern an industrializing Germany, its aristocratic elite was forced to seek allies from among the powerful industrial bourgeoisie. An age of mass politics was also beginning, so that political and economic leaders turned to new social groups for support in order to win Reichstag majorities for their policies. As the vote for Social Democracy increased, white-collar workers, especially male clerks, gained in political weight. They were well organized, their associations having about 300,000 members. And they identified themselves socially as part of the "middle estate" (*Mittelstand*), so that their political sympathies did not lie with the Left.

## The theory of estate and its dual political implications

Until the late nineteenth century there was no concept in Germany of a separate legal category of white-collar employees. The General German Commercial Code (*Allgemeines deutsches Handelsgesetzbuch* or HGB) of 1861 referred to commercial assistants in only nine articles[1] and the HGB was long held to apply only to persons working in the commercial branch of the economy. In some instances, the statutes of the Imperial Industrial Code (*Reichsgewerbeordnung* or RGO) of 1869 were considered valid for all or some white-collar workers, and the Civil Code (*Bürgerliches Gesetzbuch* or BGB) was also brought to bear.[2]

It was insurance legislation that first mentioned white-collar workers as a separate group. Bismarck's first insurance programs, designed to woo industrial workers, ignored salaried employees. But the expansion of the service sector by the end of the 1880s necessitated some provision for clerks. The Old Age and Disability Insurance Law therefore specifically mentioned "commercial assistants" when it was passed in 1889. However, by separating the discussion of clerks from the paragraph dealing with workers, apprentices, and servants, the legislation created a legal distinction between commercial assistants and manual workers and implied that clerks were members of a particular stratum of society for whom the state would provide.[3]

In 1892 the health insurance law was revised to expand its coverage to commercial assistants and apprentices earning up to 2,000 M a year. The amendment also allowed individual municipalities to increase coverage if they desired. A variety of insurance plans existed, and private insurance plans were allowed, as long as they were registered; a number of clerks' associations kept their independent health insurance programs on that basis. This amendment did not cover all white-collar employees, as the 1889 law had not; only with an 1899 amendment to the disability insurance, which provided coverage for "other white-collar workers," did recognition come that categories of employees existed who could not easily be called "commercial assistants." This amendment again emphasized that clerks were members of a particular socio-economic group, distinct from blue-collar workers, who could turn to the state for the protection of its interests.

In addition to legal definitions that served to label white-collar workers as a distinct group, linguistic usage – largely determined by the group itself – also contributed to the sharpened group identity of clerks. As office work and selling became more distinct jobs, common usage came to divide clerking into office work and sales. Despite the existence of two separate categories, however, both groups continued to consider themselves clerks. The term "commercial assistant" did not die out, although it was joined by the new term "commercial employee" (*kaufmännische Angestellte*), which again emphasized the commonality of sales and office clerks. This unity among lower-level white-collar workers was unique to Germany.

The emerging laws and language that defined some white-collar workers as members of a particular social group testify to a growing preoccupation with stratification on the part of Germans active in political and intellectual life. At the same time, economic and political trends provoked a series of related intellectual debates that also directed attention to the middle strata of German society. Sharpest was the debate between agrarians and industrializers over the future course of German economic development. Almost as intense, however, were the debates among the industrializers themselves concerning how to guide industrialization in order to assure economic growth and social and economic stability. Although socialists also argued the question, it predominated in liberal circles among thinkers who accepted the capitalist order (or foresaw only slow, evolutionary modifications).[4] These debates were of particular importance after 1888, for the death of Wilhelm I and the end of Bismarck's control made reform endeavors more vigorous; economic and political events conspired to create an intellectual climate in which both liberals and conservatives agreed on the need for social policy and social reform.

Of greatest importance to clerks was the theoretical articulation of the key role played in German society by the "middle estate." In 1897 at the Evangelical-Social Congress, Gustav Schmoller presented his analysis of German social stratification, in which he placed half the population among the middling strata. As Lebovics has noted, the categorization was in many ways nonsensical, for it grouped artists with Junkers in the upper class and placed skilled workers and foremen – often adherents of the Social Democratic Party (SPD) – in the lower middle class.[5] Schmoller's framework made sense to many Germans, however. For, as conceived by Schmoller, the middle estate offered a counterweight both to the increasing power of political and economic elites and to the vigor of the SPD and its allied Free Unions, which foresaw the revolutionary overthrow of the existing order. The existence of a strong and active socialist party and trade-union movement in Germany was central to the debates over industrialization at the end of the nineteenth century. In rejecting socialist analysis, theorists also rejected "class" as an analytic or conceptual device, and substituted the old-fashioned and nostalgia-laden term "estate." Recoiling from the socialists' prediction of revolution, they also rejected the concept of class struggle and emphasized instead social harmony. They offered a theory of balance and stability both against those emphasizing revolutionary change and those insisting upon elite domination.

Common to the various versions of the ideology of the middle estate was the notion that society was arranged in a number of "estates" (*Stände*) or strata which could work together harmoniously. If each estate was able to articulate and defend its interests, the whole nation would prosper. The state was to mediate, and a strong middle stratum was particularly important in maintaining a balance. Acceptance of this ideology cut across right/left, conservative/liberal lines, for in this form it was but a vague, defensive statement avowing little besides good intentions and fear of revolution. The ideology criticized both socialism and corporate capitalism and expected the state to bolster the position of persons in the middle.

Beyond these unclear assertions, however, corporatist ideology diverged, taking either a right or left path. For conservatives, the use of "estate" was part of a set of values presuming hierarchical and patriarchal behavior and challenging liberal individualism as well as socialism. Its use was meant to connote a backward-looking, pre-industrial society. Estates and orders implied a static society, with traditional patterns of authority and deference, and a pre-modern economy. Members of that economic group identified as the "old middle estate" were the chief proponents of this view.

However, "estate" was also part of the vocabulary among moderate, liberal, and reformist forces in Germany. Its common use by persons affiliated with these groups, in particular by white-collar organizations, does not mean that they too viewed it as an anti-modern ideology. Many moderates used "estate" as a convenient term describing different social and economic groups in a stratified society, while avoiding the term "class" and signalling rejection of Marxist social analysis. The key phrases for moderate estatists were "social policy" (*Sozialpolitik*) and social reform. The state was to provide legislation that would win the working class from socialism while soothing the middle classes by offering them status and real benefits. Social reform would win popular allegiance for the existing German state and would involve a variety of interests in Germany in political organization and legislative work, thereby assuring them that the political system was being liberalized and did indeed function with popular participation. The Society for Social Reform, headed by liberal Prussian minister von Berlepsch and supported by many members of the Association for Social Policy, led this effort.[6] Unlike their allies in the old middle estate, associations of the new tended to support a domestic policy of social reform. Clerks' organizations participated in both the Society for Social Reform and the Hansa Federation.

## Male clerks' organizations

Associations of male clerks that went beyond the local level arose in Germany in the latter half of the nineteenth century.[7] Since the economy was then essentially pre-industrial and clerking an occupational stage preceding independence, they patterned themselves on traditional guilds that united all workers in a field from apprentices to masters. These traditional clerks' associations were called "parity organizations" because they permitted employers to join on an equal basis.[8] Nevertheless, their activities focused on the interests of employees, emphasizing welfare measures and legislative reforms such as an end to the competition clause and the introduction of shorter working hours, commercial schooling, and insurance coverage. A majority rejected female employment in clerking as unfair compettiton throughout the pre-war period. The many regional groups were dominated by two large organizations that were secular and politically liberal.

A somewhat anomalous group within parity organizations was the liberal Association of German Merchants – Hirsch-Duncker (*Verein der Deutschen Kaufleute*), founded in the 1870s with strong ties to the Progressive parties. It originated with a group of businessmen interested in the plight of "young merchants," i.e., clerks, although it admitted non-clerks to membership. Its membership of 20,000 was small compared to other male clerks' associations. In its activities the association was similar to other male organizations, except that it admitted women to membership in 1906.

Parity organizations saw themselves as part of a "commercial estate" that united employers and employees and was allied with the old middle estate, an ideological position that determined much of their organizational work. Since clerks, in their view, were distinct from manual laborers, they favored legislative reforms that maintained or created distinctions between the two groups. Thus they sought new commercial courts and chambers rather than simply an expansion of the existing industrial courts to cover white-collar fields.

In addition, the parity associations tied their explanation of the declining pay, status, and promotional chances of clerks to the ideology of the middle estate. The field had changed, they insisted, because too many "unsuitable elements" – a euphemism for persons from the working class or for women – had taken routine jobs in clerking, giving the profession a bad name and limiting the chances of other employees for advancement. For this reason, parity associations sought to improve clerks' overall business knowledge through educational classes, lectures, and libraries and lobbied for educational reforms to keep out "unsuitables."

Finally, since they distinguished themselves from the proletariat, the organizations rejected striking as a form of industrial action. At their 1909 convention, the Leipzig Alliance declared: "In our opinion a strike of clerks is fully excluded in the foreseeable future," although it did not reject the strike "for all time."[9] Parity groups were wary of harming the interests of employers, both because they were organization members and because clerks themselves aspired to become employers.

Although they insisted on their non-working-class status, however, it is notable that both the concrete demands and the exclusionary tactics of the parity organizations paralleled those often used by craft unions. Craft unions also usually focused demands on better pay, shorter working hours, and better working conditions. They too sought to prevent deskilling and to improve their bargaining position by limiting access to the field through an insistence on certain educational steps, especially apprenticeship, and on certification of workers.[10]

This similarity raises important questions about class location and class consciousness. For it is apparent that even the traditional associations of male clerks had by the turn of the century decided on an organizational strategy similar to that of skilled men of the working class. At the same time, although clerks' associations borrowed the strategy of skilled workers, they continued to see themselves as members of the middle estate. In fact, the class location of clerks shifted in the period before World War I, at the very time that both men and women in clerking grappled with their self-identity as an employment group. Many elements went into the development of that sense of self-identity: the class location and self-perceptions of older generations of clerks; Germany's particular political culture; contemporary legal and political developments; and contemporary debates about how best to interpret social and political reality. It was a self-identification that was fast losing accuracy.

Parity organizations were challenged in the late nineteenth century by two new types of male clerks' groups, both of which looked to industrial workers' organizations rather than to the guilds. One type of clerks' group favored unionism, using tactics such as collective bargaining, the strike, and an appeal to solidarity among all workers. The other new type insisted that the interests of principals and commercial assistants were distinct, but rejected radical union tactics and notions of class opposition and preferred to cooperate with employers.

This second type of new clerks' association emerged with the creation of the German-Nationalist Commercial Assistants' Alliance (*Deutschnationaler Handlungsgehilfen-Verband* or DHV), which was founded locally in 1893 in Hamburg and became a national organization in 1895.[11] Its radical agitation tactics and claim to be a new union-style organization won it much publicity and many members. By the late nineteenth century Hamburg was not only an important center of commerce, but had also become a center for Free Union and socialist agitation. The twenty-three clerks who founded the group, guided by anti-Semitic leader Johannes Irwahn, were responding to the socialist Central Alliance, a rival clerks' organization affiliated with the Free Unions. Besides being anti-Semitic and hostile to socialism, the DHV was strongly nationalist, volkish, and conservative. Its leaders had ties not only to the anti-Semitic Reform Party, but also to the Conservative Party and to interest groups such as the Pan-Germans and the Agrarian Federation. Although the organization rejected union principles and referred to itself as a "professional fellowship" (*Berufsgenossenschaft*), it asserted its difference from the older parity organizations by claiming that only clerks could become members.

The parity groups claimed to be a "commercial estate"; the DHV asserted its membership in a "professional estate," a new middle estate that included all white-collar workers. It argued that the interests of principals and clerks were not identical and that, as a separate professional estate, clerks should not be organized with their employers. Rather than defining themselves in terms of economic independence, this term focused on the nature of the work process for white-collar employees and its dissimilarity to blue-collar work. It implied that clerks' work was intellectual, creative, responsible, and required an education, while manual laborers' work was physical, routine, and lacked autonomy.

Membership in the DHV was open to "all male clerks and clerk-apprentices of the German folk community." No Jews, women, foreigners, or non-commercial workers were allowed to join. Independent businessmen could join, although without voting rights.[12] The association was led until 1909 by Wilhelm Schack, a Conservative Reichstag delegate whose skills included both organizational talent and a gift for demagoguery. Under his guidance, DHV membership rapidly grew. Like the parity associations, the German-Nationalists recruited most of its members from the ranks of clerks. About 30 percent were in sales and 60 percent in office work, with fewer than 10 percent in higher positions.[13]

The DHV developed an extremely effective administrative apparatus, with active and well-disciplined functionaries, going far beyond the abilities of the older groups. It published a hard-hitting journal, and members frequently attended or leafletted meetings of their rivals. Not only was the socialist Central Alliance attacked, but the male parity organizations were also criticized for being do-nothing tools of the principals. In addition, women working as clerks and female clerks' associations faced vigorous attacks and were, along with Jews and capitalists, blamed for the decline of the social and economic position of male clerks. Like the parity organizations, the DHV established a variety of self-help bureaus, but was much more active in the field of social legislation than the parity groups. It campaigned vigorously for representation on the local insurance boards and commercial courts. By the early 1900s the association had become the largest single clerks' association; by 1910 it had over 100,000 members.

The only true union among all the competing male organizations, advocating collective bargaining, the strike, and solidarity of clerks with industrial workers' unions, was the socialist Central Alliance of Male and Female Commercial Assistants (*Zentralverband der Handlungsgehilfen und Gehilfinnen Deutschlands*), which accepted women as members from its inception. It stood in the sharpest ideological contrast to the others, supporting women's work, rejecting estatist analysis, and insisting on the proletarianization of clerking, the necessity of class struggle, and the ultimate success of socialism.

As these three organizational types emerged in the course of the later nineteenth century, they manifested some similarities. All identified themselves as associations for commercial assistants; their members were clerks in sales and office work. All developed a variety of self-help projects, turned to the state for legislative aid in pressing for reform, and favored legislation as the means to expand educational opportunities and improve work conditions.

How were women to fit into these organizational and ideological frameworks? Although male clerks denied women entry into their organizations, this did not leave female clerks without resources, for they found strength of their own in two revitalized and self-confident women's movements. Taking the analyses first articulated by male clerks and using their organizations as models, women built their own powerful clerks' associations or, in the Central Alliance, worked with the men.

Aware as they were that their members benefited from the "economic developments" to which the men so frequently referred, and having a feminist perspective, leaders of the all-female organizations had no cause to quarrel with industrialization or to reject the analyses of liberal or progressive social reformers. Female clerks' organizations drew upon estatist ideology in its less conservative form and attempted to ally both with male colleagues and with other women. Women in the socialist Central Alliance, on the other hand, relied on the economic analyses of Marxism and socialist feminism. But as each group undertook the struggle for equal employment rights and opportunities, female clerks learned that the issues of women and clerks could not always be resolved together.

# 4

# Contending strategies for women: bourgeois and socialist organization and the analysis of home and work

The women's movements of all western countries at the end of the nineteenth century comprised a variety of organizations with varying activities and strategies, and whose goals were sometimes contradictory or even opposed. Still, only in Germany were there two complete women's movements, one self-defined as "bourgeois" and the other socialist, which traveled their respective tracks with little interaction or exchange other than mutual recrimination.[1] Just as the German socialist movement and its partner, the Free Unions, were regarded as models by sympathetic observers in other lands, so too was the socialist women's movement. It was not socialist feminists who involved themselves with clerks, however, but members of the bourgeois women's movement, which had long emphasized employment and education as areas crucial to the extension of women's rights.

## The bourgeois women's movement

Middle-class women first organized to improve the status of women in 1865, when the General German Women's Association (*Allgemeiner Deutscher Frauenverein* or ADF) was founded. The ADF was led by a group of German women who had been active in 1848, especially Luise Otto-Peters and Auguste Schmidt. From its inception, the association took up the issues of female education and female employment, the most pressing in the view of many middle-class reformers. Education and employment were appealing solutions to working-class need, since they focused on self-help. In addition, they appeared suitable to the circumstances of single or widowed "ladies" who faced extreme poverty owing to their incapacity to earn a living.

In a memorandum in 1865, Dr. Adolf Lette, president of the Central

39

Association for the Welfare of the Working Classes in Prussia and a reformer with ties to the ADF, argued that attention had to be paid to the plight of middle-class and upper-class women without means of employment. He suggested the creation of various schools of vocational education, including one for "scientific" subjects that would qualify women to work in medicine as "assistant physicians," midwives, and technicians. He did not, however, advocate granting young women an education equal to that of young men at the secondary and university levels. He also emphasized the limited nature of his vision: "What we do not want is the political emancipation and equality of women."[2] As a result of his efforts, the Association for the Promotion of the Employment Capabilities of the Female Sex (or Lette Association) was founded in 1866, supported by Crown Prince Friedrich and his wife Victoria, who felt that women should expand their role in public life, achieving this through improved education and employment.[3]

The Lette Association was similar to other educational and employment reform associations, many of which developed ties to the ADF. It functioned primarily by establishing private vocational day schools and schools of continuing education for girls and women. These held day, evening, and weekend courses in basic subjects (reading, arithmetic, penmanship), advanced subjects (foreign languages, literature), commercial subjects such as bookkeeping, and in trade subjects such as needlework. Some schools also offered evening socials with lectures or discussions, slide shows, etc. Their principle was self-help; some even stated explicitly that they intended no "emancipatory endeavors."[4] In addition to educational programs, the groups often established employment bureaus, and in 1869 the Lette Association was named the central agency in the field. Some branches also set up homes for working girls and women.[5]

The ADF had been founded at the same time as the Lette Association, and its founding congress also called for better educational opportunities for women and freedom of employment. It demanded better schools, various sorts of vocational training, and access to higher education. Its statutes also proposed "the liberation of female work from all the obstacles standing opposed to its development."[6] Nowhere did the ADF demand that women receive an education equal to that of men, nor did it advocate female entrance to the university. Convinced that men's assistance was essential, it allowed men to become members with a non-binding vote, and its founding congress also called for links to, or union with, male organizations. Within a few years, sixteen local member organizations had been founded, nine with an educational focus; some had ties to male-dominated educational associations such as the Lette Association.

The emphasis on education was closely linked to the perceived necessity of extending female employment. Education would allow women greater economic (though not political) opportunities: as Otto-Peters said in 1866, "The only emancipation that we pursue for our women is the emancipation of their work."[7] Industrialization had of course only begun. In its emphasis on female employment, the ADF therefore divided its attention between middle-class professional opportunities, especially in elementary school teaching and medicine, and working-class occupations such as craft work (especially the needle trades) or domestic service. Its activities in the 1860s and 1870s reflected this dual emphasis.[8]

In 1883 at its annual "Women's Day" convention, ADF leaders called for the establishment of legal aid societies, women's self-help organizations, and female employment associations, suggestions that foreshadowed feminist activities in the Wilhelmine era. By that date, however, the effects of Bismarck's anti-socialist legislation forced a lull in the German women's movement and such projects were largely stillborn. For the repressive laws created a climate in which existing limits on women's freedom of political assembly were interpreted more rigidly. The ADF and other women's associations existed upon the sufferance of government authorities and the police, with whom organizations were forced to register their membership and to whom they had to give advance notice of all meetings. Police officers often attended meetings, where they sat taking notes at the front of the room; they could declare an assembly dissolved prior to or during a meeting. Membership in the ADF fell in this period, and the association turned toward charity and welfare work.[9]

Wilhelm I's death in 1888 marked the end of this hiatus in feminist activities and the creation of a "radical" challenge to the ADF and to the policies of bourgeois feminism.[10] With the brief accession of Friedrich to the throne, liberal and reformist forces were unleashed which did not simply disappear upon his death three months later. Restrictions upon freedom of assembly and the anti-socialist legislation were less vigorously enforced. Liberal forces were also heartened when Wilhelm II forced Bismark's resignation in 1890 and proclaimed his intention to support social legislation.

During the first years of Wilhelm's reign, several new women's organizations were founded. A number of them asserted their difference from the older associations by calling themselves radicals. These radical feminists challenged moderate and conservative feminists by demanding equality for women in all areas of life and by seeking to mobilize women to work for social and political reforms rather than to be satisfied with mere welfare activities that did not touch the bases of inequality.[11] Other new organizations continued the

ADF's emphasis on education and employment, but with new goals of legal, institutional, social, and economic equality. The moderate ADF itself became for a brief period more radical.

Central among the new radical groups was Association for Women's Weal (*Verein Frauenwohl*), which began in Berlin. Originally a women's branch of the German Academic Alliance, it was headed by Minna Cauer, a newcomer to the women's movement, although she had long been politically active in progressive concerns.[12] In assuming the chair of Women's Weal, Cauer said that she wanted to "stimulate things,"[13] although at the time she believed that if women fulfilled their duties, "then the rights will automatically devolve upon us."[14] The new association sought first to extend female educational opportunities, including vocational training, and to expand female employment. These had also been the aims of the ADF. What was new was the spirit, the intent of mobilizing masses of women for women's issues, and the goal of full equality with men. One of the first steps taken by Cauer was to help a group of female clerks to establish their own employees' association.

Feminists founded an umbrella organization in 1894, the Federation of German Women's Associations, the BDF (*Bund Deutscher Frauenvereine*). Representing both radical and moderate feminism, the BDF originally had thirty-four member groups; within a year it contained sixty-five, with approximately 50,000 members. By 1900, delegates to the BDF convention resolved that the task of the organization was to work for the "social, economic, and moral liberation of the female sex."[15]

Earlier leaders of the bourgeois women's movement had sought to improve female education to solve the problems faced by single women. The bourgeois women's movement in the mid-1890s, on the contrary, emphasized social and economic issues as a means to achieve equality for women. As Cauer wrote in 1896, "it is not narrow and merely practical issues of employment that we must place at the center of things, but the elevation of the social position of women . . ."[16] In 1896 Berlin Women's Weal used the occasion of the Berlin Exposition to arrange an international women's congress entitled "Women's Achievements and Women's Endeavors." One day of the week-long congress addressed the issue of women's work, with papers on women's position in the labor force and their low rates of pay and on the importance of state-supported female vocational education. The congress called on feminists to organize working women into occupational associations.[17] The session on women's work marked bourgeois feminists' more subtle comprehension of the issues involved in promoting female employment. The decision to mobilize employed women indicates that bourgeois feminists had moved beyond welfare measures and individual self-help to a more realistic appraisal of the needs of women who worked outside the home and of the importance of large-scale agitation on social and political issues.

By the end of the 1890s, however, a division had arisen within the bourgeois movement. Moderates wanted the BDF to work within its traditional framework of increasing female employment opportunities, providing various social and legal services, and petitioning for social and legal reforms. Cauer and other radicals argued that a broad political struggle for women's rights was essential as well. The dispute concerned both tactics and aims. The moderates, especially the ADF, emphasized participation in community work, which would slowly bring women recognition and authority and finally political rights; the radicals aimed at mass mobilization through public meetings and demonstrations to agitate for equality and reform. Cauer herself had moved away from her earlier opinion that female fulfillment of duties would bring rights. "You shall find your rights through struggle," she now urged.[18]

Despite the sharp breach between the two, both the moderates and the radicals agreed upon the central importance of female work and the necessity of improved female education in order to enable women to gain employment and to further their professional careers, and both were sympathetic to professional organizations of women. Their educational demands now included improved secondary education, especially vocational training and a reorganization of upper girls' schools to make them equal to male institutions, and unrestricted female entrance to institutions of higher learning. In the sphere of employment, the movement demanded increased opportunities for women's professional employment and equal pay for equal work. Even the "charitable" activities denigrated by the radicals – but also carried on by them – involved efforts to work with, as well as for, women of all classes. Servants, domestic piece-workers, and industrial workers, as well as professional women and clerks, benefited from the efforts of German feminists, as they established homes, legal aid services, employment bureaus, day care centers, canteens, educational and vocational courses, and evening and weekend get-togethers. Feminists petitioned and agitated for better pay and working conditions, shorter work hours, improved insurance, employees' courts and chambers, female work inspectors and female physicians at clinics, and an end to sexual harassment at work and by the police. Moderates as well as radicals supported and were active in such programs.

Where they differed was in their ultimate goal. By the end of the 1890s, radicals saw all of these activities as part of an overall strategy to emancipate women and to reform German society in a progressive democratic direction. The moderates, on the other hand, tended to

believe that such a political program was Utopian and failed sufficiently to emphasize woman's unique nature and cultural role. They
were suspicious of popular agitation and any rapprochement with
socialism, and felt that women could make their greatest gains through
long-term community work.

Behind these activities and goals, however, lay attitudes that set
limits on their achievements. Like the members of women's movements in other western lands, German feminists shared a general
set of beliefs about woman's nature that was not clearly articulated
and that contained contradictory elements. They held that women
should be granted full rights because both they and men were the
same human beings. Yet they also stated firmly that women were
essentially different from – and in some ways superior to – men, and
that since the two sexes were complementary, rights must be granted
to women in order for society to function successfully. Their belief
in innate differences led German feminists to combine their insistence
upon women's equality in education and in the labor market – in
the public sphere – with arguments that women had a special duty
in the private, domestic sphere.

Although feminists accepted woman's distinct nature, they sought
to redefine the limits placed upon her role. They granted the existence
of separate public and private spheres, but insisted that the two over-
lapped and that the womanly tasks of the private sphere extended
beyond the individual household and family. Given the changed circumstances of the late nineteenth and early twentieth centuries, feminists argued, women could no longer be confined at home, where
there was less and less for them to do. Instead they had to take their
particular female qualities – nurturance, patience, virtue – and introduce them into the public sphere through their employment and even
through socio-political activities. Like feminists abroad, German feminists argued that by bringing their maternal qualities to public life,
women would help the economy, create new values, and contribute
in a unique way to the national culture, complementing those contributions made by the other sex with its different nature.[19]

German bourgeois feminists agreed with their opponents that marriage was a woman's highest calling; only a few exceptional women
of talent could serve society to an equal extent in another role. Rather
than discussing whether a woman was justified in remaining single
when she could marry, German feminists asserted that an "excess"
of middle-class German women of marriageable age existed in the
population. Older single women, therefore, were those who *could
not* marry. But they were not to be treated with scorn: by engaging
in tasks of social motherhood, by using their innate feminine talents
for the good of their nation, single women also fulfilled their calling.

Throughout the international women's movement before World War I, the argument for women's rights based on sexual difference coexisted with one based on human equality. Certain feminists emphasized one or the other argument, but clear-cut camps cannot be identified, for the same advocate often called upon both themes. It is a mistake to hold that only conservative German feminists asserted sexual difference or that by asserting it, German feminists distinguished themselves from those in Britain or the United States. Indeed, if anything, German bourgeois feminists appear to have been more far-sighted than English and American women in the emphasis that they gave to paid female employment, insisting that it fostered individual growth and was essential to justify and underpin the extension of female rights. No other country was so successful in mobilizing large numbers of employed women in the feminist cause.

Writings by German bourgeois feminists, both moderate and radical, show clearly that both factions saw women as different from men and in some senses superior. This is so despite the fact that radical feminists *also* demanded female emancipation on the basis of Enlightenment arguments about human equality.

Helene Lange, moderate head of the ADF, stated bluntly that

today the women's movement proceeds to justify its demands with full awareness of the fact that there is a universal physical and intellectual difference between the sexes. From this fact it follows that only in mutual activities based on equality between men and women can all possible cultural progress be realized, that only in this way can a fully human culture develop out of a predominantly male culture.[20]

This did not however mean that women should be excluded from the political arena. When Minister of the Interior Count Posadowsky stated in 1904 that women should not gain political rights, Lange labeled such sentiments "male logic" and asked how women were to represent their occupational interests without engaging in political activity.[21]

Just as moderate feminists agreed that women should play a political role in order to obtain their goals, radical feminists also held that women were essentially different from and in many ways superior to men. Minna Cauer spoke of equality of rights as "desirable for the maintenance of order, manners, and morality."[22] That is, women had innate character traits that would improve society if women gained equality. Other radical feminists agreed. Frieda Radel, in a leaflet demanding women's suffrage, argued: "Woman is called to reintroduce the ethical, ideal element, to give politics once more that wide vision which leads beyond the petty struggles of parties of different hues to the solution of social and cultural problems."[23]

Women were not only more ethical, but they had a special domestic role. Minna Cauer wrote in the 1890s, explaining the goals of the German women's movement, that "the leaders emphasize over and over again that they regard the profession of housewife as one of the highest and most noble of women's life tasks . . ."[24] The International Women's Congress organized by the BDF in Berlin in 1904 included a lecture in the series on women's education on "The Profession of Motherhood."[25]

It was of crucial importance that the German bourgeois women's movement accepted the notion that women had certain innate character traits and instincts different from men and that therefore women alone were responsible for the private sphere of the home. It meant that efforts to gain equality for women in the public sphere were not balanced by any analysis of the need to reform the private. Radical feminists hinted that women could successfully combine home duties and employment, but the question of how was left unanswered (reliance on servants lurked in the background). Moderates assumed that married women, unless forced by serious economic motives, would leave the work-force. The consequences of this acknowledged "dualism" in women's lives on their struggle for equality in employment were not analyzed.

## Socialist women organize

At the same time that middle-class German women were organizing, proletarian women were both forming their own groups and fighting for their right to join working men's associations. As early as 1865 women demanded membership in the educational association led by August Bebel, and his International Manufacturing, Factory, and Artisans' Union Cooperative was open to men and women on the same basis.[26] Acceptance of female equality remained however a minority position among working men. Far more held the Lassallean view that only men should work and that they should receive a wage adequate to support the family: "To assure the man the full reward of his work means, for us, the improvement of the situation of women."[27] Delegates to an 1868 Lassallean union congress argued that allowing women to join unions would permit them to compete with men in new job areas and that women were responsible for falling wages.[28]

Bismarck's anti-socialist legislation of 1878 drove both the socialist and the trade-union movements underground, where women founded unions and self-help organizations on a local basis, as well as working in alliance with men in underground labor groups.[29] With the end of the "exceptional laws" against socialism, the SPD became more actively engaged in women's issues. Although the laws of assembly prevented women from joining the Party, male leaders from the 1890s worked with a semi-autonomous women's group which had a good deal of freedom of action.[30] The 1891 Erfurt Program demanded both "universal, equal, and direct suffrage, with secret ballot for all citizens . . . without distinction as to sex" and the "abolition of all laws that discriminate against women as compared with men in the public and private legal sphere . . ."[31]

Party congresses addressed women's issues, such as protective legislation, the need for female factory inspectors, and equality in the new Civil Code. In 1894 the Party introduced a women's suffrage bill into the Reichstag. In 1896 it elaborated an eight-point program to improve the situation of women in the public sphere through an extension of worker protection, the granting of voting rights on industrial courts, equal political rights, equal education, freedom of occupation, equal legal status, and equal pay for equal work.[32]

Male trade unionists were more willing to accept women members after the lapse of the anti-socialist laws. Union membership had declined sharply, and the recession of 1891-95 led to a mood of pessimism in which any new members were welcomed. Further, the 1895 census had revealed the great extent of female participation in the work-force. A number of leading socialist women, including Clara Zetkin, emphasized union work, both because of the theoretical importance of female employment and because laws of assembly made explicitly political work difficult.[33]

Despite the increasing proportion of female members in Free Unions (8.8 percent in 1914), neither the majority of its leaders nor the predominantly male membership was committed to female equality within the movement. Only one woman was elected to the Free Union movement's governing General Commission at the first Free Union congress in 1892, Wilhelmine Kähler. She was re-elected in 1896, but failed to gain a seat at the next election in 1899, and from then on, although a number of women stood for election, none was elected to the Commission in all the years up until World War I.[34]

Male unionists viewed neither female leadership nor women's issues as important. The protocols and resolutions of congresses reveal that attempts to discuss topics important to female workers encountered apathy and hostility. As late as 1914, men at the ninth congress insisted that female employment was "dirty competition" and that it was "unnatural" for women to work outside the home. Women's lack of interest was continually cited and then used to rationalize lukewarm efforts to agitate among women workers. In 1905 a working women's secretariat of the General Commission was established, headed first by Ida Altmann and, after 1909, by Gertrud Hanna. Although greatly increasing female union membership, it seems to have failed to end male prejudices and stereotypes about women or to aid working women to take on leadership roles within their unions, let alone to achieve equality at work or at home.

Before World War I in Germany, the socialist movement made great advances in feminist theory. Socialist theorists followed Marx; however, although Marx alluded to the family and to women's oppression, women did not comprise a particular or independent conceptual category. Their oppression arose owing to class and property relations and was exactly parallel to that suffered by working men, children, or slaves.[35]

Socialist feminist theory in Germany was largely articulated by August Bebel and Clara Zetkin. Bebel had written the first Marxist analysis of women to appear, the 1878 bestseller *Woman and Socialism*. Zetkin, editor of the socialist women's journal *Gleichheit* and author of *Die Arbeiterinnen- und Frauenfrage der Gegenwart*, largely followed Bebel. They both placed women's emancipation within the framework of economic structures. In Bebel's eyes, "all social dependency and oppression has its roots in the *economic dependence* of the oppressed upon the oppressor."[36] Both Bebel and Zetkin believed that women suffered twofold oppression: they were economically and socially dependent on men in marriage; and working women, like working men, were economically dependent as exploited and oppressed wage laborers.

The authors assumed that employed women lost any gender distinction and took on the same class position as men. "From that day when woman threw off the yoke of economic dependence on the *man*," Zetkin wrote, "she fell under the economic sway of the *capitalist* ..."[37] Wage work would therefore end sexual oppression, while socialist revolution would end class oppression. Like the man, the free and equal woman of the future would live largely in the public sphere, freed from domestic tasks with the end of monogamous marriage and owing to technological inventions such as modern and centralized kitchens and to universal child care and education.[38]

For socialists, the end was in sight, for women were by 1900 already leaving the domestic sphere as capitalism, with its drive to reduce wages, made paid work outside the home essential for an increasing number of married women.[39] As Zetkin argued, "woman herself gained from this ability *to live without the man*, it gave the *woman for the first time the ability for a completely independent life*." Clearly, women's paid employment was to be encouraged, as was public intervention in domestic tasks. Working women and men could then struggle together to overthrow capitalism and establish socialism, which alone would free them both.[40]

Socialist agitation therefore concentrated on women's public role.

Female wage labor would free women from family dependence, end female "sex-slavery," and place women in a common position with male workers, whence they would recognize their class interests and press for revolution. Socialist feminists ignored the subordination of women within the working-class family and the burden of their domestic tasks, which they assumed arose from the division of labor within the home, but would end as women became workers. Socialist feminists relied on a sort of industrialization of domestic life, through which its routines and responsibilities would be removed to the public sphere. Like monogamy, the family would wither away after the revolution. Therefore, although both Bebel and Zetkin insisted that women had been educated and socialized to play a subordinate role, neither they nor other socialist feminists analyzed the problems faced by proletarian women in the private sphere. Large-scale domestic services, such as central dining facilities, never became a serious socialist issue.

Nor were steps taken to rectify women's passive and subordinate status in working-class organizations. Accepting the orthodox position that the ultimate solution to female subordination lay in socialist revolution and that economic independence would free women within capitalism, socialist feminists had no basis on which to analyze the second-class status of working women. The fact that working women did not face problems identical to those of working men was implicitly recognized when leaders discussed the difficulty of organizing working women and women's desire to marry and leave the work-force. Leaders invariably assumed that the problem stemmed from women's "slavery in the home"; but since the form of the family was determined by social forces, the difficulty would disappear with socialism. Socialists contended that women accepted domestic slavery because they saw themselves as women rather than as workers. The solution therefore was to agitate and organize them as workers in unions; developing their sense of class consciousness and solidarity would combine personal independence and self-assertion.[41]

Although within the Social Democratic Party socialist feminists insisted upon a measure of autonomy, within the unions they were unwilling to organize special programs to develop women's self-esteem or ability to assert themselves. Few of the aids offered by bourgeois women's groups were made available to working women. Zetkin and other socialist leaders proved hostile to attempts to offer women special services (such as women's columns in union papers or all-female union schooling) that could result in more independent and assertive behavior. When, for example, Else Lüders – a left-liberal radical feminist – offered a series of educational proposals to feminist unionists, she met withering criticism.[42] Lüders noted that during a discussion class at the Berlin Workers' Education School, the women had "shyly and quietly held back" and not once taken part. On the basis of this observation, Lüders proposed special discussion courses for competent trade-union women, to be taught by a woman with solid socio-economic knowledge and skilled in "the tools of running an association" and including small-group involvement. Lüders also suggested that union papers include a "woman's corner" in order to increase female interest in union affairs, covering topics such as union work, public affairs, and working women's lives.

For the socialist women, such an approach threatened permanent second-class status. Ida Altmann, head of the women's secretariat of the Free Union General Commission, responded with sarcasm and hostility toward any hint of separatism within the unions.

Union women's courses are supposed to be necessary to overcome the shyness of working women. The wonder of this logic! Because "thousands of years of educational mistakes," deficient education, deficient equality – i.e., exactly because of the separation of human communities on the basis of sex – have made women shy, shyness will be fought by again practicing separation on the basis of sex . . .[43]

Women who learned to speak in small groups at women's courses, Altmann contended, would once again fall silent in a larger circle containing men. Likewise, a "woman's corner" in newspapers would encourage women to read only that and would reinforce men's prejudices that women's affairs were of little importance and only for "dumb dames." The two sexes would lose any chance of "mutual understanding" or sense of the identity of their needs and goals. Clara Zetkin had responded in a similar way in 1897 to Lily Braun's suggestion for women's agitation groups. "The task of the socialist women's movement," she maintained, "should be to awaken female proletarians to class consciousness, to tranform them from any indifferent or obstructing force to a propelling one, to educate them to become conscious socialists."[44] Party and Free Union women, then, were to work in solidarity with male colleagues and to attempt to raise the level of class consciousness among women, enlisting them in the ranks of the socialist movement. This alone would lead to human – including female – emancipation.

## Relations between bourgeois and socialist feminists

Since radical bourgeois feminists had come to believe that social and economic issues – and not simply lack of work and education – were central to female inequality, a number of radical leaders sought contact with socialist women. In 1899 a national Women's Weal convention rejected the notion that a split should exist between middle-class and working-class women and sought to win working women to its chapters and to work with blue-collar organizations.[45] At the same time, however, even the most sincere radical women held rather patronizing views of working-class women. Minna Cauer wrote in her diary in 1896: "We must, as the cultured and better-advantaged, understand the struggle of those lower [down the social scale than us] and build bridges by dealing with [the socialist women's] demands in an understanding way ...,"[46] which betrays a certain tone of *noblesse oblige* from which bourgeois feminists were never able to free themselves. Indeed, they did not seem to be aware of their patronizing attitude. On balance, the bourgeois radicals seem to have been critical of capitalism, concerned with the plight of working-class women, but far from seeking an egalitarian "sisterhood" that might abolish a stratified society.

By 1900 the entire bourgeois women's movement was considering an alliance with socialist feminists, both because of individual feminist efforts and because the SPD was the only political party consistently championing female equality. At meetings between 1900 and 1905, bourgeois feminists debated working with socialist women and with blue-collar women.[47] At its 1905 convention, the BDF resolved that members had a duty to spread the ideas of the women's movement to all classes and groups and to develop the concept of a solidarity of interests among all women.[48]

But difficulties stood in the way of working together. Socialist leaders, in particular Clara Zetkin, opposed cooperation with the bourgeois women's movement. Middle-class feminists were supposedly interested solely in charity and welfare work within the capitalist order. In 1896 Zetkin spoke in Berlin at the public meeting called by socialist feminists as a counter to the bourgeois International Women's Congress taking place. She explained that while socialist women and bourgeois social reformers had many demands in common, socialists insisted on ending "the class-slavery of the proletariat." She insisted that "the lack of rights faced by women on the basis of sex is no bond that would be strong enough to close the yawning gap; the class interests stand above the sex interests." The bourgeois feminist goal of women's right to individual fulfillment, Zetkin felt, remained a chimera within capitalism. As she said in 1896, "The woman of the upper 10,000 is free because she possesses a fat purse; this purse allows her the possibility of developing her individuality, her skills in all areas of knowledge."[49] As another woman socialist wrote in criticism of the Hamburg ADF on its founding in 1896, "we want our rights, which is why we must join the fighting organizations of our male comrades and work with them side by side, so that we won't just place bandages on wounds, but rather that the social body will be healed thoroughly from the inside out."[50]

A second bar to cooperation lay in the unwillingness of female industrial and domestic workers to collaborate with bourgeois women when they attempted to organize them, which can be traced both to their sympathies toward socialism and socialist trade-unionism and to the structural problems inherent in home-based employment.

Finally, moderates within bourgeois feminism remained suspicious of socialism. Anna Pappritz at the 1904 Women's Congress could "recognize the services of social democracy, but declared that the basis of the bourgeois women's movement was to work within the existing state."[51] Gertrud Bäumer contended in 1905 that, although the German women's movement should ideally be unified, socialist women made this impossible by placing class struggle above feminist unity, thereby ignoring women's need to work together for particular female interests,[52] a charge that was certainly correct.

For middle-class feminists, the failure to engage in common work with socialist women meant that they were never forced to analyze class as opposed to sex as a cause of the discrimination faced by women, nor were they challenged to overcome their acceptance of a hierarchical social ordering with different privileges assigned in accordance with rank. Socialist feminists, for their part, never acknowledged causes of women's oppression that were not based on economic dependence.

Two competing feminist theories and two rival women's movements thus contended in Germany. Both emphasized reform of the public sphere of work and politics, but they developed quite different views on female employment and its role in women's emancipation. Neither theory devoted more than rudimentary analysis to the private sphere of marriage and family, but implicit in the bourgeois tenets was an evaluation of domestic life as central to a woman's being, while socialist feminists clearly expected it to disappear. Neither perceived the interaction between the public and the private, between women's lives at home in the family and abroad at the workplace. They both expected the transformation of the public sphere to carry over into the private and were optimistic about the possibility of that public transformation occurring. Organizations of working women were an obvious place to turn theory into practice.

# 5

## Putting bourgeois feminism into practice: the founding of all-female clerks' associations

### The first associations

In February 1889 an advertisement, placed in a number of Berlin newspapers, sought "all ladies who are employed at a fixed salary as office workers, cashiers, saleswomen, directresses, expediting agents, etc., and who would like to participate in founding an aid association . . ."[1] The result was the first female clerks' group, the Aid Association for Female Salaried Employees in Commerce and Trade. The organization provided a model for future organizing and became a bulwark of the female clerks' movement. The radical feminist Minna Cauer was active in its creation, as was Julius Meyer, a bank clerk who participated in a variety of progressive issues.[2] This relationship to the bourgeois women's movement affected both the tactics and the goals of the association.

When the Clerks' Aid Association was officially founded in Berlin in May 1889, it had already recruited 600 members. Its board was headed by Meyer and Cauer and contained a number of businessmen and merchants, including representatives of the local chamber of commerce, and a sizeable number of businessmen were extraordinary members who contributed talent or funds. Regular membership was limited to female clerks and educated craftswomen (seamstresses, directresses, draftswomen, etc.).[3] By the end of the first year, the association had enrolled 1,147 regular members.[4]

After a few years of local activity, the Berlin organization began working to establish clerks' associations in other German cities. Cauer traveled extensively in order to expand the organization, as did Agnes Herrmann, one of the few leading officials who was herself a clerk. Josef Silbermann, a man active in progressive circles who served as general secretary after 1895, took part as well. In founding a new local group, the visitor first sought persons in the area willing to work actively; often feminists or local philanthropists volunteered. After speaking at a public meeting on a topic of interest to female clerks, interested women were recruited on the spot by arranging an organizational meeting and asking new members to serve on the executive board.[5]

Feminists in cities throughout Germany also acted independently to establish clerks' associations, sometimes using the Berlin Clerks' Aid Association as a model.[6] In Frankfurt Friederike Broell, a clerk active in the BDF, presided over an organization founded in 1895.[7] In Cassel in 1897 Johanna Waescher, a feminist and the wife of a local merchant, organized and led a local group.[8] In Königsberg Eva von Roy, active in the local Women's Weal, established a clerks' association that same year.[9] In Munich, a bookkeeper established a local group, which then sought affiliation to the BDF.[10] Once they had taken root, many groups then expanded to nearby towns, as the Berlin association had.[11] By 1900 there were at least twelve independent female clerks' associations in cities throughout Germany.

In Hamburg a leading radical feminist, Lida Gustava Heymann, founded an important all-female clerks' association. A woman of independent wealth, she sought to realize the feminist principle of sisterhood by providing services for young working women. Her first effort, a lunch room in her home, served an average of 170 girls each day by 1899. She then added bathing facilities, a library and reading room (complete with piano), and "evening socials" twice a week. Most of the young women who came regularly were salespersons, which may have encouraged Heymann to turn her attention to clerks.[12]

In late 1897, Heymann decided to found a clerks' organization, whose model was to be the Berlin Clerks' Aid Association. The new group, Industria, was open to men and women interested in supporting "female white-collar workers in commerce and trade," and actively sought the participation of female clerks.[13] The organization offered members career advice and information, employment listings, courses, lectures, and reduced-price admissions to cultural events. Its goals were similar to those of the Berlin Clerks' Aid Association and emphasized solidarity as well as self-help, asserting that "through courses, lectures, entertainments, etc., it hopes to make members more competent in fulfilling their professional obligations, and to bring them closer together on a human level."[14] The statutes established a new category of membership, so that women without the necessary professional qualifications to join could become social members, indicating Heymann's deep desire to foster solidarity among women of different classes. By the end of 1898, 284 persons

had joined Industria, and a year later membership stood at over
400.

Feminists were also influential in the establishment of local Roman
Catholic clerks' associations, but Catholic organizations also emerged
from lay and clerical efforts to counter the SPD and the Free Unions
and to maintain the spiritual and political allegiance of the Catholic
population. In the 1880s and 1890s, Church-led workers' groups were
established within an organization named Workers' Weal, which
emphasized self-help and developed a bureau for "social welfare,"
intending to found groups for servants and shop assistants as well
as for workers.[15] Craft Associations also dated from this period, which
had close ties to the Church hierarchy, as did the less conservative
Christian trade unions, which sought Protestant members and tried
to limit clerical control.[16]

A more political Catholic organization, the People's Association for
Catholic Germany (*Volksverein für das katholische Deutschland*), was
founded in 1890. It used modern techniques of agitation and soon
had a powerful mass base. The People's Association was strongest
in the Rhineland and was associated with the "Cologne wing" of
lay Catholicism that favored social reform. Activists from Workers'
Weal participated in the People's Association, as did Reichstag deputy
Trimborn, who formulated the new organization's goals of countering
the SPD and furthering "proper" social relations, which recognized
that employers and employees had common interests and a relationship of mutual duties.[17]

The People's Association, modern as it was in its political methods,
held that women's primary duties lay in the home. This led to difficulties with the Catholic Women's Federation, founded in Cologne in
1903 on the initiative of a local women's organization in which Frau
Trimborn was an active member. The group believed that the
"healthy" ideas of the German women's movement should be
accepted and adapted to Catholicism. Geared to middle-class and
upper-class women, the Federation emphasized female education, the
equality of women in employment, and women's role in public life.
It distanced itself from the secular bourgeois women's movement and
refused to join the BDF, but worked with it on specific issues, such
as female education.[18]

The first Catholic female clerks' associations must be viewed within
the context of these Catholic endeavors. The Alliance of Female Commercial Assistants of Mönchen-Gladbach was founded in 1893, and
a similar group was created in Cologne in 1894.[19] The Cologne
Alliance, founded by the Cologne Catholic women's organization,
grew out of a home for salesgirls. A cleric headed the new Cologne
clerks' association, but Frau Trimborn was a leader in its affairs.[20]
Within a few years, a number of local groups had been founded,

especially in western Prussia, the same area in which the People's Association and the labor groups were active. All had clerical leadership and were aided by highly placed Catholic women. Non-clerks always remained a strong presence in local chapters, to a much greater degree than in the secular organizations. In 1905, for instance, 610 female clerks were members of the Cologne Association, with 310 supporting and honorary members. The executive board was composed of "eleven commercial assistants and in addition five ladies and gentlemen."[21]

In 1901 the local associations banded together as the Collective Alliance of Female Catholic Commercial Assistants of Germany. Like the secular groups, the Catholic Alliance favored self-help and support services for its members, establishing an employment listing and a health insurance plan. Like the secular groups, most chapters established employment listings and courses for their members and worked on issues such as eight o'clock store closing. Occasionally, chapters campaigned on a particular issue in conjunction with local secular clerks' groups. The locals were also centers for social activities. Unlike the secular associations, many activities had religious goals; some of the locals, indeed, were Marian Societies for clerks, and meetings were frequently planned after mass.[22] Yet the Catholic groups too had some feminist goals, for they sought female equality in employment and attempted to educate women clerks about the principles of Roman Catholic feminism.[23]

The Catholic Alliance faced a problem not experienced by the secular female clerks' groups, for it had been organized for and remained committed to the support of Catholic religious values. The tension between the contemporary values of Roman Catholicism and the goals of the bourgeois women's movement, however, led the Catholic Alliance to offer feminism but tepid support. Alliance leaders agreed that trends in modern society had changed the nature of housework and created a new positive valuation of individual freedom and fulfillment. They asserted that these developments, coupled with the demographic fact that not all women could marry, had created a climate in which women sought new employment opportunities and demanded access to educational institutions. The Catholic Alliance journal registered its support for many demands of the women's movement and favored "granting women all the rights and duties that men have, and taking all means of education as aids" in the task, so that women could eventually be active in public life and the professions on a level of equality with the men.[24]

The demands of secular feminists for equal education and free choice of profession were, however, only accepted as legitimate "within the natural limits of the female," and political emancipation for employed women only was deemed "theoretically justified, although far off in practice."[25] The Catholic Alliance did not consider equal pay for equal work a valid demand, arguing that women's lesser strength, lower "resistance," and lesser motivation for professional excellence would always exist. Nevertheless, employed women had the right to equal vocational training and should organize to represent their interests to overcome "artificial" pay differentials.

Although they seemed at first sight to be little more than friendly societies, local organizations of female clerks were feminist in their activities and agitation, their theoretical orientation, and the goals toward which they worked. The secular groups worked closely with local feminist educational and social groups and with national organizations such as the ADF, Women's Weal, and the BDF.[26] The Catholic Alliance worked with Catholic women's groups and with the Catholic Women's Federation. Active feminists such as Minna Cauer, Eva von Roy, and Frau Trimborn led associations while working to bring clerks into the leadership. Leaders who were themselves clerks participated in feminist campaigns. Issues of the women's movement became clerks' issues, and questions that clerks raised were taken up by the bourgeois women's movement. This clear interrelationship remained until 1906, when the Berlin organization, the largest and most important group, insisted that professional unity took precedence over women's solidarity, splitting the secular women clerks' movement into two rival factions. Until that time, the partnership between bourgeois feminists and clerks' organizations raised hopes that it could succeed in improving the work conditions of female clerks, increasing their feminist awareness and elevating the status of women in Germany as a whole. Only after 1905 were feminists forced to moderate these ambitious goals.

### Female clerks' associations and their feminist allies: campaigns for improved working conditions

By the close of the 1890s, spurred on by the radical women's movement, clerks' organizations had moved beyond the concept of individual self-help to that of solidarity and representation of professional interests. Public pressure and legislative reform were perceived to be essential, and leading women's organizations collaborated with clerks' groups on a number of issues to mobilize public opinion.

The earliest campaign co-sponsored by clerks and other feminists sought a law requiring shop owners to provide chairs for salespersons. This campaign began in Berlin in 1896 when representatives of local feminist organizations (led by Women's Weal and including the Berlin Clerks' Aid Association) joined together to demand seating for saleswomen. They sought both voluntary compliance by shop owners and legislation. They directed their appeals to women, who were asked to sign a petition supporting the right of saleswomen to sit when they were not waiting on a customer.[27] From Berlin other cities picked up the issue. The Health and Welfare Committee of Hamburg's ADF introduced the tactic of boycott, circulating a petition stipulating that the undersigned would only shop in stores that had adequate seating. The ADF insisted that "only through ladies, as consumers, showing a lively and continuous interest in the well-being of saleswomen can they fulfill their social duty to these sisters of sex . . ." By May over 5,000 persons had signed.[28]

Legislation followed, both an ordinance in 1896 and an amendment to the Industrial Code in 1900. But even when legally required to install seating, most stores either failed to provide chairs or had policies forbidding employees to use them. Feminists began new petition drives, and in 1902 the BDF Commission for Clerks recommended that German women only buy in stores with adequate seating. Representatives of female clerks' associations spoke at the BDF convention. Friederike Broell insisted that women's groups had to work actively for the cause to prevent reprisals, and delegates responded by passing a motion that BDF member organizations work to guarantee seating for saleswomen.[29]

This issue was later often joined to demands for male and female "commercial inspectors," whose work would parallel that of factory inspectors, and to campaigns for an earlier store closing and a shorter workday. Unlike the campaign for seating, the issue of early shop closing had been raised by male clerks' organizations, and in many cities committees for early closing were established with members of both sexes. When female clerks' associations took up the issue, however, they again allied themselves with the women's movement.

The Berlin Clerks' Aid Association began a campaign for earlier shop closing in 1897. The strategy of the campaign, which asked store owners to sign a petition in favor of an eight o'clock store closing, was to show both shopkeepers and government authorities that a majority of store owners favored earlier closing hours.[30] At the same time, consumers' societies organized a campaign, supported by the bourgeois women's movement, urging consumers to "buy before eight p.m." (later this was tied to an appeal not to buy on Sundays). Female clerks' associations publicized the demand and sought allies among feminists in other organizations and in other cities.[31]

In the campaigns for seating and earlier shop closing, organizations of the bourgeois women's movement allied themselves with women clerks' associations, and women were reminded of their ability to unite across class lines. Married homemakers were asked to help employed women out of a sense of solidarity. Other campaigns had a broader thrust, explicitly connecting the problems and inequalities faced by employed women to the general status of women in German society. They were more radical in their potential, for they did not simply ask women to unite on issues not directly affecting them, but demanded that women recognize that all members of their sex suffered from the same discrimination and injustice.

*Female clerks' associations and their feminist allies: discrimination facing clerks and all women*

The most radical campaign of the Berlin Clerks' Aid Association was directed against sexual harassment on the job. Leaders in female clerks' associations joined other feminists to focus public awareness on the issue and to press for legal and social reform. Sexual and moral issues had become well-articulated planks of the radical feminist program by 1896.[32] From a focus on prostitution, their interest broadened to include the issue of sexual harassment at work, so that the radical association Youth Protection, headed by Hanna Bieber-Böhm, began to offer legal aid to employees who experienced harassment. In 1897 alone, six cases were brought to court in Berlin.[33]

Agnes Herrmann, secretary of the Berlin Clerks' Aid Association, also took up the question. In a prominent progressive journal she described the difficult situation female employees faced with sexual harassment. Since a civil suit for insult was their only legal recourse, women usually either tolerated employers' advances or quit work, thereby losing their source of income and the chance to obtain a favorable reference. Herrmann contended that sexual harassment was not an "uncommon exception" on the job although the public remained unaware because women clerks feared publicity and because, witnesses not usually being present, there was often no evidence besides the victim's word. She demanded that harassment become a criminal offense like rape.[34] That same year, Herrmann spoke at the International Women's Congress in Berlin on the working conditions of female clerks, stating that they were subject to "immoral attacks on the part of numerous superiors."[35]

By 1897 the Berlin Clerks' Aid Association was taking active steps against sexual harassment. Firms whose managers or owners were suspected of improper behavior were removed from its employment list,[36] and the association journal discussed methods of dealing with the problem and reported harassment suits brought against employers.[37] The association also offered the services of its legal bureau to press civil suits against offenders. The issue was a volatile one, however. When one case was lost in court, Berlin newspapers seized upon it, confusing the Aid Association and Youth Protection and claiming rather hysterically that the clerks' group was a "workers' association with socialist tendencies."[38]

The "Köppen case" brought the issue of harassment to national attention. Here feminists, including leaders of the Clerks' Aid Association, linked the issue of prostitution to the general question of the status of women. The Köppen case began in late 1897 when the teenage daughter of a coachman was arrested by Berlin police on suspicion of prostitution after she had complained to them about being pestered by a man.[39] During her time under arrest, the girl was forced to submit to a medical examination for venereal disease, which very much distressed her. The bourgeois women's movement seized upon Frl. Köppen's experience, for it seemed to provide clear evidence that the indignities suffered by prostitutes were but an extreme example of the indignities faced by all women. Radical feminists also pointed to the teenager's working-class background, emphasizing the class prejudice that had led the police to discount her story (the socialist press did not take up the issue, merely commenting that such police behavior was to be expected in a capitalist state).[40]

To publicize the issues, Berlin Women's Weal called a public meeting in January 1898. Among the speakers was Frl. Markowsky, a clerk, who spoke on the topic of sexual harassment in the workplace. She claimed that "the gentlemen have persecuted the girls, often with immoral propositions" and she called upon married women to manifest greater support and understanding toward their working sisters. She concluded by demanding that the Criminal Code be changed to protect female clerks against harassment and to permit men and women to play an equal role in public life.[41]

The Köppen case soon moved beyond the morality issue, as it was bound to do once feminists connected prostitution, sexual harassment, and women's low status. Conservatives came to the defense of the police and of established policies. Feminists launched a petition to the Reichstag demanding legislation to raise the age of majority to eighteen (to protect teenage girls) and to amend the legal code to punish employers who sexually exploited or condoned the harassment of female blue-collar and white-collar workers and apprentices. Clerks' associations also held meetings to discuss the topic, with Minna Cauer warning of the "great moral dangers" present in clerking.[42] Although the Criminal Code was not changed, the revised Commercial Code of 1900 made employers reponsible for sexual harassment at the workplace and permitted victims to resign with several weeks' pay.

The Berlin Clerks' Aid Association continued to believe that harassment was regularly occurring and that women should be protected from it. The organization soon chose, however, to disassociate itself from the faction-ridden morality campaign and to withdraw public attention from the issue of harassment at the workplace. The issue was not dropped entirely, however, but rather kept within clerking circles.[43] In the following years, the journals of the secular clerks' associations reported cases of sexual harassment, and some groups, including Berlin, kept lists of undesirable employers. The journal of the Catholic Alliance also reported cases of sexual harassment, although this reflected the fears of the Catholic Church regarding the dangers faced by women in public life more than the concerns of the bourgeois women's movement. Besides reporting its existence and admonishing young women to be alert to its dangers, the Catholic Alliance did nothing.[44]

By the end of the 1890s, radical feminists and leaders of the clerks' associations sought not only social and economic reforms, but greater political rights for women as well. Feminists pressed for an end to the limits on the right of assembly,[45] and some radical feminists, including Minna Cauer and Lida Heymann, founded a women's suffrage movement. The demand for women's suffrage found a parallel in the demand by clerks' associations for female voting rights on commercial courts. Male clerks' organizations first proposed the creation of commercial courts in the 1890s, arguing that clerks should have access to a facility similar to the industrial courts that resolved disputes between workers and employers. In 1899, National Liberal leader Bassermann called for commercial courts, whose members, chosen by election, would represent clerks and employers in equal numbers. Once it appeared that the government was drafting legislation, the Berlin Clerks' Aid Association took up the issue so that women would not be excluded.[46] The organization demanded that women be granted both the right to elect members to the courts and the right to sit on the bench.

By 1903, feminists in and out of clerks' associations had mobilized to press for women's right to vote and sit on the courts. Suffrage organizations and local clerks' associations held public meetings at which they cited female clerks' disenfranchisement from the commercial courts as an example of the political powerlessness of women.[47] The more reticent Catholic Alliance supported the position of bourgeois feminists who favored female voting rights on the commercial courts and who opposed legal limits on women's right of assembly. Its journal argued that since the Commercial Code placed men and women on an equal footing before the law, female representation on the courts was the only just course and that limits on women's right of assembly limited their ability to work for their social and economic interests.[48] However, the organization took no steps beyond its expression of support.

In 1904 the legislation to set up commercial courts reached its third reading in the Reichstag, and feminists renewed their pressure by writing articles and sending petitions to the Reichstag and to the predominantly male German Alliance of Commercial Associations.[49] They asserted that women engaged in many important public activities and that men could not not represent women in public affairs. Women had shown their equality on the job and should therefore receive political rights on the courts. The German government, however, flatly informed the Reichstag that it would refuse any law that included female rights, for that would grant the principle of female political equality.[50]

The 1904 International Women's Congress, organized by the BDF, met in Berlin just as the Reichstag approved legislation establishing commercial courts that excluded women from voting rights. Agnes Herrmann explained the vote to the congress and predicted bitterly that women's exclusion would put them at "men's mercy."[51] While the Congress was in session, a nation-wide alliance of female clerks' associations called a mass meeting to demand voting rights on the courts. Feminists from Europe and America attended the meeting, chaired by Minna Cauer and Friederike Broell, and passed a resolution that women were fully competent to serve on the courts, declaring that "a decision that makes the right to vote dependent in a one-sided way on one's sex must further be viewed as a clear expression of an inferior evaluation of the German woman."[52]

Throughout 1904 and 1905, female clerks' associations and feminist organizations continued to agitate on the issue. Some local groups used women as experts to bring testimony before the courts,[53] when municipalities allowed, but that was the extent of female participation on the commercial courts until the Weimar Republic.

## Women's interest in the all-female clerks' associations

By 1905 there were at least thirty-five female clerks' associations with approximately 17,600 members, and within ten years the number had doubled.[54] These are surprising figures in light of the oft-stated reluctance of women to join labor unions and the accepted difficulty of organizing white-collar workers. One important factor stimulating white-collar organization is the concentration of employees,[55] but in pre-1914 Germany most women were employed as clerks in small firms. What factors, then, influenced women to join a clerks' association, granting that many joined a group only to drop out shortly afterward?[56]

There were a number of objective factors hindering female participation in clerks' associations. Women were not concentrated in the workplace (with the exception of department-store sales personnel). Their long work hours gave them little time to make contact with organized colleagues, to attend meetings, or to participate in organizational activities. Difficulties also arose because of the public disapproval faced by young women who attended meetings at restaurants or taverns or who travelled home from meetings alone late at night. Although quite a number of businessmen viewed clerks' associations with favor or took a neutral stance, many were opposed to employees' organizations, especially small shop owners in the food and tobacco trades where many saleswomen were employed. Hence, female clerks often justifiably feared loss of employment should they join a clerks' association.[57]

To some, this direct threat to their livelihood was coupled with a less tangible political threat. Although female clerks' associations repeatedly avowed their apolitical stance, their activities included legislative demands, placing them within the broad definition of political associations which it was illegal for women to join before 1908. Throughout the period, clerks' groups were supervised and sometimes harassed by the police.[58] Seeing a policeman take notes of speakers' points and knowing that details of the association were filed at police headquarters would daunt many a young clerk, even a woman with high motivation.

Besides such external factors, there existed many reasons within the clerks themselves, in their socialization, in their sense of identity, and in their expectations, which hindered their ability to organize.[59] Parents commonly showed no sympathy for any attempts made by their daughters to improve themselves professionally, since they expected the girls to marry and leave the work-force after a brief period of employment. Young clerks themselves often viewed their occupational life as a transitory stage preceding marriage. In speeches, articles, and even leaflets, organization leaders complained about women's lack of any "professional consciousness," which led women to tolerate low pay, routinized work, and wretched work conditions.[60] Clerks might complain of their miserable circumstances, but leaving the work-force remained the solution for many, rather than refusing to accept such employment or joining an organization to agitate for change.

Many young women clerks might also have found the leadership and goals of clerks' associations unattractive because leaders were so different from them. Members were young and planned to marry. By contrast, women in executive positions were aging and single. For the women who became involved with female clerks' associations before 1900 often remained as leaders into the Weimar Republic, and married women were rare within the leadership except in Catholic groups.[61] The organizations tried to minimize conflict by challenging the stereotype of the eccentric spinster. They attacked the notion of the "old maid" and contended that womankind had to be freed from the "ominous" image of a woman in "old-fashioned clothing and of a peculiar, uncertain appearance, whose femininity has a somewhat ridiculous effect, who passes her life uselessly and without satisfaction and who, intellectually dull, lives without noble human goals."[62] Despite their efforts to create sympathy for the career woman, at least some young women must have experienced difficulty identifying with organizations whose leaders were both older than they and had different life plans. At times they must surely have felt that the leadership did not understand their interests, priorities, or goals and that the leaders' emphasis on careers was not relevant to them.

A lack of organizational and of feminist consciousness often accompanied clerks' lack of professional consciousness. Young women clerks often did not feel any solidarity toward their female co-workers. Coming from a society marked by rigid class and status rankings, it is little wonder that the women had scant sense of female solidarity. Clerks from the "higher estates" shunned contact with women from "lower orders." One member noted indignantly that some of her colleagues would not attend association functions because "that wouldn't suit the ladies; they don't come to the sort of association activities where they come into contact with all the elements brought together by the association."[63]

To these obstacles must be added the fact that nineteenth-century women had had little organizational experience. Isolated in their homes and taught to shun any public role as inappropriate, young women found that organizational work in the public arena was alien and involved personal risk. To organize meant that some women had to assume responsible leadership positions, while the entire female membership was expected to decide policy issues and to speak out – to engage in forms of behavior that society deemed unladylike and aggressive.

Given the obstacles to organization, it is remarkable that so many young women did join clerks' associations. The primary motivation seems to have been the women's desire to gain individual help finding employment, for employment listings were the greatest single drawing card of the clerks' associations. Contemporaries were well aware of this,[64] and even the weakest clerks' associations, which offered their members little beyond entertainment, maintained employment lists. The opportunity to attend evening courses was an incentive to join for young women who sought to improve their vocational skills or their career opportunities. Courses were popular, most young women enrolled in subjects like stenography a keeping that could easily be learned,[65] indicating not so m fessional consciousness" as an individual desire improvement in job skills.

Support facilities were so central to the associations that members who did not use them sometimes felt cheated. One woman wrote to the Berlin Commercial Alliance that she wanted to resign her membership, having "no inducement to support the interest of your Association by paying the yearly sum of 26 M. I have scarcely used [the resources of] your Association in all the years, so I have had no advantage to speak of from my money."[66]

Social activities also offered a strong incentive to join. Members were always willing to serve on the associations' entertainment committees, and evening socials, holiday shows and parties, and weekend excursions were usually well attended.[67] Indeed, the leadership often complained that members were interested in nothing but entertainment, and that they expected the organization to offer benefits to them while doing nothing in return.[68] The desire for entertainment testified more to girls' wish for a circle of acquaintances than to a desire for escapist leisure, however. Instead of going to the cinema or window shopping, young women clerks relaxed with group activities such as hiking, visiting cultural or historic sites, and holding recitals, songfests, and parties.[69]

Since most women clerks were isolated at work, employed as they were in small firms or among a predominantly male staff, the associations provided one of the only ways of meeting other working women. Personal bonds seem also to have played a role in recruitment, for women sometimes joined clerks' groups owing to direct personal contact. Members of the publicity committee of the Catholic Alliance, for instance, sent leaflets about the organization to non-members, then visited the young women.[70] In all organizations, leaders rotated the duty of attending weekly get-togethers to introduce newcomers to members.[71]

The presence of older career women may have attracted some young clerks. As women with life-long careers, older single members were doubtless those clerks with the greatest interest in organizational activity and those with the greatest professional, feminist, and political awareness. They may not have provided most clerks with a role-model for future life, but they could nevertheless have served as guides for job behavior and life outside the family. Members were sometimes quick to rely on board members for advice and aid; the Confederation referred wryly to the frequency with which members "approached members of the board for help in all possible sorts of occurrences."[72]

Other factors could also counter at least some of the obstacles to membership. Despite the heated opposition of many businessmen toward clerks' groups, some business support did exist. Shop owners and other employers were active in local associations or supported them with donations, rebates, or by signing their petitions. Retailers' associations and chambers of commerce attended the conventions of female clerks' associations and publicly supported some of their demands. At times, community leaders, local philanthropists, and political figures espoused their cause as well. This lent an aura of respectability to clerks' associations and, along with leaders' disavowal of union tactics or direct political aims, helped to distance the associations from the taint of socialism, radicalism, and low status.

Although some parents did not encourage participation, others encouraged membership. Parents who were themselves in clerking or manual work were those most likely to favor their daughters' organizational activities.[73] Since blue-collar unions and male clerks' associations had long existed and had large followings, those parents were most able realistically to assess the benefits of a clerks' association for women. As a good proportion of girls entering clerking had fathers in blue-collar and white-collar fields, it is possible that at least a few daughters received sympathy and encouragement at home.

In addition, Catholic clerks had a religious motive for their membership. For some, joining the Catholic Alliance was indistinguisable from membership in a local girls' devotional society. For others, social or professional concerns no doubt weighed more heavily, with the religious bond merely reaffirming the social and cultural ties of Catholicism.

This is not to say that no young women joined a clerks' association for professional, political, or feminist reasons. About forty-five members, a good-sized audience, attended lectures on women in employment given in Hamburg.[74] Large numbers of women attended mass meetings demanding reforms such as shorter work hours or female participation on commercial courts. The evidence indicates, however, that the young women who overcame the many obstacles to membership in clerks' associations did so primarily for personal motives. Although they were joining feminist organizations whose leaders were aware of the need for wide-ranging reforms in German society, new young members seem to have thought less about broad social issues and more about their personal lives.

This discrepancy between the aims of the leadership and of the majority of the members suggests that the bourgeois women's movement faced a substantial difficulty in its attempt to win employed women to its cause. Simply to organize employed women was clearly not sufficient to raise their consciousness. Once organized, leaders had the task of developing a feminist awareness among members. Yet in an occupational organization, that could never be the primary goal. An examination of the work of the clerks' associations in the Wilhelmine era indicates that feminists had set themselves no easy task. Class and professional interests often clashed with the demands for unity among women. In the early years of the female clerks' associations, however, feminist aspirations predominated and feminist hopes ran high.

# 6

# Professionalization or feminism: alternatives facing female clerks' organizations in the new century

## Emerging tensions

As the all-female clerks' associations grew and gained self-confidence, their organizational goal of improving the circumstances of their members began to clash with their feminist goals of sisterhood across class lines and equality for all women. This occurred in particular owing to leaders' emphasis on a strategy of professionalization as the best means to improve women's position in clerking.

Leaders in clerks' associations drew on a number of sources to formulate their analysis. Both socialists and bourgeois feminists had noted that modern economic trends had removed productive work from the home, causing women to seek employment although they lacked the level of education and training that men had.[1] At the same time, leaders were impressed with comments by male clerks' associations about the changed nature of clerking at the turn of the century, especially the deskilling and routinization of tasks and the increased division of labor in the field. Male commentators blamed these changes on the too rapid expansion of office and sales work, which had allowed unqualified applicants to gain positions. They assumed that these "unsuitable elements" were female and lower class. Being poorly educated and improperly trained, the new employees were only capable of carrying out routinized, segmented work. With no professional standards, they were content with low salaries and demeaned the professional estate.[2]

The strategy of professionalization relied upon regulation of entry and on job control, both standard craft-union strategies. Leaders in female clerks' associations accepted the need to prevent "unsuitables" from entering clerking and looked primarily to education to limit entry to the field. They insisted that girls successfully complete general and vocational programs and an apprenticeship before beginning employment and expected thereby to eliminate "unsuitables" and reduce the number of clerks. If professionalization succeeded, they believed that women in clerking would be so highly skilled that they would no longer be limited to routine, segmented tasks, and the status and pay of female clerks would rise.

Clerks' associations both pressed for legislation to ensure professional status for clerks and employed certification procedures themselves. Only girls passing an entrance examination were admitted to most of the commercial day schools established by the associations.[3] Many local groups imposed criteria for membership or for the use of their employment bureaus.[4] Self-help and support measures were now viewed by leaders in the clerks' associations – and by the women's movement in general – as tools through which to strengthen the organization and to professionalize clerking, and their range increased. Employment bureaus were now favored, for instance, because they served to attract new members and to prevent poorly trained women from applying for choice jobs and were a means to press employers for better pay and work conditions.[5]

Job counselling, a service offered both by feminist organizations and by female clerks' associations, also became part of the campaign to professionalize.[6] Middle-class feminists agreed that "unsuitable elements" should be guided away from clerking, while they laid great stress on the benefits of domestic service for working-class girls.[7] The Berlin Clerks' Aid Association instituted job counselling in 1894, clearly hoping to discourage unsuitable girls from clerking. Letters to local Evangelical ministers were followed by yearly appeals to elementary school principals. Soon the Berlin Association suggested that girls be directed elsewhere, claiming that there were excellent opportunities in craft work and in "well paid" industrial jobs. These less than subtle hints were followed in 1900 by booklets on occupational guidance that were distributed throughout Germany.[8] Parents' evenings were also held to discuss girls' employment opportunities. Both laid great stress on the importance of secondary education if a girl was considering clerking. Other local female clerks' groups embarked on similar programs.[9]

The shift away from self-help to professionalization led the Berlin Clerks' Aid Association to change its name in 1903 to the Commercial Alliance for Female Employees, announcing the change to members in a journal article entitled "Unity Gives Strength."[10] Insisting that leaders of the women's movement agreed with clerks' associations that only a strong professional organization could achieve better pay and working conditions for female clerks, Berlin now stressed that an individual's contribution lay in organizational support and adherence to professional standards. This would help women of coming generations and give the association a powerful position in public life.[11]

The Catholic Alliance joined the secular female clerks' association in its belief that professionalization was essential to improve the conditions of female clerks. Despite its interest in maintaining spiritual values, professionalization became an ever more important goal of the organization, to be achieved through better education and a stronger organization. By 1904 the Catholic Alliance identified itself as a "social union favoring reform legislation."[12] However, the Catholic Alliance was much more conservative in approach than were the secular associations. It engaged in little agitation, relying on the Center Party to represent its interests. Any activities that did occur were initiated by individual local chapters.

The strategy of professionalization was at once progressive and conservative. It was progressive in going beyond individual self-help measures and in seeking professional equality for female clerks, which would then provide a stepping-stone for more complete social equality. As Berlin's association wrote concerning its goals, it hoped to improve not only female clerks' employment situation, but also "to bring about the actual recognition of the complete equality of women's work."[13] But it was conservative in that both female and male clerks wished to elevate their estate at the expense of "unsuitables" from below who, in their view, were degrading the profession. Although middle-class girls were in reality just as likely to enter clerking with inadequate vocational training, association leaders always assumed that only working-class girls were unfit clerks. Agnes Herrmann argued that because daughters of the "higher estates" were not entering the profession, "capable personnel with good language competency . . . was lacking."[14] Even so radical a feminist as Minna Cauer shared this opinion. Speaking in Hamburg when Industria was founded, she argued that one problem faced by women in commercial life was that girls of all classes sought to enter the field.[15] The emphasis on professionalization therefore directed feminists working with women clerks away from their original avowal of sisterhood.

The emphasis created tension in another way as well. For legislation to improve the clerking estate came to seem more urgent to association leaders than did female solidarity and broad campaigns for equality in society. Leaders had to woo and bargain with male colleagues, as fellow members of the estate, in order to achieve goals of professional development, however hostile the men were to their female co-workers. Class as well as gender had become important to the analyses of the clerks' groups, so that sisterhood vied with estate

as tools to mobilize female clerks and to agitate for reforms. The ultimate result was a split in the ranks of the secular all-female clerks'
associations.

## *Gender versus estate: the creation of the Confederation of Commercial Associations and the transformation of the Berlin Commercial Alliance*

To the leaders of certain female clerks' associations, particularly the
Berlin Commercial Alliance, the strategy of professionalization suggested that allies from above had as little place as undesirables from
below. Where they had previously followed the male parity organizations and included clerks in a "commercial estate" that ranged from
apprentices and clerks to merchants, their new framework was drawn
from the activist DHV and assumed a "professional estate" of white-
collar workers alone.[16] As estate was reformulated, employers and
other non-clerks (including feminists) were perceived to have interests
different from or opposed to those of its members and could therefore
not be allowed a voice in the organization.

This new definition of estate led the Berlin Commercial Alliance
to sever its ties to businessmen allies and to feminist groups. In early
1905 employers were denied the right to sit on the executive board
and the statutes were altered to read that the Alliance was "an independent organization of clerks" – a clear indication that the group
planned to limit non-clerks' participation.[17] By 1907 it had become
a centralized "professional organization" composed only of clerks,
with the leadership seeking social reforms that would benefit all clerks,
male and female.

A number of factors motivated the Berlin Alliance to move away
from feminism and toward the notion of a professional estate, a shift
which prompted much debate.[18] The increasing number of women
clerks on Berlin's executive board gave weight to those who wanted
to focus on employment issues as against those who saw the Alliance
as a part of the radical women's movement and desired to emphasize
larger women's issues.[19] Since many feminists had come to hold that
organizational strength and agitation for reform were essential to help
women clerks, it followed that the larger issues would lose emphasis.

Leaders were also aware that contact with the radical women's
movement could hinder professional reform. Agnes Herrmann had
seen at first hand the danger of too close a link, for she and the
Berlin Clerks' Aid Association had faced a good deal of unfavorable
publicity in 1898/99 when its connection to Youth Protection and the
morality movement was exposed in Berlin newspapers. Attacks on
feminist leaders were frequent and intemperate. Identification in the
public mind of clerks' associations with radical causes – socialist as

well as feminist – meant that they would lose members and would not be taken seriously by the authorities, in which case they could not press for the reforms in education and work conditions that the leadership was coming increasingly to emphasize.

Class tension between working women clerks and well-to-do feminists also contributed to the shift, for it led to resentment and rejection of them as allies. In the period up to 1905 there had been a fruitful alliance between the two, both in executive and advisory positions and at the level of mass participation in campaigns to improve working conditions for sales clerks. Feminist leaders were quite concerned that they effectively aid and encourage working women; as Cauer remarked, they hoped "not to allow class differences to count."[20] But although some feminists insisted that occupational organizations be led by the employed women themselves, most middle-class activists still expected to play a role in the leadership of women's professional associations. When the BDF convention of 1900 entered into a long debate about the relationship between the women's movement and clerks, the head of its Commission for Clerks, Ika Freudenberg, urged the BDF to create a central organization for clerks' associations that would "rely on the bourgeois women's movement."[21]

Many female clerks appreciated the support they had received from the women's movement and accepted the leadership of bourgeois feminists. In 1903 a Königsberg clerk asked members to "think, my ladies, who called our group into life, who leads it? We ourselves cannot for various reasons; we lack influence, funds. It is people who have positions in society, who have money. They come without looking down on us ..."[22] Likewise, an anonymous clerk in Hamburg in 1905 defended the efforts of radical feminists "filled with true love of others." She insisted that "we employed women should support such people whenever we can, for they struggle for our rights as well."[23]

Tensions nevertheless arose between clerks and non-clerks in the secular organizations. Some clerks had always been suspicious of "better-situated" women, "society ladies" who, they believed, patronized and dominated them. Contacts between female clerks and professional women or women of independent means were sometimes quite bitter, although differences were minimized until 1906. In 1898 when Lida Gustava Heymann announced plans to establish Industria, an indignant young clerk wrote to a local newspaper that working women did not need outside help: "What then do the ladies think who foist themselves upon us ...? Are we so in need of saving, have we then no parents and other relatives ...? If they cannot help us, then neither can any philanthropist with soothing speeches and tea and cake!"[24] In 1907 an Alliance speaker commented bitterly: "Even refined ladies who fight in their associations for the moral protection of female clerks avoid any social contact with them."[25]

Even clerks who had worked closely with feminists from other classes could view them with suspicion. In early 1906 Paulina Franck, a Hamburg bookkeeper who had become chair of Industria, published an open letter to Anita Augspurg and other radical feminist leaders. Franck took this step after Augspurg published an Industria petition in *Frauenbewegung* with the editorial comment that she was "not responsible for its stylistic peculiarities." Deeply affronted, Franck asked:

What could lead Dr. Augspurg, a woman who seeks to occupy a leading position in the women's movement . . . to wound our sense of honor in such a way?
Even if we were truly not successful in meeting Frl. Dr. Augspurg's taste with our style, there was still not the least cause for her to take us to task in public. We clerks have certainly shown in our work that we have advanced beyond infancy and can indeed accomplish our own work without the help of influential and privileged ladies.[26]

Why indeed should Augspurg have insulted a group of women to whom she had earlier turned for support in her suffrage campaign? Her tactless comment can only be understood with an eye to the patronizing view held by middle-class feminists – despite their proclamations of female solidarity – toward working women of other classes. Even so tolerant a woman as Minna Cauer, writing in 1914 when she had moved quite far to the left, remarked in her diary that "one can essentially view [female clerks'] development only with joy. Wonderful, how these girls of the people and of simple schooling educated themselves in economic and legal affairs better than many women with the Ph.D."[27]

Finally, the presence of particular men in the leadership may have played a role in the board's decision to become an organization solely of clerks. After 1900, Franz Schneider joined the Berlin group after leaving the DHV; at the same time he began to work with the socialist Central Alliance. He took the notion of a professional estate from the DHV and combined it with Central Alliance stress on unionism and joint male–female organizations. By 1905, Schneider was arguing in the Commercial Alliance journal that a common male–female clerks' association must be the ultimate goal of those working to elevate the position of women in the estate.[28] Dr. Josef Silbermann may also have sought to change the direction of the organization. His writings indicate that he firmly believed it essential that economic and professional groups have their interests represented politically in order for national life to flourish.[29] In 1907 the annual convention of the Commercial

Alliance unanimously granted Silbermann life tenure as general secretary, a clear indication of his importance within the organization and a sign of the victory of his policies.[30]

Efforts to create a professional organization of clerks on the part of the Berlin Commercial Alliance and its predecessor, the Clerks' Aid Association, were coupled with attempts that began in the 1890s to centralize and to expand its influence throughout Germany. The change in name from Aid Association to Commercial Alliance in 1903 reflected in part its intention to expand beyond Berlin, and indeed from that date the organization began active measures to found chapters in other cities. Some independent associations of female clerks accepted Berlin's argument that organizational strength demanded unity, and they became affiliated. Hamburg's Industria became the Berlin Commercial Alliance, Hamburg Chapter, chaired by bookkeeper Paulina Franck, who had long been active in the organization.[31] Lida Gustava Heymann retired from the board, and the association office was moved from Heymann's home. By 1905 there were twenty-one chapters of the Berlin Commercial Alliance, with over 19,000 members.[32]

Although a number of independent groups were willing to accept Berlin's leadership, others valued their autonomy and had strong bonds with other local organizations. It sought to influence these associations indirectly. The first opportunity arose in 1901 when the Frankfurt female clerk's association called a conference to discuss merging employment services for clerks and uniting independent female clerks' organizations. The Berlin Clerks' Aid Association supported the idea on the assumption that it could dominate any national organization that might result. The fourteen groups present at the conference created the Confederation of Commercial Associations for Female Employees. Julius Meyer of Berlin headed the new organization, supported by Friederike Broell of Frankfurt, with Eva von Roy and Johanna Waescher among the board members.[33] Once founded, the Confederation pledged itself to work to improve female clerks' educational and employment opportunities, to encourage organization, and to work together on "issues of the estate." The great differences that existed among local groups in composition, tactics, and strategy resulted in a weak organizational structure, however, with Berlin unable to dominate. Each association kept its independence, sending delegates to yearly conferences solely to exchange ideas and discuss pertinent issues.[34]

As the Berlin Commercial Alliance moved to establish an organization composed solely of female clerks and expanded to accomplish this, relations with the Confederation of Commercial Associations became strained, for a majority of its members favored policies of local independence, feminism, and participation by non-clerks. In part the difference was regional, for the Confederation was strong in southwestern Germany, where class antagonisms were not as sharp as elsewhere, especially Prussia. Differences came to a head in 1905 when the Commercial Alliance resigned from the Confederation and refused offers of compromise, apparently in the belief that the Confederation would disintegrate without its participation.[35]

After its break with the Confederation, the Commercial Alliance moved to exclude non-clerks from the membership, marking the culmination of its drive to become the dominant professional organization representing the clerking estate. At its stormy 1906 convention in Erfurt, the Commercial Alliance took a number of key decisions. Franz Schneider was forced to leave the organization when he refused to sever his connection to the socialist Central Alliance of Clerks. Minna Cauer and Reichstag Deputy Schrader were asked to resign from the executive board, as non-clerks were no longer welcome in the organization. Two clerks on the board, Margarete Lucke and Erna Wönckhaus, resigned in protest against the removal of non-clerk feminists from the organization.[36] They wrote a joint letter to the Alliance journal claiming that they were "radical in the union sense"[37] – indicating that they were not opposed to the removal of employers from the group – but that they nevertheless demanded that the bond to the women's movement be kept. Their resignations provoked a long discussion about the relationship between the women's movement and female professional organizations. As a result, Cauer was named honorary chair and Schrader became an honorary member.[38] Cauer was not placated by the distinction. She wrote with bitterness in her diary: "Seventeen years of unremitting work, and such a conclusion."[39]

The other important step taken at Erfurt was the elaboration of a "Social Program." This completed the transformation of the Berlin Commercial Alliance into a professional organization dedicated to the elevation of the white-collar estate. The opening lines conceded that antagonism existed between employers and employees, but rejected the idea that commercial assistants were proletarian or should adopt the idea of class struggle. Instead, the Program declared that the Commercial Alliance "represented the professional and status interests of female commercial assistants, whom it views as an essential element of the white-collar estate."[40]

The Commercial Alliance defined its new stance as unionism, but traditional union tactics, including the strike and collective bargaining, found no place in it, and the convention defeated a motion to include within the Social Program "wage struggles" – the contemporary Free Union term for those tactics.[41] The Social Program of the Berlin Commercial Alliance, rather than introducing a new, more radical, unionism, simply formalized policies and strategies that had already been developed and pursued in the 1890s. Professionalization and agitation for legislative reform were the means the organization would employ.[42] Leaders of the Commercial Alliance hoped that its new self-definition as an association of the professional estate would give it a central role in the "white-collar movement."

## Re-evaluating ties to the bourgeois women's movement

When the Berlin Commercial Alliance took up its new policy of representing the clerking estate, the organization did not completely reject feminism. Rather, it limited its feminist concerns to those related to employment and made women's issues subordinate to those of the estate. This was nevertheless a major re-evaluation of feminism, which placed the group closer to the moderate wing of the German bourgeois women's movement and distanced it from the radical feminists who had previously been its staunchest supporters. Leaders demanded an end to limitations on the freedom of assembly for women, for instance, not as a step toward full female emancipation, but merely as a tool to enable women clerks to achieve "the equalization of woman and man with regard to their public participation in questions of profession and estate."[43] The larger questions that had been of central concern to radical feminists were now placed outside the province of a professional organization of the clerking estate.

The Berlin Commercial Alliance criticized the Confederation by claiming that it failed to represent the white-collar estate. Berlin stressed the presence in local Confederation groups of employers and philanthropists, implying that middle-class feminists fell into the latter category. It labelled feminists in the Confederation as coming

largely from the stratum of people who look down on female clerks, who do not always succeed in eliminating their differences of estate – despite their good intentions, which we do not doubt – so that something of the nature of a "lady–patron" relationship gets mixed in.[44]

Rejecting any role for women non-clerks, the Commercial Alliance insisted that "a professional organization connotes that the members of the profession have the determining voice, that they do most of the work."[45]

For its part, the Confederation countered with evidence that clerks played an important role in the organization's work and that the activities of persons outside the estate promoted the interests of clerks.[46] It also moved to develop its own social program, establishing a set of guiding principles for socio-political work in 1908, declaring itself willing to join male clerks for common work on issues affecting the estate.[47] Since it continued to allow shop owners and employers to participate, however, the Confederation continued to refer to the "commercial estate" and remained a parity organization.

As the rivalry with the Berlin Commercial Alliance continued, the Confederation began increasingly to define itself as a "women's group" that put female solidarity above unity with male colleagues, insisting on its membership in the German women's movement. It sent delegates to a range of women's conferences (including both radical and moderate organizations) and encouraged its locals to join feminist associations.[48] The Confederation emphasized that its priorities were the opposite of those of the Commercial Alliance, for it was a women's organization first and a representation of all clerks second, and it welcomed outside help in the enormous task of organizing female clerks.

Imbued with that strong feeling of solidarity – to which we hope to educate contemporary women – we do not understand the narrow-minded view that construes participation by women who are not clerks as indicating a relationship of dependency and believes that independence is impaired when women help one another . . . Women's movement and female clerks' movement are dependent on one another, and they both can achieve the goal for which they both struggle – equality of rights and status – that much more quickly if they work together in the closest contact . . .[49]

Unlike the Alliance, the Confederation insisted that women clerks sought the full social and political equality demanded by the bourgeois women's movement. Although granting the need to work with male colleagues, it emphasized that in addition, "shoulder to shoulder with women of all professions and all social classes, we must do battle for the common interests of the whole world of women."[50] In 1908 the Confederation joined the BDF, shortly after that organization published a progressive statement of principles that devoted a section to employment issues in which it demanded equal pay for equal work and full female participation in all public agencies serving employed women (such as commercial courts).[51]

This statement was used by Johanna Waescher to justify the Confederation's decision to join the BDF. Stressing "the urgent necessity of concerted action by all women to achieve the goals which both have set," she insisted that employed women in particular had benefited from the women's movement and that the reforms desired by the BDF would have wide-reaching effects on all women's lives.[52] Her clear feminist declaration characterized the stance of the Confederation throughout the pre-war period.

The Berlin Commercial Alliance found itself somewhat trapped by its new theoretical position. On the one hand, its attempts to destroy the Confederation had failed, leaving it with a rival that drew strength from its enduring bond to the bourgeois women's movement, a bond that the Commercial Alliance had relinquished. On the other hand, the Berlin Alliance now faced competition from the socialist Central Alliance and the Hirsch-Duncker Association of German Merchants, which had both male and female members and could claim to represent the interests of clerks better than a single-sex organization. The Commercial Alliance was therefore forced to define itself as an all-female organization which, however, refused to allow non-clerk feminists to work within it. It argued that because men and women were not yet equal, only an all-female association would consistently press for women's employment equality.[53]

After a period in which it ignored the bourgeois women's movement, Berlin began to rebuild its ties to feminism by devoting many lectures and articles to feminist issues, including a 1908 series of articles on feminist organizations. Unlike Waescher's article for the Confederation journal, the Alliance series drew no connection between clerks' issues and organizations and the activities of the women's movement. This gave the series a curious, disembodied quality, as if the articles had strayed by chance to the pages of a clerks' journal. The article on the BDF ignored its 1907 statement of principle and failed to comment on any benefits clerks might gain from a commitment to feminism, implying that the BDF functioned only as a clearinghouse for particular interests rather than as a sponsor for general feminist demands.[54]

The Berlin Commercial Alliance rejoined the BDF in 1910.[55] Rapprochement had become easier because the bourgeois women's movement had become more moderate. Radical feminists found themselves more and more isolated, both within the women's movement and within the liberal and progressive political parties from whom they sought support in their drive for female equality and political reform.[56] Josef Silbermann justified the renewed ties between "profession and the women's movement" by arguing that "the employed woman is foremost in creating the basis for all the demands of the women's movement right up to women's suffrage ... [She] makes the first breach in ossified prejudices and opens a clear path for the entire sex."[57] His vision reversed Waescher's, for she asserted that fulfilling the goals of feminism would enrich the lives of working women, while Silbermann implied that employment equality and other piecemeal reforms were the very stuff of social emancipation. In the more conservative view of the Berlin Alliance, the BDF and bourgeois feminism had simply to coordinate the variegated special interests of women. Emancipation, defined as legal equality, would come in incremental steps as individual interest groups pressed for particular reforms within the existing order.

The executive board of the Commercial Alliance pressed its chapters in 1910 to work with and join local and regional women's organizations. Many chapters responded and got support from women's groups on issues such as mandatory commercial continuation schools for girls or Sunday shop closing, as well as help in campaigns to elect clerks to insurance boards. Chapters held joint lectures and cultural events with other women's organizations. In 1912, the Alliance established a Committee for the Woman Question, whose task was to maintain and extend relations between it and the women's movement.[58]

That same year, the Commercial Alliance participated in a women's exhibition mounted in Berlin that had the patronage of the Empress. The earlier 1896 congress had challenged German society to recognize "women's endeavors" and had emphasized the goals women sought to obtain. The 1912 show presented "Women at Home and at Work" and simply praised the achievements of women in the private and public spheres with no mention of the discrimination and inferior status they still faced. During the opening week, the BDF held a women's congress, at which Gertrud Israel of the Commercial Alliance spoke. She emphasized the importance of professional organizations for employed women, summing up the Commercial Alliance position. To be effective, Israel asserted, professional women's organizations had to be limited to members of the estate, and leaders had to be drawn from within its ranks, for employees' interests were different from those of employers, although "struggle" between the two was not necessary.[59]

The changing relationship between the Commercial Alliance and the bourgeois women's movement highlights the difficulties faced by all organizations of employed women, especially in Germany before World War I. The Catholic Alliance, which engaged in few activities, had little difficulty balancing its allegiances, but the secular associations found that it was not easy both to represent women and to improve the situation of clerks. The Confederation placed feminism first and found it difficult to gain a hearing from male clerks' associations. The Berlin Commercial Alliance placed the estate first at the expense of its earlier feminist vision. Both organizations were constrained by the fact that their male colleagues expressed little interest in reforms aimed at meeting the needs of female clerks or providing equality for women in clerking.

# 7

# Class and gender in the socialist Central Alliance

## Socialism, Free Unionism, and clerks

The all-female clerks' associations did not offer the only organizational option, for a socialist clerks' union with men and women members also existed in Germany before World War I. From its creation, this group maintained ties to the Social Democratic Party and to the SPD-affiliated Free Unions, and it rejected any alliance with white-collar associations that identified themselves as part of the middle estate. The all-female clerks' associations looked to the bourgeois women's movement and to male white-collar groups when formulating theory and policies. The Central Alliance, on the contrary, drew on socialist analyses regarding the situation of wage workers and of women, and its policies were those of the SPD and the Free Unions.

The first German clerks' unions were established in Berlin and Hamburg in 1883. The Free Organization of Young Merchants in Berlin offered the familiar measures of self-help and mutual support, including an employment service, legal aid, and health and burial insurance.[1] But it was also the earliest organization to insist upon state intervention to aid clerks, and it elaborated a program of reform including apprenticeship regulations, shorter working hours and Sunday rest, old age and disability protection, and "questions of pay." Its assertion "that the interests of the young employed merchants in many cases collide with those of the principals . . ."[2] soon alienated local parity groups, and some employers even denounced the group as an SPD ally and as "inflammatory." By 1887 financial difficulties and business and government hostility led it to disband.

Friedrich's ascension to the throne in 1888 created a new political climate, and the Free Alliance of Merchants arose. It openly acknowledged its ties to the SPD, which "has until now represented our interests most effectively." By the end of 1892, nineteen groups corresponded throughout Germany, and most accepted female members. They insisted upon the opposition of interests between employers and employees and emphasized the need for state regulation and legislative reform. Unlike the unsuccessful Free Organization, they ignored self-help measures.

From 1894 to 1898 conflict arose concerning both the union's relationship to the SPD and the possibility of centralization. The first issue was resolved in 1896 when the group refused to identify or join with "apolitical estatist associations," but rather to ally with the SPD. A year later the second dispute was resolved with the creation of a national organization.[3] The new Central Alliance of Male and Female Commercial Assistants was based in Hamburg owing to that state's liberal law of assembly (which was especially important given female participation). The organization joined the Free Union General Commission, and by 1898 the remaining independent unions had joined.

Centralization brought radicalization. The executive board claimed to represent "those male and female commercial assistants who do not recognize a harmony of interests between principal and clerk . . . those clerks who stand by the principle of class struggle." In taking this stance, the Central Alliance was adhering to a Marxist analysis of the situation of low-level white-collar workers and rejecting any notions of a "new middle estate." To the union, it was obvious that the development of capitalism was causing the field of clerking to become deskilled and its tasks routinized, and that clerks faced a proletarian future. It therefore insisted on solidarity among all paid employees, standing "shoulder to shoulder with the workers organized in unions."[4] Leaders emphasized that they were not lackeys of Social Democracy, but that the SPD best supported the interests of clerks. Socialists often spoke at Central Alliance meetings, and some individual locals joined the Party.[5]

The Central Alliance pursued many of the same policies as other male and female clerks' associations, especially the more modern DHV and the all-female groups. It continued to demand legislation in a number of areas, such as regulated work hours, commercial inspectors, commercial courts, and additional state insurance programs and benefits, paralleling the demands made by other clerks' groups. But it also began to offer self-help measures, including employment lists, legal aid, and unemployment insurance, which had been neglected until local leaders complained that they could not compete with rival associations in their absence. However, the union remained suspicious of self-help measures because they aided individuals rather than changing the structures determining the working lives of all clerks. It thus rejected the idea of offering vocational or educational courses to its members.

The policy that most clearly distinguished the Central Alliance from other clerks' associations was its willingness to engage in strikes, coupled with its belief that collective bargaining was necessary in order to achieve better working conditions and uniform and higher pay for clerks. It directed and participated in a number of strikes, especially in the years 1903–4.[6] Its attempts to negotiate contracts were hampered because collective bargaining was illegal before World War I, and hence it had few lasting successes except with consumers' cooperatives, a number of which had a closed shop and hired only union members. The cooperatives were the main recruiting ground for the Central Alliance; at the end of 1905, the organization had 5,815 members, with 2,211 employed in consumer cooperatives.[7]

## Women in the Central Alliance

Although the leadership of the Central Alliance remained firmly male, the organization made serious efforts to recruit women, to address issues important to them, and to work toward women's equality. From the 1880s women had joined local Free Union clerks' groups and found appeals to them for membership in union journals. As early as 1896, the union coordinating committee demanded that women should receive pay equal to that of men.[8] In part, the response to female issues was pragmatic: Alliance leaders were aware of the increase in female employment in clerking and of male hostility to women's "dirty competition." The first published annual report of the Central Alliance, indeed, claimed that women were difficult to organize because "they believe that they will soon be able to leave work by a speedy marriage, and also because of the greater lack of participation by the female sex in public affairs."[9]

But it was not pragmatism alone that led the Central Alliance to include women's issues. For the organization accepted Bebel's and Zetkin's analyses of economic development and believed that the degradation of clerking and increased female participation in the white-collar work-force could not be hindered.[10] They therefore encouraged female clerks to organize as a part of that general politicization of all workers that would lead to human emancipation.

Under the guidance of Max Josephsohn, the national Central Alliance actively recruited women, primarily using the Free Union's tactic of "plant meetings." Local unions invited sales staff at a single department store or all saleswomen in a particular retail branch to attend meetings to discuss grievances or poor work conditions, at which a woman often spoke. Women at the meetings learned about working conditions and pay, the history of women's work, and the importance of female organization and solidarity.[11] Attending meetings sponsored by the Central Alliance, young saleswomen could get to know their colleagues, discuss grievances, and establish support networks. Meetings could also provide an opportunity to work with a female leader or to organize workers' committees that dealt with particular demands.

Many union educational activities were designed to bring both sexes to a better understanding of issues of female employment and of the "woman question" in general. Some were geared to female members or to unorganized female clerks, but others were clearly intended to influence men. Lectures and journal articles traced the history of sales work and explained the trends within capitalism tending toward concentration; others described the poor conditions faced by sales workers, especially women, and insisted that only organization could bring justice to employed women. Topics attempting to reach men emphasized the economic circumstances that drove women to seek employment and the need for both sexes to express solidarity and work together in the same union.[12] They countered male prejudices and stereotypes, placed women's issues within the framework of socialist theory, and showed the necessity of a joint male–female clerks' organization.

Some individual locals of the Central Alliance tried to involve women in the local leadership, and a number of them elected women to their committees and executive boards.[13] Regina Krauss was hired as the second paid functionary of the Central Alliance and soon became an important union recruiter, speaking both on women's issues and on issues of general concern to socialist clerks. In 1914 she was the only woman on the eight-member national board.[14]

The question of women's particular needs was a difficult one for the Central Alliance. Some leaders were strongly committed to the goal of female emancipation, while others either rejected it or at least felt unwilling to take active measures to promote it. The issue was not simply one of poor or prejudiced leadership, however. Part of the difficulty lay in the theoretical framework within which women's issues were discussed. Socialist feminism did not allow for consideration of gender distinction either on the job or within the organization. Indeed, the issue of discrimination against women in the union was ignored entirely. As a consequence, women played only a passive role within the Central Alliance. There were few women in responsible positions, and there was no effective female support network. The emphasis on class struggle made leaders unwilling to establish any separate female activities in the locals or any "woman's corner" in the journal. In addition, the emphasis on solidarity and the betterment of the group made leaders hostile to programs that stressed individual advancement, so that they were unwilling to offer the sort of self-help information and measures that were so important in all-female clerks' associations.

Many of the same data used as examples of Alliance interest in women also testify to the failure of the organization to achieve equality between the sexes within it. That it addressed women's issues was important; that it did so rarely given the proportion of the membership that was female is also noteworthy. Few delegates to Alliance conventions were female, and protocols indicate that the female delegates often failed to speak throughout the sessions. When Paul Lange reported to one convention on "The Clerks' Movement and Social Policy," he ignored women and the all-female associations. It took male delegates to suggest that Lange might have "given more details about women's work in commerce and about pay issues" and to point out that the report on clerks' associations had ignored the all-female Commercial Alliance.[15] Neither woman delegate addressed the issue. A man, Max Josephsohn, was even selected to represent the Central Alliance at the 1904 Bremen Conference of Social Democratic Women.[16]

We may also question whether women were adequately represented when they held only approximately 10 to 30 percent of the local offices. Not only could women continually be outvoted, but male predominance led women to acquiesce in decisions and to voice few opinions at all. It was rare for female members to speak. In Dessau at a members' meeting in 1912, "Mr. Colleague Neumann raised the question of the present pay situation at Rosslauer's, in the name of the female colleagues working there."[17] In Bremen that same year, "Mrs. Colleague Schweida, [addressing] primarily the women, asked [them] to please agitate for the association, if not publicly, then at least personally among acquaintances."[18]

Furthermore, the proportion of speeches and articles pertaining to women was not very high. A 1910 survey showed that the journal devoted only 1,021 lines to "women's issues," which put the topic on a par with historical topics or discussions of political parties, while "professional questions other than pay" received 15,121 lines.[19] When the subject of a talk or essay was not specifically addressed to women, they were usually ignored. Most references to the clerks' movement therefore treated it as all-male despite the spirited competition for members between the Central Alliance and the all-female associations.[20] A journal article entitled "The Suppression of the People in Prussia" attacked the limited manhood franchise, but was silent about women's lack of voting rights.[21]

The general insensitivity of male Central Alliance leaders is under-scored by the decision taken at its 1912 convention to remove the word "Female" from the title. A motion to this effect had first been proposed in 1908 in order to shorten the title, but had failed by a great margin.[22] In 1912, the executive board proposed the change, both to shorten the title and as a "radical modernization." There were a number of opponents, despite the absence of any female delegates. One man pointed out, in a bit of an understatement, that "things are different with us than other organizations that take no women, for we have a very large number of women members." Another dele-gate asserted that it was important for agitation purposes "that female clerks are also named in the title," and a third proposed that the word "Germany" could be stricken to shorten the name. The change was approved, however, by a small majority.[23]

Since socialist feminists rejected female separatism within unions, there was no particular organization of women members of the Alliance. Some locals offered "cheery social evenings," but none was held for women alone. Discussion evenings as well were open to all members, with no opportunity for women to develop their speak-ing skills or assertiveness in debate in an all-female environment. Since socialist feminists expected economic independence alone to liberate women, no attempt was made to encourage women to develop personal assertiveness or independence through travel, education, or leisure activities. On the other hand, neither was there any talk about women's "natural profession" of marriage and motherhood, for the Central Alliance predicted paid employment for all married women. The Alliance aimed to raise women's consciousness concern-ing employment issues, the need for organization and solidarity, and the importance of class struggle and socialism. Beyond that, politiciza-tion did not occur. Women were urged to vote in state-insurance elec-tions, and lectures were given on the importance of female civic rights, but abstract rights were never connected to the political activities (or lack of them) undertaken by women in the union.

## The Central Alliance in Hamburg

Hamburg's Central Alliance local provides an example of socialist diffi-culties in dealing with women's issues despite a leadership committed to the emancipation of women. Hamburg was one of the largest union locals and served as the national headquarters until 1912. The local began as Association Forwards in 1892 and accepted female members from its inception. In 1896 it had fifty-two members.[24] Although female interest was low, the local spoke directly to women's concerns, includ-ing the "regulation of the woman and apprenticeship question" as a goal of the organization.[25] By 1899 female attendance began to increase from under 5 percent to about 25 percent of the audience at meetings. Women responded when Max Josephsohn organized department-store saleswomen and recruited members from the consumer cooperatives, which hired almost entirely female sales personnel.[26]

Leaders in Hamburg directed many campaigns at single firms or retail branches, using the technique of plant meetings. Early in 1902 the union sought to recruit employees at the consumer cooperative New Society.[27] It was quite effective in gaining women's attention; at one meeting to discuss grievances, about 40 percent of those attending were women.[28] By 1908 the Hamburg Central Alliance was ready to organize saleswomen in department stores and began a series of campaigns aimed at specific businesses. By 1909 the local represented saleswomen in three different department stores and it negotiated as well for the employees of four cooperatives.[29]

Besides plant meetings, the Hamburg Central Alliance held numerous general meetings and lectures through the years for female clerks. Sometimes the organization invited outside women speakers such as Regina Krauss and prominent socialist feminist Luise Zietz, who spoke in 1901 on the history of women's waged work.[30] Most lecturers followed a fairly standard pattern. They acknowledged that the flow of women into the labor market did lower wages and that women sometimes did compete with men for the same jobs, but asserted that it was capitalism that was at fault, not individual women – after all, men too competed with each other. The solution to the problem was not to blame women but to organize them into common union organizations with the men so that they could struggle to achieve better pay and improved working conditions.[31]

The local also sought to win female members with a brochure distributed throughout the city in 1909 that showed considerable skill at public relations. The pamphlet detailed the low pay and poor working conditions faced by women in retail sales and explained that the Central Alliance was working "to alleviate the *misery* of commercial employees and where possible to *end* it." In conclusion the union argued: "YOU COMPLAIN – BUT HAVE YOU THE RIGHT TO COMPLAIN?" Even if female commercial assistants "toil and moil the whole day" under difficult work and pay conditions, they were nevertheless cowardly to complain unless they had "used all means to resist the enemy powers," especially by joining the union to fight "shoulder to shoulder with female colleagues."[32]

The Hamburg Central Alliance differed in theory and in approach from the all-female clerks' associations. In line with its socialist and unionist beliefs, the organization accepted the proletarian nature of clerking and, rather than emphasizing steps fostering individual career opportunities, it campaigned to improve conditions for all employees. It insisted upon actions against the employer as well as those aimed at wresting reforms from the government. Like the all-female associations, however, the Central Alliance asserted that employed women had the right to equal pay and work opportunities, and to equal legal status.

Sympathetic to socialist feminist theory, Central Alliance leaders in Hamburg tried to increase female involvement in the union, pressing women to attend meetings, agitate for new members, and hold executive positions. In the decade before the war, women held a number of positions in the Hamburg union, including some on the board. Two women sat on the agitation and election committees in 1901 and three sat a year later. In 1910 Martha Groth, who had given lectures for the local, was elected second secretary. All of the activist women for whom information exists were single, and a number were daughters of men active in the union local.[33]

The data indicate that the Hamburg local consistently sought to educate women and men about female employment issues, to recruit women into the union, and to include women in the organization's leadership, communicating its essential commitment to equal rights for both sexes. It is none the less the case that Hamburg, like the Central Alliance as a whole, failed to ensure female equality within the organization, despite the fact that by 1910 male leaders themselves seem to have felt uncomfortable about the low level of female involvement in the group.

On two occasions in 1911, the board publicly sought female nominations at elections to responsible positions, while at the same time suggesting that most women would be inadequate for the job. On the first occasion, the chair expressed his regret that no woman had stood for election to the executive board, but added that "only those should be nominated who are really prepared and capable of working with us."[34] At the end of the year, the chair said that he would "greet it with joy" if a woman were elected, but only if he was convinced that she was "able to fulfill the duties of office in every way."[35]

Male leaders were apparently ambivalent about the role they wanted and expected female members to play. They recognized that female leaders were essential to an organization half composed of women and desiring to recruit more. But giving women responsible positions was still an uncomfortable novelty. The women evidently sensed this. In all the reports of discussions at meetings throughout the years, there were few occasions on which women ventured any opinions, and the women who did speak were those same few women who held office. Sometimes when they spoke, they were dismissed patronizingly. When Frl. Storch criticized the executive board in 1908 for failing to support employees in one consumer cooperative, the chair denied the validity of her charges in a manner suggesting that she was at fault, so that a month later, a chastened Storch felt called upon to explain that she had not meant to attack the board but "to explain the benefits of a workers' committee."[36] Rather than seizing its opportunity to involve Storch in organizational efforts, the board embarrassed her.

Nor did the Hamburg local offer any structures that addressed women's particular difficulties, on the job or in the organization. Unlike the all-female clerks' associations in the city, Industria and the Association of Female Office Workers, the male-dominated Central Alliance local provided few opportunities (such as women's discussion groups) for women to learn skills essential to advancing in the public sphere: the ability to speak in public; to express opinions authoritatively; to formulate policies; to assume authority or to hold office. Its "cheery evenings" were never solely for women.

The difficulties faced by Central Alliance leaders, on both local and national levels, reflect the intractable nature of the problems arising in an organization that recognizes inequality between men and women but fails to perceive its nature. Since the union accepted Zetkin's contention that woman must be subsumed by worker and that female employment and concomitant financial independence placed women in identical circumstances to the men of their class, the Central Alliance was blind to the fact that men and women clerks had an identical situation neither on the job nor in the organization. The Alliance did not see its task as teaching individual self-improvement, but as a consequence, neither the Hamburg local nor the national union offered women a chance to learn effective work or organizational behavior. Since the Alliance concentrated entirely on women's employment role, it never discussed waged work within the perspective of women's entire lives, even though its female members typically left the labor force to marry. The Central Alliance insisted that men and women clerks must march together "shoulder to shoulder," but ignored the fact that the women walked at the rear of the parade.

# 8

## *Jobs or marriage: contradictory messages in socializing women clerks*

While the socialist Central Alliance assumed that working women and men were in the same situation, the all-female clerks' associations accepted a sex-distinct feminist theory that insisted upon the primacy of women's domestic responsibilities and upon the special character of women. In their view, emancipation was a matter for the public sphere. These male/female and public/private dichotomies however led to serious contradictions. First, association members received contradictory images of themselves. They were to be independent career women before marriage, the full equals in employment of their male colleagues, and their equal companions in societal affairs. Yet homemaking still remained women's natural and primary career, so that outside employment ended with marriage and home tasks became women's sole occupation – despite the fact that feminists justified single women's employment by arguing that there was now less housework to do.

In addition, the all-female clerks' associations offered members a number of policies at cross-purposes with one another. On the one hand, their major goal was employment equality for women. To compete successfully with men in the workplace, female clerks required equal education, training, and career opportunities – for which the female clerks' associations fought tenaciously. To achieve those objectives, they had to exist as forceful organizations, inspiring loyalty and professional awareness in their members and convincing businessmen, the public, and the government that employed women should be granted career opportunities equal to those of men. On the other hand, the associations also insisted that women had "dual careers," first in paid employment and then in homemaking, and that employment would remain secondary for most women. This gave weight to opponents' claims that female training and promotion wasted resources, since women typically left the work-force within ten years, perhaps one-third of the time for which a man would use his employment skills and advance his career. In addition, it meant that organizations lost many long-term members – those most dedicated and knowledgeable – when they married. Leaders in the all-female organizations found no solution to these dilemmas; clearly there was no solution, granting the premises that women were both equal to men and yet innately different from them, that women should share equally in employment tasks yet alone be burdened with domestic responsibilities.

### Independence, assertion, and equality: the socialization of the new public woman

The all-female clerks' associations used the related strategies of sociali-zation and politicization to increase women's loyalty to the organiza-tion and to the workplace and to improve their career opportunities. Their tactics were to elevate women's self-esteem, to teach them skills, attitudes, and behaviors necessary to a public or employment role, and to offer women a new image of femininity and of male–female relations.

From their inception, female clerks' organizations schooled their members in assertive, independent behavior. Occasional articles in the journals reported trips and tours taken by members, offered advice on how to travel alone or with another woman, and exhorted women not to be intimidated into remaining at home.[1] Other essays reported the experiences of clerks temporarily working away from home or abroad and encouraged women to seek jobs in new areas and to act more independently.[2] Josef Silbermann justified female independence with arguments rooted in theories of liberal individualism, claiming that girls had the right to develop their individual talents to the fullest extent and pleading that it was natural that "the daughter does not wish to have others feed her, but desires to be valued as an indepen-dent personality ... With a man, this is totally clear. A man who cannot feed himself is not accepted fully. No wonder that the woman yearns for the same evaluation ..."[3] Even the Catholic Alliance insisted that women should have free choice of occupation and equal educational opportunities owing to "the air of individualism that today wafts through humanity, the general demand for personal autonomy and economic independence."[4]

Organization leaders criticized women's "unawareness of their own needs" (*Bedürfnislosigkeit*), which resulted from their dependence on their families and fear of individual self-assertion. One leaflet widely distributed by Hamburg Industria, for example, contended that women were satisfied with inadequate salaries and poor working conditions because of a "lack of self-esteem and a contentedness [with little] cultivated by the family and by education. Think! You stand in the midst of a struggle for existence and not in a salon!"[5]

Female clerks' associations also sought to change members' work attitudes and behavior, noting that although clerks complained of their miserable circumstances, most left work rather than refusing jobs or joining an organization to agitate for change. In the eyes of organization leaders, female clerks lacked "professional consciousness" owing to the inferior evaluation they made of themselves as clerks. This was an obstacle to women's advancement to equality with men in clerking, for it made them willing to accept lower pay than their male colleagues, to work primarily in clerking positions that were routinized and degraded, and to expect never to move upward into a position involving the supervision of men. To awaken their members to professional consciousness, association leaders stressed their need to assess themselves professionally, learn about employment issues, and even study social and political affairs. To foster this, association chapters often held lecture or discussion evenings with titles such as "Happiness at Work" or "Satisfaction in Professional Life."[6]

The teaching of employment skills and behavior was seen as very important by the female clerks' associations. Every chapter offered evening courses teaching skills such as typing, stenography, or bookkeeping. Stories, articles, and lectures encouraged women to improve both their job skills and their educational level, to be punctual, and to work efficiently.[7] Arguing that women could well learn from men, one journal article stated that male clerks had "*'discipline'* and *'esprit de corps'*" and that women too needed the valuable work habits that men had learned in school and apprenticeship.[8] The Catholic Alliance urged its members not to treat their employment responsibilities lightly.[9] Organizations also published booklets containing information useful to female clerks, covering topics such as laws and regulations affecting clerks, details of insurance coverage, and tips on job performance. They also commonly offered advice to their members on proper dress and behavior for job interviews and at work.[10]

Leaders of clerks' associations expected women to increase their self-esteem and become more competent on the job once they learned appropriate employment attitudes and behavior. In part, the notions of propriety were those of the middle class. Since a growing proportion of young working-class women was entering clerking after the turn of the century, leaders of clerks' associations feared that women from "better circles" would flee the field and undermine their strategy of professionalization. For them, "the honor of our social stratum"

(*Standesehre*) dictated that working-class clerks learn correct – middle-class – behavior.

But the issue was not one of class alone. Since young women were educated apart from men and taught only to prepare themselves for marriage, it was appropriate that the organizations resocialize them and prepare them in appearance, attitudes, and behavior for the workplace. The standards of the public sphere were not those of the private. It was seen as important for girls from middle-class as well as working-class backgrounds to receive advice on appropriate dress and behavior for the job.

Female clerks' associations not only expected their activities to result in a new, equal, employment role for women, but believed that the responsibilities undertaken on the job and the self-esteem gained through employment would affect the private sphere, creating new female roles and altering male–female relationships to provide the basis for a new type of marriage.[11] The leaflet distributed by the Hamburg group, calling upon women to improve themselves, asserted that "the more you know, the more sought after and independent you are, the greater will become your freedom to select the man of your heart yourself and to stride through life at his side, a free companion. For life today, more than ever, demands capable women."[12] At one lecture for clerks, the speaker insisted that employment made a woman a "happily creative and resolute personality without losing her femininity," allowing her to become an "understanding companion" to a man. As a result, selfishness and brutality would disappear from men's interactions, and dependence and superficiality would disappear from those of women.[13]

## Organization and involvement: the politicization of the new female clerk

Female clerks' associations also attempted to politicize their members. They impressed upon them the importance of working actively for the chapter, recruiting new members, and supporting organizational policies. Further, the associations expected women to enter the larger political life, to vote in the few elections open to them, to discuss political issues, and to join political reform groups such as the Society for Social Reform.

The leadership continually insisted that members participate in organizational affairs and recruit women to their chapters. "Our greatest enemy," lectured Johanna Waescher in 1908, was not male opposition but female apathy and lack of interest; organization was essential.[14] Essays detailing the circumstances of female clerks – their low pay and poor chances of promotion, for example – emphasized that women needed to act to improve their lot. As the Confederation *Yearbook* claimed:

The power of organization has proven itself everywhere ... What were they before? Female clerks without esteem, without social position ... What are they now? Clerks who have fought for respect, whose dedication to duty and ability are respected, and who are also more valued economically.[15]

Stories appeared in clerks' journals to make the same point. When "Miss Smart," "Miss Peter," and "Miss Sweet" met on the train, Miss Smart learned that although Miss Peter was a member, she was not interested in her clerks' association. "To run there every week and listen to lectures about eight o'clock closing, commercial chambers. – What we are and what we should be ... Isn't that a bit boring? Do people even show up?" After Miss Smart explained the excitement of the meetings ("you've definitely never seen so much intelligence in one place!") and recounted a list of organizational activities, she won the allegiance of both Miss Peters and Miss Sweet – who had "never dared to go" to a discussion evening – and they promised to attend the next meeting.[16]

Many association members who did attend meetings were nevertheless loath to take on leadership roles. Organizations had continually to repeat their pleas for greater member participation in their activities and to emphasize the importance of an active role in the association in preparing women for larger public and political life. The Commercial Alliance insisted that organizing had a particular importance for women.

For them, excluded as they are from public life almost everywhere, organization is the basis upon which a sense of solidarity can be developed, upon which personalities can be strengthened. Here the fresh wind blows, unleashing all the forces that have lain dormant during the thousands of years in which women have been trapped in the home.[17]

The associations sought to train women by offering courses in public speaking and in chairing a discussion.[18] They also mobilized their members to vote or stand for office in elections to local health and pension insurance boards.

The lectures and discussions that clerks' associations offered their members extended to cultural, political, and socio-economic affairs as well. In the mid-1890s, women in Berlin could hear talks on topics such as "The Legal Position of Women" or "Rights and Duties of Clerks." Ten years later, they could attend discussions of "The German Constitution" or "Feelings of Solidarity."[19] Although the Catholic Alliance held few lectures on general cultural or political topics, it suggested in 1910 that "social courses" be established to educate members, pointing to the example of its Danzig chapter, which held a course focusing on general issues of female employment. Its topics ranged from a discussion of "What does 'social' mean? What are social issues?" to lectures on women's legal rights and their employment and educational opportunities.[20] No chapter responded to the proposal, however. In 1912 the Berlin chapter of the Commercial Alliance began its own course in "social training," with a program of three evening lectures covering economic theory, German political parties, and socio-political affairs. The chapter asserted that "thinking women" would gain "rich profits for their education and heightened understanding for the meaning of our organizational life."[21]

Members were not only expected to become more politically active individuals, but to show a greater sense of solidarity among themselves. One Alliance member appealed to her colleagues to support each other at work:

I know very well from my own experience that it's a great temptation to please the boss by excelling in everything and by getting praise at the expense of the other employees. And yet it should always be a rule of wisdom with us to stick together in collegial unanimity . . . [22]

A Confederation member also criticized women's lack of solidarity on the job.

When for example a colleague says "I could never take a position where I would have a female supervisor," or another, "I would much rather seek advice from a man because he knows so much and can give me better information," then I am always hurt. Such statements are not at all rare, and indicate very well the relationships women have with each other.[23]

A book celebrating the first fifteen years of the Alliance joined the themes of self-esteem, improved working conditions, organization, and solidarity. As women became aware of themselves as members of an important estate, asserted the author, they would gain a sense of self-worth.

No one shall dare to approach too closely because of their sex, no one shall in future regard women clerks as fair game, no one look at them ironically or askance or with a disrespectful eye. Things that one wants must be fought for, including respect. The only way to fight for it is by showing solidarity, that is, by joining a professional organization.[24]

Association leaders expected heightened female self-esteem and equality in the workplace to improve women's legal and political status. Since women were equal to men on the job and had the same employment responsibilities as men, they argued, women were entitled to civic rights, a point they frequently reiterated. As the Confederation angrily insisted: "Equal duties! Women pay taxes like men, yet they lack the same rights to administer city affairs and to participate in the legislation of the state and Empire!"[25]

## Passivity and dependence: the contradictory message

At the same time that organizations encouraged women to be assertive, career-minded, politically active, and life companions for their husbands, they also asserted that that was but one half of women's dual role and that their essential difference from men made the tasks of wife and mother their "natural profession." In addition, clerks' groups used those gender characteristics to justify certain types of employment and job behavior, which restricted women at work and thus affected their public as well as their private behavior. Women were told to be both independent and dependent, active and passive, assertive and docile.

This message did not contradict the avowed feminism of leaders of female clerks' associations, but rather sprang from the acceptance by most bourgeois feminists that women were essentially different from men. Association members therefore frequently heard or read that married women did not work and that women's "highest profession" was that of wife and mother. Numerous articles referred casually to marriage as the point at which women left clerking.[26] In one story, a young clerk dreamed that if she remained single, she could "open a little typing office." If "she should become spouse to a beloved man and own her own home," then she would attend to her family.[27] The Roman Catholic Alliance journal justified different treatment for men and women on the basis of eternal "natural sex differences" and insisted that marriage and domesticity were divinely ordained for women and would in future remain "the characteristic and sole activity and satisfaction . . . of the overwhelming majority."[28]

Radical feminists had sometimes argued that married women should be allowed to continue their professional lives, but leaders in clerks' associations viewed it as a "double burden" that most women could not bear.[29] Rather than this doubling of work, feminists in the clerks' associations favored "dual careers" for women, meaning sequential careers spanning a woman's lifetime. They envisaged a female life cycle comprising a career outside the home while single, followed by a domestic career after marriage and motherhood, and perhaps a return to outside employment if widowed.

The Berlin chapter of the Commercial Alliance went so far as to establish courses for marriage-minded clerks. In 1907 its regional newsletter announced cooking and hygiene courses "for colleagues who want to get married."[30] Agnes Herrmann described the pupils as "young employed girls who work to earn their bread in commercial establishments ... who are planning to marry and want to prepare themselves for the profession of housewife."[31] The cooking course was an instant success, the hygiene course less so, prompting Herrmann to emphasize its importance to women.

The employed woman, especially the clerk, is called upon to help create change in this area through her example. She has prepared herself for her employment, she is used to carrying out her duties seriously; she should be the first to realize that the profession of housewife and mother – the most responsible one – also demands preparation from her.[32]

Since leaders in the all-female clerks' associations believed that married women belonged in the home, they faced difficulties in justifying the rights of unmarried women to employment and employment equality, for critics of female work pointed to women's shorter career lives and the secondary importance of any career to women as serious professional obstacles justifying discrimination. Leaders were therefore reduced to citing economic and demographic trends that necessitated employment for single women. They explained that housework had become easier, so that daughters no longer had to remain at home to help, and that family circumstances often required additional household income, so that a girl's paid employment became essential. Further, employment outside the home could allow a young woman to save money for her marriage, allowing it to occur sooner.[33] Although older unmarried women were to be respected for their achievements, the journals always implied that spinsterhood was rarely a woman's choice, but was foisted upon her owing to the excess of middle-class women in the population. "The girl who gets no man is usually one who has no worldly goods. She therefore has no choice but to look for a profession that will provide her daily bread."[34] That the leaders of clerks' groups expected women to marry and leave work was bound to be confusing for their members. Why seek a career, or strive for long-term professional excellence, if marriage was around the corner and spinsterhood an admission of failure to interest a man?

The associations' identification of "woman's nature" with traditional notions of feminine passivity, dependence, and powerlessness was even more confusing. For although the female clerks' associations contended that women should be assertive and independent, they also presumed that "feminine" characteristics were important both in marriage and on the job. Rather than arguing that both sexes were suited to the same tasks, female clerks' associations insisted that middle-class women were especially suited to clerking owing to certain innate female traits. They brought to their jobs "selflessness and a denigration of their own personal needs" and a "talent for adjusting."[35] One Commercial Alliance article commented that a woman would have a greater interest in the firm's business than a man "because she would work from the one specific female characteristic, from her feelings." She would also be more tractable than the male.[36] The Catholic Alliance took an even more conservative position. In its view, the only professions appropriate for women were those using women's nurturant abilities, their inborn aesthetic sense, and their instinct for cleanliness and order.[37]

Besides insisting that women were innately passive and deferential, the associations reinforced the message by teaching female clerks the importance of submissive work behavior. A brochure published by the Commercial Alliance, encouraging specialized training for young saleswomen, emphasized that the girls must learn "pleasing business demeanor," "how to act with propriety," "self-control," and "loyalty."[38] The Catholic Alliance claimed that saleswomen had to be "willing to please, charming, undemanding, modest, and patient."[39]

Despite the fact that women clerks were being urged by their association leaders to increase their self-esteem, to be more independent, and to gain the respect of their male colleagues by their competence, then, women were also expected to continue many traditional behaviors that were quite the contrary. The reader does well to ask what comprised the "new" woman's independence and self-esteem. Despite those traits, she was to remain docile, obedient, quiet, and delicate. Such passive qualities do not offer much scope for such important job characteristics as seizing initiative, taking responsibility, making decisions, or supervising others.

Subtly, female clerks' associations reinforced the notion that women's working lives were secondary and that, although they might be loyal employees who deserved promotion, women were not really suited to managerial positions; their role in clerking would remain different from men's. The associations' image of the fulfilled older career woman was that of a woman in a minor supervisory role, loyal to her employer, and with a complete grasp of the routine affairs of the firm, but with no great responsibilities, no creative input, and no executive role. The Commercial Alliance edited a girls' magazine, which told the story of a new young clerk working under Frl. Bernt, who

has already been in the firm for many years and has the full trust of her boss. She is conscientious over the smallest things. Since she is responsible for payments, she checks to see that every unnecessary expense is avoided. [In the case at hand, the item of expense was ink pads.] For this reason, every new colleague feels she is pedantic. But they soon notice that Frl. Bernt is a hard-working and conscientious person, who truly acts in a supportive way and from whom one can learn an awful lot of things pertaining to one's career and to many other things.[40]

The portrait is sympathetic, but Frl. Bernt supervises mostly trivia. One can imagine young male clerks reading a parallel didactic tale, but the portrait would be quite different. The male supervisor would no doubt take matters out of his boss's hands, dream up schemes to reorganize office affairs, and end the story by being promoted.

The all-female clerks' associations, unlike the socialist Central Alliance, recognized that they had to change women's attiudes and behavior concerning their employment and organizational lives. The associations' policies gave individual women skills and self-confidence, helping them to achieve better positions at work and to assume a more active role in public life. However, those gains were limited, for the all-female groups failed to recognize the interrelationship between work and home, just as the Central Alliance had. Although the latter group relied on socialist feminist theory, while the all-female associations accepted that of the bourgeois women's movement, each assumed that equality for women in employment, and in all public life, could be achieved independent of domestic roles. The socialists expected women's waged work to end "sex slavery" both inside and outside the home, while bourgeois feminists regarded the home as immutably women's domain, so that equality between the sexes could be achieved in the public sphere without a changed division of domestic labor. As a result, the Central Alliance ignored the subordinate position of women in clerking and in the union, while the all-female groups ignored the fact that as long as women alone had "dual careers," no firm basis for employment equality existed.

# 9

## Campaigns for improved commercial training: the boundaries of the estate

Commercial education had become an issue of widespread debate by 1900 for a number of reasons. First, the deskilling of clerking and its separation from more responsible forms of white-collar work meant that a growing number of clerks came to their jobs from working-class backgrounds, with fewer skills and less education than the entrepreneurial, higher-status clerks of the mid nineteenth century. Yet clerking still demanded literacy and numeracy, as well as values such as loyalty and punctiliousness, which working-class boys and girls in overcrowded elementary schools often failed to acquire. The need for competent personnel led businessmen and government authorities to demand some sort of commercial training.

Clerks' organizations also recognized the changes affecting the field of clerking. They too sought commercial education and training, but for different reasons, for they expected a higher level of skills and knowledge to halt routinization and segmentation and to preserve clerking as an occupation of the middle estate. Male clerks' groups emphasized boys' commercial training, and either proposed to limit girls solely to menial clerking tasks or to exclude them from clerking entirely on the grounds that it was they who caused the degradation of the field. The all-female clerks' associations, on the contrary, regarded commercial education for girls as central to their goal of employment equality for women.

The women's organizations agreed with many of the men's criticisms. They acknowledged that female clerks had less training than their male colleagues, that they earned less, and that they often exhibited a disturbing lack of career interest and a disinclination to organize to improve their situation. Too many female clerks, they conceded, were recruited from the working class, further lowering the status of the profession. But they offered a different solution from that of the male associations, for they insisted that it was both unfair and unrealistic to expect women to leave the field. Instead, both women and men should receive the same opportunities for commercial training. They assumed that giving women the same education as men would successfully eliminate "unsuitables" from clerking, since incompetent (i.e., working-class) girls would fail to complete their schooling. The demands of both male and female clerks would thereby be met, for the women would truly be equal to the men in employment matters and would no longer depress pay, lower the skill level of clerking, or take jobs away from their male colleagues as cheaper unskilled competition.[1] As a result, the field would be professionalized and both male and female clerks would regain status and responsibility.

The socialist Central Alliance, alone among clerks' associations, rejected the strategy of professionalization and the role of education within it. Viewing clerks' descent into the proletariat as inevitable, the group insisted that attempts to professionalize were illusory, for any return to the days when clerking had been a multifaceted and responsible profession was impossible. Rather than emphasize education and individual effort, the socialist Central Alliance contended that only union organization and union tactics in alliance with manual workers could lead to better work conditions and pay within the field.[2] Education was envisaged as an instrument to awaken the proletariat politically and to establish social equality rather than as a tool to raise either individuals or the profession. The Central Alliance therefore favored educational reforms to give boys and girls the same schooling, preferably in the same coeducational classroom, and to assure working-class children an equal chance of attending secondary schools and universities.[3]

The all-female associations offered women clerks a more precise and appealing theory than their socialist counterpart. Their emphasis on education allowed members to take some control over their lives, for young women could use schooling or an apprenticeship as a means of individual advancement. They also offered young women pride in skilled, well-paid, high-status work and equality in attainment between men and women, a more attractive vision to many female clerks, whether from the middle class or from upwardly mobile working-class families. Finally, the all-female organizations demanded reforms within the existing state rather than class struggle and its overthrow. Even in their attacks on exploitative apprenticeship programs, the all-female groups chose not to focus upon the employers' role in creating and maintaining those programs, but rather to insist upon state regulation of apprenticeships. The state was the agency

of reform, mediating among the interests of different estates and introducing balanced legislation to ensure social harmony. The polity
would not become further polarized by women's crusades, class not
set against class; Germany would not become a proletarian society.
Rather, reforms would secure equality for female clerks, and women
would gain greater opportunities to become full and equal participants
in Wilhelmine society.

The feminism of the leaders of female clerks' associations was that
of moderates in the bourgeois women's movement, for they accepted
social stratification and class inequality: female clerks were to become
equal only to the men of their class. This class- or profession-bound
feminism became increasingly powerless when the interests of the
estate and those of feminist equality led in different directions. The
all-female associations found that they could successfully implement
educational reforms only when other economic interest groups and
political leaders, acting from motives far removed from those of feminists, favored them. The goal of educational equality fell prey to the
contradiction between a class-based politics of professionalization and
a gender politics insisting on the rights of all women.

## *The key to professionalization and equality: the campaign to improve girls' commercial schooling*

The first educational campaign of clerks' groups was undertaken to
regulate commercial apprenticeships, for both male and female clerks'
associations were aware of the exploitative and inadequate conditions
in which many apprentices worked. Girls faced in addition drastically
shortened programs or total exclusion from apprenticeships. Leaders
in female clerks' groups and other feminists were quick to note that
this caused a division within the profession, with women relegated
to the less skilled positions and condemned to routinized work. By
limiting or abolishing apprenticeships, they argued, employers
created a deskilled work-force, to the detriment of male clerks as well
as female.[4]

However, the German government took no interest in regulating
the field, and employers ignored demands that they improve their
programs. The all-female clerks' groups therefore turned their attention to commercial schooling. This involved three interrelated campaigns: to regulate privately owned commercial academies or
"presses"; to establish private commercial schools for girls; and to
expand part-time public education for girls in commercial subjects.
All three were seen as elements in the process of professionalization
that would exclude "unsuitable" girls from clerking and make women
clerks equal to their male colleagues.

"Presses" had sprung up in the late nineteenth century to cater to young men and, more especially, young women who sought to enter clerking, and by 1900 they had become the primary institution training female office workers. Although some offered a wide range of courses, most presses emphasized the quick and easy acquisition of a limited number of skills, hired poorly trained staff, and were unscrupulous in their advertising, claiming to produce "fully accomplished" clerks in one to three months.[5]

The Berlin Clerks' Aid Association denounced presses in 1896, with other female associations soon echoing its charges.[6] It warned that attending short courses in typing, stenography, or bookkeeping gave women the false impression that they could become "accomplished" without thorough schooling, so that they rejected longer, more rigorous educational programs. Prepared only for routine, segmented work, they then joined the lowest stratum of clerks, earning a pittance and with no chance of upward mobility. In this way incompetent, unsuitable elements gained a foothold in the profession and brought discredit on all female clerks.[7]

The all-female clerks' associations sought Imperial legislation or, failing that, state or local ordinances to regulate private academies. After lobbying failed, the Berlin Commercial Alliance launched a petition drive to several German state legislatures and city councils in 1907, which received widespread publicity. It demanded that governments license private academies, check the competence of the head and teaching staff, set a standard curriculum, and bar pupils without elementary school degrees.[8] In its campaign, the Commercial Alliance sought and won support from business interests and, for the first time, from male clerks' groups. Business circles attacked the presses as a "cancer of German vocational education,"[9] while male clerks' associations demanded government regulation of "so-called commercial academies."[10] The men's motives however differed from those of the all-female clerks' associations, for they favored regulation not only to prevent deskilling, but as a means to limit female access to clerking as well.[11]

The campaign succeeded in moving the Prussian Minister of Commerce to give instructions in 1907 that private industrial and commercial schools could only be opened with permission, and that local councils should control school activities.[12] These measures did not satisfy the Commercial Alliance, which claimed that the edict left "sufficient holes through which unsuitables can still slip."[13] The real problem was that the organization sought more than the regulation of the presses. Male clerks' organizations, business circles, and government authorities all regarded regulation of the presses simply as a means to ensure minimum educational standards for clerks. The all-female associations sought in addition to prevent women from becoming a segregated and secondary labor force in clerking. Only the Commercial Alliance, therefore, demanded that private schools be prevented from offering short courses in specific skills that fostered the division of clerking into various "segmented and routine" tasks or that they set entrance requirements that would limit access by working-class girls.

At the same time that they fought the presses, many local female clerks' associations established courses and opened private commercial day schools (*Handelsschulen*) for women. Reputable programs offered a fixed curriculum for a minimum of one year to pupils who had completed elementary or junior high school. Subjects included commercial mathematics, business German, typing and stenography, letter writing, geography, "product science," and foreign languages. Pupils had to pay an enrollment fee and buy their own books. The day schools were intended to provide an education equal to males' at all levels of study and to provide a model for female commercial education. Organizations expected graduates to move into clerking positions as the full equals of male colleagues who had completed either secondary school or a three-year clerking apprenticeship, and thereby to contribute to the professionalization of the field.[14]

Female clerks' organizations quickly learned, however, that private schools were costly to operate, that many young women could not afford to pay fees and postpone employment, and that in any case these full-time schools could reach but a fraction of the girls who entered clerking each year with only an elementary education. Leaders therefore soon concentrated their efforts on legislation to create girls' commercial schools of continuing education (*Fortbildungsschulen*).

Commercial continuation schools enrolled teenagers apprenticed or employed in clerking, who attended four to six hours a week. The curriculum encompassed basic commercial subjects, with civics and religion explicitly included to inculcate young people with appropriate values and political views. Although a few commercial continuation schools had been established by chambers of commerce, clerks' associations, or women's groups, they were usually funded by state and local governments. The all-female clerks' associations hoped that if these schools became mandatory for all teenagers in clerking, they could provide a mass basis for professionalization. They reckoned that continuation classes would weed out "unsuitable elements" whose literacy and behavior did not meet bourgeois standards, and that girls who failed the required continuation courses would leave clerking, making the estate more homogeneous and elevating its status. Further, they expected the schools to give their pupils sufficient education to enable clerks to take on responsible and complex tasks and to make women the equals of men in the field.

The revised Imperial Industrial Code of 1891 permitted muncipalities to establish boys' commercial schools of continuing education with required attendance. In addition, the laws of several German states required municipalities to establish obligatory boys' continuation schools, and Baden's law extended to girls as well.[15] With state support, boys' commercial schooling increased greatly, although the number of schools still lagged behind that of industrial continuation schools with working-class pupils.[16] Female clerks' associations first agitated at the state and national levels for legislation allowing municipalities to require attendance at girls' schools.[17] After 1900, when the Industrial Code was so amended, local clerks' groups pressed city councils to establish girls' schools, while the national organizations sought Imperial legislation to create a nation-wide school system of girls' commercial continuation schools with mandatory attendance.[18]

In their battle, the all-female clerks' associations sought to capture public attention and to win allies. A number of organizations within the bourgeois women's movement immediately took up the issue and demanded girls' schools of continuing education with mandatory attendance as part of its educational policy.[19] The high point of the feminist campaign occurred in 1907 when the Prussian government sent a bill to the Diet requiring all towns with over 10,000 inhabitants to establish continuation schools for boys (municipalities were permitted to institute them for girls should they desire).[20] The Berlin Commercial Alliance – joined by over sixty women's organizations throughout Germany – petitioned the Diet to demand that communities be required to establish commercial schools for girls. It then sponsored a public meeting in support of the petition.[21] Neither was successful.

On this issue, even the Catholic Women's Federation joined secular feminists. With the local branch of the Catholic Alliance and secular female clerks' associations, it co-sponsored a large public meeting in Munich in 1909 on "Burning Issues for Female Clerks." Leaders of the bourgeois women's movement, including Ika Freudenberg and Eva von Roy, spoke and called for obligatory commercial continuing education for girls.[22]

The female associations also won male allies. In their arguments, leaders emphasized the danger to all clerks posed by a secondary labor force of poorly educated and poorly paid women. The German Alliance for Commercial Education, one of the many special interest groups arising at the time in Germany, was the first to respond. From its creation in 1895, the organization had presented the public with a steady stream of information about the benefits of commercial schooling for business and the state. After Josef Silbermann lectured on girls' continuation schooling to the group in 1899, it dealt regularly with issues relating to female education and established a committee for female commercial education, chaired by Johanna Waescher.[23] Male clerks' groups and business interests also expressed support for female education, to the extent that they wrote and petitioned government authorities.[24] Businessmen and government authorities recognized that for clerking it was necessary to attain a modicum of literacy and commercial knowledge beyond the elementary education that was the extent of schooling for an ever-increasing proportion of female clerks, while male clerks' associations feared that by excluding women from vocational schooling, they would remain a cheaper, less skilled competition to male clerks.[25] Mayor Beck of Mannheim, one of the first cities to require obligatory commercial continuation schooling for girls, found the schools essential because "ever more persons invade the commercial estate from the lower estates, and because the division of labor is ever more thorough."[26]

The campaign for widespread and equal girls' commercial continuing education was only of modest success. Neither the Empire nor the states enacted legislation requiring schools to be established, let alone schools with mandatory attendance. Some municipalities, however, did act. In 1903 there were only five cities with girls' commercial schools of continuing education requiring attendance; in 1906 there were nineteen cities. In 1907 only twenty-nine girls' continuation schools existed; by 1912 there were 115 schools.[27]

In all of the education campaigns by the female clerks' associations, we find the same policies, the same tactics, and the same mixed results. Emphasizing legislative reform, the all-female groups joined forces with a broad array of other interests, from businessmen to reform societies. This suited their plan to be mass organizations representing the estate in German political life. Yet the all-female clerks' associations failed to recognize that they were not simply another lobby. Women held a distinct and inferior position in the clerking labor force, and although they expected educational reform to rectify that, they were alone in that belief. Male colleagues, businessmen, educators, and government authorities who supported girls' commercial schooling did not seek equality for women in the clerking work-force, but acted because they wanted to provide the business world with women adequately trained to accomplish routine tasks. They envisioned a hierarchy of clerks, with women – well-trained, suitable women – at the bottom. Owing to this, when the all-female clerks' groups sought feminist goals in education, demanding for girls the sort of preparation that could contribute to employment equality, such as apprenticeships, thorough commercial education, and mandatory continuation schooling, their male supporters disappeared.

The socialist Central Alliance ignored campaigns against presses and never sought to establish commercial courses, for it rejected notions of individual improvement and insisted that the deskilling of clerking could not be reversed. The union did, however, favor obligatory continuation schooling for all boys and girls in clerking under eighteen, which it regarded as an element in the socialist demand for improved public schooling for all children beyond the elementary level. The union therefore insisted that classes should be held twelve hours a week, twice the standard time.[28] Like the all-female associations, the Central Alliance pressed for legislation and sometimes petitioned local governments. However, it never made educational reform a key issue as the estatist associations did. Its arguments were ignored by everyone excepting socialists, who supported legislation for continuation schools in all fields.

## Saleswomen's courses: working-class girls and the estate

The growing interest in separate schools or classes for saleswomen best illustrates the conflict between feminism and professionalization within the all-female clerks' associations. The associations developed plans for "salesgirls' schools" (*Verkäuferinnenschulen*) in conjunction with their other educational proposals. The schools were to offer salesgirls a particular curriculum, which would teach skills essential to retail sales work *and* instill bourgeois values and habits. Although leaders encouraged private commercial schools to offer such a curriculum, they were especially keen to establish salesgirls' schools within commercial continuing education.

The all-female clerks' associations justified the need for salesgirls' schools with the claim that employers could not find qualified sales personnel because of the increasing proportion of saleswomen who, coming from lower-class families, had inadequate education and deportment. Special sales schools would counter this, they argued, for these incompetent salesgirls would fail or drop out of the courses, while middle-class daughters would enter the field owing to its heightened prestige and selective standards. Leaders also expected the presence of middle-class saleswomen to result in working conditions commensurate with the clerks' higher status and expectations. The long-range goal was to make the field of clerking a bourgeois profession for women, as it had been in the early 1890s.

At the heart of these proposals was the assumption, common to bourgeois feminists, that working-class women were sisters, but across a divide. Equality meant for them simply the opportunity to advance into the middle estate on the basis of merit. Leaders in clerks' associations followed moderate feminists such as Josephine Levy-

Rathenau, active in youth employment counselling, who favored a "regulated vocational education" to increase the number of "socially valuable elements" entering a field, while serving "to frighten off the unsuitable elements," girls "at war with their mother tongue, who are able neither to spell properly nor to write clearly."[29]

This attitude explains why the Confederation, despite its more consistent feminism, also expressed disdain for working-class saleswomen who could not adapt to bourgeois patterns. Eva von Roy spoke of the "dubious elements" flocking to sales work.[30] She and Johanna Waescher asserted that unsuitable girls "would block the higher development of the entire estate and lessen its reputation," and justified their lack of feminist solidarity by claiming that it was in the best interests of the girls themselves, who "would find no satisfaction in commercial professions."[31]

There was an additional, pragmatic reason for professionalizing sales work. Since the majority of female clerks worked in retail sales, leaders of the all-female organizations recognized that they had to recruit saleswomen in order to succeed as mass organizations. Agnes Herrmann saw the winning of saleswomen as crucial, for the Berlin Commercial Alliance "was not planned as a Ladies' Professional Association, but as a mass organization with a broad basis."[32] Leaders assumed that professionalization would increase "career consciousness" and organizational strength. And if sales work were a bourgeois preserve, rivalry with the Central Alliance could be overcome.

The first separate sales course was established by the Berlin Clerks' Aid Association in 1901.[33] The organization only came to emphasize special sales schools after 1906, however, when its program placed the needs of the estate above feminism. Both the Berlin Commercial Alliance and the Catholic Alliance, with their professional emphasis, favored separate salesgirls' schools. This policy undermined both the principle that all clerks receive the same training in order to prevent the emergence of a "clerking proletariat" and the demand for equal education for both sexes, for there were no plans for salesmen's courses. Women in sales were left therefore as the poor sisters of male clerks and of women in the more prestigious and better-paid field of office work. The organizations seem to have accepted this owing to a fear that without measures taken to upgrade saleswork, clerking would become entirely divided on gender lines, with female office workers identified with their uncouth sisters in sales. This might have meant a loss of membership and organizational strength as well as the sacrifice of public respect and political influence.[34] Without a strong pressure group, equal rights for women would become an even more distant goal.

The Confederation, with a policy that placed feminism and sisterhood across class boundaries above estatist goals, accepted the need for sales training while attempting to avoid a split among women clerks.[35] Elisabeth von Mumm, a Confederation expert on continuing education and its representative to the predominantly male German Alliance for Commercial Education, suggested that separate curricula would increase the segmentation of clerking and was particularly unfair when many girls were unsure whether they would work on the sales floor or in the office.[36] Johanna Waescher, who headed the female clerks' committee of the German Alliance for Commercial Education, convinced that organization to oppose separate curricula for sales and office workers in continuation schools. The Confederation did not oppose better schooling for sales personnel, but as Waescher argued, "the goal to be kept in mind is that the saleswoman be given an education equal to that of the office worker."[37] At its 1913 convention, the Confederation chose to broaden the scope of its policies regarding sales work, recommending a whole set of proposals to "elevate the situation of saleswomen" that centered upon legislation to improve pay and working conditions in sales.[38]

As had been the case with other educational proposals by female clerks' associations, a variety of male allies came to the support of sales courses. Beginning with a few entrepreneurs who established sales courses for their female department-store employees, the idea of systematic salesgirls' training began to receive wide attention from retailers' organizations and businessmen.[39] Here as elsewhere, their motives differed greatly from those of the associations. Both department stores and retail shops hired untrained elementary school girls, paid them little, and offered scant career mobility. They nevertheless railed against poorly trained working-class girls without proper work habits. One retailer bemoaned the fact that "daughters from the better circles, who learned good manners and proper speech at home, as well as excellent taste," were prejudiced against sales work.[40]

Although businessmen disliked the increased presence of working-class women in sales clerking, they did not halt the flow of "unsuitable" working-class girls into retail sales work. Rather, they sought ways to make them "suitable." Entrepreneurs did not seek to ameliorate the plight of women in clerking, they simply wanted to obtain qualified personnel without resorting to increased salaries and better apprenticeship training, both of which cost money. This led them to support the female clerks' associations in demanding schools for salesgirls. The solution brought educators and government bodies into the debate. By about 1910, both directors and teachers at commercial schools of continuing education had become convinced that special courses for salesgirls were needed, as did their professional organizations.[41]

All parties agreed about the nature of the proposed course. Since saleswomen were primarily considered unsuitable owing to their working-class backgrounds and their consequent inability to perform clerking tasks according to middle-class standards (poor spelling, inappropriate use of language, lack of proper taste and manners), the sales curricula all emphasized "lessons in taste" or "lessons in propriety."[42] As one businessman explained, "it's not at all easy to get a young girl who's just come from elementary school to grasp who should be addressed as 'If you please, Madam,' and who as 'Yes, Mrs. X'"[43] Elly von Rössing, who taught at a Berlin girls' continuation school and worked with the Confederation, proposed a similar curriculum. As an exercise to develop pupils' taste, von Rössing suggested that they criticize their own and one another's clothing and homes.[44]

How are these saleswomen's programs to be evaluated? They denoted an awareness on the part of the leadership of female organizations that saleswomen had to gain some general commercial knowledge and vocational skills if the estate were to continue to enjoy a degree of unity and if clerks' associations were to function successfully as pressure groups in German society. Further, a necessary pragmatism was embodied in the view that, within Wilhelmine society, working-class salesgirls had to take on certain middle-class patterns of thought and behavior in order to enjoy success in their careers or to move up a career ladder.

Yet there is no doubt that to encourage separate sales schooling implied an acceptance of the existing white-collar division of labor and of the hierarchies of both class and sex. The courses meant that women alone would be groomed for retail customer contact; men could continue to aspire to wholesale sales work or to store management. The gap between sales work and office work for female employees would be increased rather than bridged, limiting female professional mobility. Finally, the courses – emphatically designed to weed out "unsuitables" – reflect the organizations' acceptance of the class structure of Wilhelmine Germany, in which the working class was presumed to remain on the lowest rung of the socio-economic ladder in perpetuity. Only a few talented working-class girls would complete the necessary schooling and adapt to bourgeois codes of behavior in order to step up into clerking, a profession of the middle estate. Sales courses were expected to encourage well-bred girls to enter the field while hinting to working-class pupils that they would do better to lower their ambitions.

The Confederation, with its more consistent feminism, was willing to sacrifice some of its interest in professionalization in order to foster female unity within clerking. But it failed to move beyond that limited aim. It too accepted the socio-political status quo and assumed that the goal of equality avowed by bourgeois feminism would be achieved through equality of opportunity; thoughts of unity among women were not to be wasted on unsuitable elements.

Neither the Confederation nor the Commercial Alliance analyzed the motives of the business interests that took up the issue. They failed to consider the long-range implications of a dual curriculum, although the entrepreneurs had. With no thoughts for female equality in clerking, the businessmen recognized that sales courses would allow them to recruit employees from the pool of untrained working-class girls, to continue to pay them low salaries, and yet to be able to benefit from the middle-class cultivation foisted upon the girls at continuation schools financed by the state.

*Home economics courses: the relegation of women to the domestic sphere*

Leaders in female clerks' associations and other feminists had found support among males in clerking, business, and government for their plans to establish state-supported commercial schools and for sales-girls' courses. They accepted male support without question. By the end of the first decade of the twentieth century, however, the associations were forced to recognize that male support had not been motivated by any desire for female equality, and that the same groups that acted to provide girls with commercial schooling also favored separate and non-equal education.

From the late nineteenth century, many advocates of girls' vocational education sought it in order to prepare girls for domesticity; pupils would learn morality and home economics. They assumed that working-class girls came from inadequate families and began work in childhood, which prevented them from learning necessary homemaking skills.[45] The state had therefore to teach domestic skills in order to create a stable family environment in the next generation and to contribute to working-class docility.

Industrial continuation schools for girls commonly included domestic training, but as commercial continuation schools arose, they usually omitted such courses. When statistics revealed that a growing proportion of female clerks had working-class backgrounds, however, pressure mounted to introduce domestic training into the commercial curriculum. Even some moderate feminists agreed, accepting that woman's ultimate goal was marriage and motherhood.[46] The DHV, which sought to remove women entirely from clerking, seized on the notion and touted the suggestion that women be trained for their life's domestic work.[47]

As discussion became more widespread, the Berlin Commercial Alliance challenged proposals that home economics be included in commercial continuing education. The Alliance conceded that marriage and motherhood were women's highest calling and that some domestic training was useful to women. But it vehemently denied that continuation schooling was the proper place to teach domestic skills. If girls had fewer hours of instruction in commercial subjects, leaders argued, they would receive an inferior vocational education and would continue to trail behind men in pay and work achievement, while "unsuitable" girls were less likely to be eliminated.

To underline her point that domestic training was valuable, outside the vocational curriculum, Alliance leader Agnes Herrmann established voluntary "marriage courses" in Berlin in 1908. "These marriage courses show women how to do justice to the double career of the employed woman and yet to avoid half-measures," she wrote, insisting that girls needed a thorough vocational training when they began clerking, and that domestic training could follow when marriage approached.[48] Herrmann also claimed that domestic training was inappropriate for clerks because middle-class girls learned those skills at home.

Home economics should be used where the mother of the family – who provides the best education for marriage – fails to teach homemaking. The issue of obligatory home economics is a question of life importance for the lowest classes in the population, whose family life is threatened by dissolution owing to the mother's employment. Female clerks, however, come from the so-called middle estate to an extremely great degree and are daughters of officials, teachers, merchants, artisans. Here one finds domestic order in even the smallest matters; the mother sees her life's value in raising the children, caring for the household with the aid of her growing daughters ... Such schooling by the mother has been seen as sufficient up to now, and it ought to satisfy now as well, given the simplification of domestic responsibilities by modern technology.

As an alternative, Herrmann recommended teaching home economics in the last year of elementary school.[49] Another Commercial Alliance leader proposed in 1909 to divide continuing education. Commercial schools would have no home economics in the curriculum, industrial schools would devote one-third of the curriculum to home economics, and unskilled workers, servants, and unemployed girls would attend domestic training schools.[50]

The Confederation also proposed a ninth year of elementary school for all girls to concentrate on home economics and "further spiritual–moral education." It too expressed a sense that working-class girls were neglected at home, that family supports were dwindling, and that the schools had to step in to replace guidance no longer provided at home.[51] The Catholic Alliance at first accepted the need for home economics within continuation schooling, but by 1910 it also sought to exclude it from the curriculum, arguing that if girls received an inadequate education, opponents could justify discrimination in clerking on the basis of female inferiority. Believing that domestic training was important for all girls, the Catholic organization proposed teaching home economics during elementary school.[52]

In 1911, after the matter had received much popular attention, the Prussian Ministry of Commerce decreed that both male and female commercial continuation schools must have the same number of weekly teaching hours and an equal course length. However, their curricula differed, for girls were required to take home economics. "Instead of civics, [girls should receive] a life schooling which, above all, takes account of the position of woman in home and family, in profession and in charity work."[53]

The female clerks' associations immediately attacked the ruling, which they were certain would damage women's professional opportunities.[54] With a pragmatic eye to compromise, and more interested in professionalization than feminism, Agnes Herrmann suggested that girls go to school for eight hours a week rather than six, so that they could receive domestic training while still completing the same vocational coursework as boys. The Confederation, by contrast, insisted on complete educational equality, with no home economics at any point in the curriculum, and called Herrmann's proposal a setback for feminism.[55] But even the Confederation criticized the course because it provided an inadequate "training for the profession of housewife" and because it excluded unemployed girls, which would not be the case if home economics were taught in elementary school.[56]

The Alliance and the Confederation joined forces in 1914 to convene a conference on female careers that urged full equality between girls and boys in any vocational education.[57] They and other feminist groups circulated a letter to German chambers of commerce that opposed home economics courses in continuation schools and asserted that middle-class girls learned domestic tasks sufficiently well at home.[58]

Male clerks' organizations had supported women's efforts to improve girls' commercial schools because they feared that an uneducated female clerking proletariat could lower the status of the field and cost men their jobs. The same men sought to include home economics within the female curriculum, hoping that women would, as a result, leave the labor force to marry. Other male supporters of female education approved of home economics courses simply because they regarded women's sphere as the home. Since they viewed women as having jobs, not careers, they saw no reason why their vocational education should equal men's. Even the various commercial education lobbies, usually so supportive of the efforts of female clerks' associations, favored home economics. As one speaker noted, women needed adequate professional training, but "the way to her natural profession as housewife, mother, and educator must at all times remain open." Continuing education had therefore to include home economics.[59]

The campaign to introduce home economics into girls' commercial continuation schooling finally alerted the leadership of the all-female clerks' associations to the fact that their allies in educational reform did not seek female equality in clerking. By then, however, the female clerks' associations were trapped by the contradictions of their own statements, which demanded both that women be seen as a separate employment group having "dual careers," yet also that women be treated completely equally in employment matters. The organizations did not therefore point to the absurdity of teaching women their "natural" profession or call for an end to all home economics courses. Accepting innate sex differences, the associations did not challenge assumptions about women's nature, women's roles, or the secondary nature of women's employment lives. But nor did they openly proclaim that women were not men's equals in employment owing to their special domestic role and develop strategies based on difference rather than equality. Instead, they contended either that home economics courses belonged elsewhere or that middle-class girls did not need domestic training. They still aimed to professionalize clerking and to exclude unsuitable elements in order to assure women equality with men in the middle estate.

The educational campaigns of the all-female clerks' associations and the more limited proposals of the socialist Central Alliance both illustrate the tension between the interests and goals of feminism and those of class and professional interest. Leaders of the female groups had the feminist goal of raising female clerks to parity with their male colleagues. But their strategy of professionalization, with vocational education as its linchpin, meant that equality would come at the expense of working-class women who could not fulfill the professional requirements, so that sisterhood did not extend beyond the boundaries of class. With the campaign for sales courses, leaders ignored even the limited principle of equality for all women within the profession. The Central Alliance, for its part, dismissed any arguments that women required special attention, and formulated its educational policies only on the basis of the perceived interests of the working class.

The strategy of professionalization emphasized the common interests of men and women in clerking. Female clerks' organizations won a number of male allies, and owned their legislative successes to them rather than to support by the women's movement. Yet the educational campaigns of the all-female associations only succeeded to the extent that male interests predominated, as the instance of home economics courses most clearly showed. The successes came because business-men and government authorities hoped to produce well-trained women for low-level white-collar positions and because male clerks' associations sought to prevent the further deskilling of clerking, which they associated with an increase in female employment in the field, and not owing to any male interest in gender equality in clerking.

# 10

## *The needs of women versus the estate: white-collar insurance*

In the emerging welfare state of Wilhelmine Germany, pensions became a major public issue, for pension insurance divided workers into different categories and thereby strengthened or undercut their self-perceptions concerning class location. Given their insistence on professionalization, it is not surprising that both male and female clerks' associations sought to create a state pension insurance program solely for white-collar workers. Nor is it surprising that the socialist Central Alliance saw that campaign as a major threat and attempted to prevent the creation of a separate insurance fund.

The success of clerks and other white-collar workers in securing legislation to create a special insurance fund of their own has been seen as a victory for the conservatism and status-hunger of Germany's "new middle estate."[1] Yet evidence supports the view that the insurance program was rather a victory for professionalization. The "collar line" was indeed important to these men and women, as Kocka insists, but their strategy of preventing any further loss of skill and responsibility in clerking was equally important. Leaders of clerks' associations expected the establishment of an independent insurance program to assure the professional recognition of the field and by distinguishing themselves from blue-collar workers to hinder its continued routinization. The issue of status was certainly important to this project, but that status was a component of economic strategy rather than an element in class identity.

Both the Berlin Commercial Alliance and the Confederation worked actively for the reform, which exposed the cross-cutting loyalties faced by female clerks. The Alliance tried to balance women's needs against its awareness of the limits of pragmatic possibility and of the necessity of male support. The Confederation took the more consistent feminist position, as it had on other issues, insisting that the insurance plan meet the particular needs of women clerks and questioning insurance support for non-working wives. As with other proposed reform measures, the Central Alliance asserted the unity of interests between white-collar and blue-collar workers and failed to mobilize significant support.

## White-collar workers raise the issue of state insurance

The state disability insurance program, which provided pension insurance and survivors' benefits, was expanded in 1893 so that many white-collar workers were included. A variety of male white-collar organizations felt that coverage was insufficient, however, claiming that even the highest pension paid was neither adequate for their needs nor commensurate with their status. They were particularly unhappy about the low rate of widows' pensions and about disability coverage, which did not include "professional disability." As a result, a pension was only paid when the insured person became incapable of all work, not simply white-collar tasks. They also noted that the insurance only covered persons earning under 2,000 M a year, which was less than the average male salary.[2]

After individual efforts, most of the large white-collar associations joined forces in 1901 to create the Main Committee for State Pension and Survivors' Insurance for White-Collar Workers, referred to as the Main Pension Committee, which had soon established chapters in over 150 cities. Although the Berlin Commercial Alliance joined and sent Josef Silbermann as its delegate,[3] in its early years the Committee chiefly represented the interests of married male white-collar workers and ignored the somewhat different concerns of single persons, especially women. Indeed, some members at first expected the insurance to exclude certain categories of female clerks from coverage by defining their work as "mechanical" and therefore blue-collar rather than white.[4] Men in the Main Pension Committee soon realized however that excluding women from an expensive state insurance program would make them attractive job candidates to employers who sought to avoid paying its premiums.[5] From that point on, the Committee adhered to a policy of professionalization that included women and insisted on the unity of clerking, fighting any division of the field or its workplace into primary and secondary sectors.

As with the campaigns to reform commercial education, the clerks' campaign for white-collar pension insurance should be viewed as part of their efforts to prevent deskilling and loss of control over the work process. Two types of benefits were expected from the separate fund.

First, by emphasizing the distinct legal status of clerks and other white-collar workers, the legislation was expected to aid organizations in preventing the dilution of the clerking work-force and the fragmenting of its tasks. In addition, the program would give real material advantages to its members. At the same time, however, the policy hindered clerks' recognition of their changing class position and prevented them from allying with the socialist Central Alliance, not only because the union asserted that white-collar workers were members of the proletariat, but also because it accepted the deskilling of clerking, with the routinization of work and loss of income that that implied.

By 1903 the Main Pension Committee was so well organized that it could investigate the circumstances of German clerks. It distributed a questionnaire and received over 150,000 replies, which it turned over to the Imperial Ministry of the Interior for statistical analysis.[6] When the government released its report in 1907 and proposed high premiums to cover costs, white-collar leaders rejected the government's draft. The reinvigorated Main Pension Committee was chaired and dominated by the DHV,[7] which used its control of the executive Commission of Seven to dominate the insurance issue, lending credence to its claim to lead the "white-collar movement" and pushing other clerks' organizations in a conservative direction.

At the end of 1907 the Main Pension Committee split into two factions on the question of whether to expand the existing state pension and disability insurance program or to create a separate white-collar plan. The flexibility displayed up until that point indicates that material concerns and strategies based on group interest were of greater urgency than issues of status. The majority of organizations, guided by the DHV, insisted on a separate plan. The minority, composed of the socialist Central Alliance and other Free Union and Hirsch-Duncker white-collar organizations, sought to reform the existing – largely blue-collar – program. When the DHV barred the minority faction from publicly expressing its views, it walked out and constituted the Free Alliance for Social Insurance for Private Salaried Employees.[8] Neither male faction sought support from the female clerks' organizations.

It is of particular note that the Central Alliance aimed its arguments almost entirely at men. Since most female clerks earned under 2,000 M a year and were therefore obliged to join the existing government pension plan, the Free Alliance might well have won their support, yet the group made no overtures to women.[9] Indeed, in one article the Central Alliance appealed directly to male prejudices against employed women, predicting that the proposed white-collar insurance would cause women to flock to clerking.[10]

## Women and white-collar insurance

Before 1907, although the Berlin Commercial Alliance had joined the
Main Pension Committee, it showed little interest in white-collar pension insurance. With salaries under 2,000 M a year, female clerks were
covered by the existing state program, and widows' pensions pena-
lized them. Eva von Roy, however, head of the independent Königsberg clerks' association, saw feminist potential in the issue. At the
1904 Confederation convention, she suggested that female clerks'
organizations force the Main Committee to meet the needs of women,
and proposed that widows' pensions only be paid to aged or disabled
women. Most delegates, however, were unfamiliar with the whole
matter, and accepted Agnes Herrmann's contention that von Roy's
proposal was "particularistic" and "asocial," and that the Commercial
Alliance adequately represented women on the Pension Committee.[11]

When the government released its report in 1907, von Roy again
pressed the Confederation – now a rival to the Berlin Commercial
Alliance – to participate in the insurance debate. The organization
appointed von Roy to investigate the issue and then confer with other
feminist organizations and with the Pension Committee's executive
Commission of Seven.[12] The Confederation also sought support from
the BDF executive, which responded eagerly, seeking the views of
its members as to whether it was equitable that "all private officials,
even *single* ones, contribute to the costs of survivors' benefits . . . or
is it more appropriate to exact special fees for the widows' and
orphans' insurance?" The BDF also insisted that in any insurance
plan, "female participation in all administrative bodies must be
assured."[13] What is remarkable is the willingness of German bourgeois
feminists to insist upon the needs and rights of single working women
when they ran counter to those of married women and the family
unit.

The Confederation worked throughout 1907 to formulate and publicize its program, soon widely known as the "women's demands,"
which rejected widows' pensions and substituted "wives' insurance."
This well-argued but poorly received proposal is the single example
of consistent and radical feminist policy on the part of any clerks'
association in the pre-war period. The Confederation took a political
opportunity created by male white-collar workers and attempted to
mount a major feminist campaign. It articulated a theory of the economic role of housework, confronted woman's dual role at home and
in professional life, and raised questions of equity between the sexes
in insurance matters that have only re-emerged in the past decade.[14]

Von Roy proposed that white-collar pension insurance have two categories, "mandatorily insured" persons and "those needing provision."

It was out-dated, she asserted, to equate the latter category solely with widows and orphans, for that ignored the needs of single persons who supported relatives; this was especially true of women.

The burden of caring for dependents unable to work is usually left to single women, with no further ado; one sees this often enough in daily life. The minute the son marries, he is busy with his family; it is then the daughter's responsibility to support other dependents.[15]

Von Roy therefore demanded that all needy relatives, not just wives, receive survivors' benefits.

On the other hand, von Roy challenged the view that all widows – not simply aged or invalid women – should receive a stipend. "The need faced by a capable widow is no greater than that faced by each girl or woman who depends upon the work of her hands," wrote von Roy, who assumed that all women should be regarded as free individuals, each having to make her way without privilege. It was also a plea to recognize the worth of single employed women and to address their problems. However, her proposal ignored the fact that many middle-class women had received no employment skills, having assumed since childhood that their adult lives would center upon marriage. Von Roy simply remarked that employment among single girls was increasing, assuming as a result that education and vocational training would solve the problem.[16]

Von Roy's feminist demand for work skills was not meant to denigrate the role of housewife. On the contrary, she had a shrewd appreciation of the low status of that feminine role, despite the lip service paid to woman's "natural profession." In her view, the single career woman could either continue outside employment with "homemaking specialists" hired for domestic tasks, or she could embark on a career as a salaried homemaker. She commented that a woman's

role as housewife and mother is not considered her professional work – although on the other hand it is always extolled as the single true and natural profession of the woman – and has thus far not been included in insurance. The activity of the housewife and mother is not rewarded monetarily today, but rather viewed as a sort of honorary work . . . If however her energy or good will fail, then the nurse or housekeeper who takes her place must be paid.

Von Roy contended that a revolution in domestic life was underway in which wives would come to be paid for their services, assuring them "economic independence in marriage."[17]

In the field of insurance, therefore, von Roy insisted that no widows' pensions should exist (although survivors' benefits for truly needy dependent relatives, including widows, would be part of the coverage). All women would work before marriage and receive employees' insurance. Upon marriage, rather than resigning from the program, a woman would continue her insurance as a homemaker. The fees would be paid by the woman herself out of the "salary" she received from her husband. In practice, as critics indignantly noted, von Roy's proposal meant that married men were to pay a double insurance fee (or triple, since the employer's payment would also have to be met by him). This charge did not trouble her. Men were no longer the sole breadwinners of the family, she replied, and husbands who wanted the luxury of unemployed wives – most likely for status reasons – should be willing to pay for it.[18]

Farsighted as it was, von Roy's analysis still suffered from an inability to see beyond her own middle-class milieu. The female life cycle she posited, moving from home to workplace to home, was not that of proletarian or peasant women, who were both responsible for homemaking and child care as well as for work outside the home – without the aid of "specialists." Like the Confederation's educational plans, the insurance proposal was appropriate only to the middle estate. Yet even there her suggestion was unworkable, for it failed to challenge the view that domestic work was "natural" for women and therefore their sole responsibility. If the rules and actors in the private and public spheres were distinct and different, there was no logical reason why a married woman should remain employed and hire domestic help and no grounds on which she could demand a salary for her "natural" family duties.

The Confederation worked during 1907 to publicize von Roy's proposal and to win allies, raising the "women's demands" at regional conventions of white-collar organizations[19] and convincing associations of female teachers and nurses to join the Main Pension Committee and support its women's demands.[20] Finally, the Confederation challenged the Committee and its executive Commission of Seven to address the needs of female white-collar workers and to seat women on the Commission.

Neither the Main Pension Committee nor its executive Commission, however, proved sympathetic. Secretary Schack (DHV) of the Commission offered to admit a Confederation representative only to executive deliberations pertaining to women, which the Confederation rejected as tokenism.[21] The full Committee showed no interest in discussing the Confederation's proposals, with one DHV delegate commenting that "this is not the time to involve ourselves in women's issues." Although the Committee agreed to send the Confederation demands to the government along with its own proposals, the Ministry of the Interior never received any of the Confederation material.[22]

Owing to the conflicts within the white-collar ranks and to the pre-eminence attained by the Confederation with its women's demands, the Berlin Commercial Alliance began to formulate its own position. Up until the end of 1907, the Alliance held that an expansion of existing state insurance was sufficient to meet women's needs.[23] It took this position not because it was a progressive organization, but because it feared that male white-collar organizations would use the new insurance program to downgrade certain female clerking fields (especially warehousing and sales, but possibly also stenotyping). In opting for the expansion of the existing state program, the Commercial Alliance was not rejecting the notion of a white-collar estate but, rather, acting to assure female clerks a place within it. However, by the end of 1907 it was clear that only a minority of male clerks – identified with unionism and socialism – favored expansion, leading the Commercial Alliance to identify its interests with those of the Main Pension Committee and to press for separate white-collar insurance.[24]

The question of women's demands was more difficult for the Commercial Alliance to resolve, for the association wanted both to work with male organizations of the middle estate and yet to claim that it best represented the interests of women. The organization rejected as "antisocial" the Confederation proposal to create separate pension categories for employees and wives, remarking that it would burden men and "limit the possibilities of marriage." It also dismissed the alternative suggestion that women pay a lower insurance fee (since they received no widows' benefit), contending that since the employers' contribution would then also be lower, employers would hire a preponderance of women.[25]

But although the Berlin Commercial Alliance did not support the demands of the Confederation, neither did it offer its own vision of the relationship of home and work in women's lives. Feminist analysis was again sacrificed to the perceived needs of the professional estate and to the organization's desire to work on an equal footing with male clerks' associations. As the executive board noted, "we wanted to maintain the previously established standpoint of professional solidarity between the sexes."[26] Berlin's own modest set of demands emphasized formal equality between male and female members regarding insurance obligations and benefits. It proposed that all relatives economically dependent on the member be given survivors' benefits, including illegitimate children; that if a female member married, her insurance be transformed into an old-age pension; that she be allowed to re-enter the full program if later re-employed; and that if a woman continued full coverage throughout her marriage, her widower and children receive survivors' benefits.[27]

At first glance, these provisions seem both to establish equality between the sexes and to meet the special needs of women leaving the work-force upon marriage. But the impression is misleading. Few married women worked in clerking, so that few female clerks would use the provision for widowers and children. Nor would many single clerks bear and raise illegitimate children. Only the plan to expand coverage to include all dependent relatives offered benefits to a majority of women in clerking. But the Confederation had already considered that proposal and rejected it owing to the enormous cost.[28] The Commercial Alliance therefore offered women a formal equality which might even prove detrimental to them, for the insurance was much more expensive than the existing plan to which most female clerks already belonged.

In 1908 the Confederation called a conference of female white-collar organizations. The Berlin Commercial Alliance attended, but rejected most of the Confederation proposals, agreeing only to co-sponsor the demand that women be seated on the Commission of Seven, which the Main Pension Committee again refused.[29] In this atmosphere of stalemate, the government intervened.

*Gender and estate*

In 1908 the German government published a second proposal for white-collar pension insurance, which attempted to meet the objections of clerks' organizations. In addition to lower fees, female employees would receive certain special provisions in order to redress the imbalance in benefits.[30] By this time, a number of outside pressure groups had seized on the issue. The Society for Social Reform discussed the issue at its annual convention, creating widespread publicity and public support for the measure. A number of industrial and commercial pressure groups also acted, including the Alliance of Saxon Industrialists, the Alliance of German Department Stores, the Central Alliance of German Industrialists, and the Hansa Federation.[31]

At the same time, the Main Pension Committee changed its composition and its tenor. The minority faction of the Committee resigned in 1909 and established an independent organization. Reichstag Deputy Schack, DHV chief and secretary of the powerful executive Commission of Seven, resigned after the public exposure of his unsavory sexual affairs.[32] The new secretary, Bechly, was a more moderate DHV member and introduced Clara Mleinek to the executive Commission as the representative of the Berlin Commercial Alliance.[33]

With its new stature as a Commission member, the Commercial Alliance went over to the offensive and criticized both the Confederation plan and its view of women's roles. The Confederation, in defense, shifted the grounds of its argument and became even more radical. Both associations publicized their positions and attempted to win support in the press and among Reichstag deputies, professional organizations, and other interest groups.[34] Their brief debate had little impact on the final form of the insurance program, although the existence of female white-collar organizations with well-articulated demands did lead the government to include some provisions for women in its legislation.

The Commercial Alliance claimed that the Confederation women's demands were unworkable and attacked the Confederation view that married women should work. Clara Mleinek argued that "it really isn't a praiseworthy goal to alienate women more and more from the home. Nor is respect for the work of wives and mothers increased by outside employment. We should work much more to enable women to fulfill household duties."[35] Eva von Roy, drawing on the results of the 1907 census, responded by describing the "double burden" of the married woman worker. In a demand that she termed both "reasonable and practical," she asked that "every adult person, whether man or woman, married or unmarried, should stand on his own feet in our economic and employment world, independent from others if possible." From her earlier analysis, which suggested that housework deserved respect and remuneration, she now asserted that married women should work outside the home rather than be "nailed fast to homemaking tasks."[36] What had begun in 1907 as a careful analysis of the difficulties women faced in their two roles became a radical attack on women's limitation to the domestic sphere, but a curiously unproductive one, for the interests and experiences of von Roy's constituents were not those of working wives. It was not enough to assert that all adults should work; in order to win converts, von Roy needed to suggest practical means by which women could work and still fulfill domestic obligations. Thrown on the defensive by the Berlin Commercial Alliance, von Roy moved away from her earlier, more careful, analysis and was left with a policy that appeared Utopian, impractical, and irrelevant.

In 1910 the Confederation made a final effort to win support for its radically new approach to insurance by extending its women's demands to all government programs. It petitioned the Reichstag asking that coverage in all government insurance programs extend to spouses and that parents and siblings of single members receive health insurance and burial stipends.[37] However, the Confederation proposals were ignored, and by the end of the year it acknowledged its failure. The organization dropped its proposal for wives' insurance, although it continued to advocate survivors' benefits for which only the needy were eligible.[38] Early in 1911 the government finally laid its legislation before the Reichstag. Neither the Confederation proposal nor the Commercial Alliance suggestions appeared in the draft. Although male white-collar groups criticized points in the legislation, none mentioned its discrimination against women. The Berlin Commercial Alliance was silent as well about discriminatory provisions, and it dropped its own demands.[39]

Unlike the Commercial Alliance, which had chosen to ally itself with the male organizations and to accept discrimination against insured women, the Confederation was shaken by its failure to win better provisions for women in the insurance legislation. At its 1911 convention, delegates debated whether to resign from the Main Pension Committee entirely and to reject the draft legislation. At a meeting marked by great conflict, a majority voted to remain, at the same time sending its own proposal to the Reichstag and Bundesrat. A number of Confederation locals resigned from the Committee, and Johanna Waescher replaced Eva von Roy as the Confederation delegate.[40]

After the insurance legislation had been passed, the Confederation and the Commercial Alliance each took credit for the few concessions that the law offered women.[41] Each was only partially correct. It was surely owing to the work of Confederation leaders, especially von Roy, that public attention was drawn to the fact that women faced discrimination in the insurance proposals. The final law, however, embodied the modest suggestions offered by the Commercial Alliance rather than the radical restructuring demanded by the Confederation, for it granted widowers of insured (i.e., employed) women the same pension as widows, and it gave survivors' benefits to illegitimate as well as legitimate children. Women who married received a payment or an annuity.[42] If a feminist analysis had drawn attention to the inequity of the original insurance plans, it was the pragmatic and conciliatory set of proposals made by the Berlin Commercial Alliance that gained women concessions.

## Women and the elections to the white-collar insurance administration

With the passage of the white-collar pension insurance law, women achieved the right to participate in its administration, winning both active and passive voting rights on most administrative bodies – no small concession in the era of conservatism after 1910.[43] This gave female clerks' associations an opportunity to win members to the organization and to mobilize them for political activity. It also provided a chance to show the wider public that women took their civic duties seriously. The associations here followed the example of the Free Unions, which had been the first group to recognize that elections to insurance boards could politicize workers and testify to their civic concern and competence.[44]

Electoral activity did not begin with the white-collar insurance, for both the Central Alliance and the all-female clerks' associations had campaigned to seat representatives on the boards of the German community health plans (OKK) established by Bismarck, which granted voting rights to women. By 1910 approximately 140,000 female clerks belonged to the OKK,[45] and the Confederation had successfully campaigned in a number of communities to elect female representatives to their boards, where they pressed to hire women as claims inspectors, etc.[46] Some worked in conjunction with other female professional organizations and with organizations of the women's movement.[47] The Berlin Commercial Alliance was slower to mount election campaigns, but it too worked with local women's groups to elect female OKK representatives.[48]

Once the white-collar pension insurance law was passed, both the Confederation and the Commercial Alliance worked vigorously to elect women to its administrative bodies. They hoped for high female voter participation to ensure female representation on the insurance board "to make use of a new right and to offer evidence that women are mature enough for it, that they possess understanding for the demands of the day."[49] They also expected election campaigning to arouse the interest of unorganized female clerks, who would become aware of professional issues and perhaps join an organization.[50] Even the Catholic Alliance was anxious to participate in election campaigns, although its motive was as much to halt socialism as to encourage female voting rights.[51]

The Commercial Alliance sent campaign guidelines to chapters, suggesting that they unite with local women's groups, especially professional associations, in order to research local conditions and propose a slate of women to stand for election.[52] In large cities, female white-collar organizations ran joint "women's slates."[53] In most smaller towns, however, Confederation locals and Alliance chapters joined male organizations belonging to the Main Pension Committee, including the DHV. Some local organizations combined to present a single Pension Committee slate (with candidates chosen by lot), others offered separate women's and men's slates, with the understanding that each would receive the other's preferences.[54] Although the socialist Central Alliance had consistently championed female voting rights on all social bodies, while the DHV had been implacably hostile to women in clerking, none of the female clerks' associations mounted a joint campaign with the Central Alliance.[55] Once again, unity among members of the white-collar estate received priority over feminism.

In the election campaign that followed, the Central Alliance emphasized that the Confederation and the Commercial Alliance had both thrown in their lot with "enemies of women's work."[56] There was ample truth in this. In some cities where women ran a separate slate, the DHV distributed pamphlets urging men and women not to vote for it. However, the Free Alliance itself rarely nominated women, or it listed them so far down the ticket that they had no chance of election.[57] The all-female associations criticized this and contended that their work with the DHV was merely tactical. Clara Mleinek of the Berlin Commercial Alliance reassured members at an election meeting that "women have always been aware of the [DHV's] hostility toward women," but that to ensure passage of the white-collar insurance, "all particularistic interests had to be relegated to the background."[58] Her view of women's interests as "particularistic" is telling; it reduced sex discrimination to the level of a minor grievance within the white-collar estate. In the first white-collar insurance election, a high percentage of women voted, and sixty-nine women white-collar workers became trustees of the insurance.[59] This set the new strategy; women would work within the estate, with the aid of their male colleagues, and press for reform.

The 1911 white-collar insurance law was of fundamental importance for male clerks. Its effect on female clerks was far-reaching as well. A majority of the women, like the men, had become part of a bloc of white-collar workers, their associations committed to a strategy of professionalization that set them apart from blue-collar workers. The thrust of their organizational efforts was directed at the government, which they expected to prevent the deskilling of clerking and to provide them with benefits commensurate with their perceived status as important new members of the middle estate.

But the women were affected in other ways as well. The debate over insurance provisions for women resulted in the most thorough attempt by feminists in clerks' associations to analyze women's employment and domestic roles and to apply that analysis to policy proposals. The failure of that attempt had a long-range effect on the all-female associations, for it gave the lead to the Commercial Alliance, now prepared to compromise with male organizations – even the DHV – and to ignore pressing feminist issues. From an auspicious beginning in which they sought equality for women throughout the public sphere, leaders of the all-female clerks' groups narrowed their sights to concentrate upon winning concessions for the white-collar estate, overlooking women's second-class status within it. At the same time, the Central Alliance became more marginal, for it had failed both to convince white-collar workers that their interests were identical to those of blue-collar workers and to persuade women that it could represent their interests. An analysis based on estate triumphed over analyses based on class or gender.

# Conclusion

Before World War I clerks' organizations with female members achieved a number of reforms, both alone and working with their male colleagues. Evening store-closing hours, commercial courts, a wide network of girls' commercial continuation schools, and white-collar insurance were all reforms owing much to the members and leaders of the organizations. With their belief in the need to increase the political role of the middle estate, the all-female associations could point with satisfaction to their ability to ally with other white-collar workers and with business interests to win government support for reforms. Gertrud Israel, a Commercial Alliance leader, wrote of the pride and sense of community experienced by delegates at its 1912 convention, for they represented women who had "not allowed the waves of destiny to break passively over them, nor let others do their work for them, but – with confidence in their own power – put their hands to the task, so that by working together each could help herself."[1] The socialist Central Alliance, for its part, could point to legislative reform that it had supported, as well as to employment contracts it had negotiated that improved saleswomen's working conditions and pay scales.

Clerks' organizations aided their female members on an individual basis as well. Members of the bourgeois all-female associations benefited from the services their groups offered, the courses in vocational and educational subjects they ran, and the cultural events they sponsored. The women also learned from the associations' socializing and politicizing messages, which taught them the importance of self-assertion, independence, and civic participation. Although the Central Alliance did not aim at individual betterment, it nevertheless offered members a sense of solidarity and a support network, both of which could help women clerks adjust to the world of work.

The achievements of the clerks' associations, however, were limited. Neither the legislative reforms affecting all women clerks nor the programs serving individual members led to employment equality for women in clerking. Nor did they improve the general lot of clerks *vis-à-vis* other salaried or wage workers in the German economy. Although the all-female associations and the Central Alliance each sought to raise the status of women and to help women achieve economic independence, neither questioned female subordination in the private sphere, which meant that neither recognized that women comprised a particular employment grouping. It also meant that leaders in the Central Alliance, however well meaning, did not perceive women's second-class status within the organization.

This study has argued that clerks' associations with female members were hampered in a variety of ways, making the achievement of feminist and professional goals impossible at the time. One set of difficulties arose from the particular problems faced by women in the world of work. Women in clerking were a new employment group, without traditions of organization or professional awareness. Women worked for a relatively brief period of time and viewed their employment lives as secondary. Both men and women – including most feminists – believed that women alone had domestic duties and responsibilities, so that marriage and a career were incompatible.

In addition, both bourgeois and socialist organizations failed to generate theories of female emancipation that recognized the conflict in women's lives arising from the contradictory roles, attitudes, and behavior expected of them in the public and private spheres. Both the all-female clerks' associations and the socialist Central Alliance insisted that female equality in society was essential, but they encouraged members to believe that women's employment problems were solely an issue pertaining to the public sphere. They were convinced that overcoming discrimination in the public sphere would entirely emancipate women.

Both theories viewed paid employment outside the home as central to redressing female subordination. The bourgeois women's movement had long expected education and employment to liberate women. Work before marriage would allow each woman's unique personality and talents to unfold, making her more intellectually assertive and economically independent and allowing her to enter marriage a full partner to her husband or to remain unwed and work for the community at large. Socialists offered a very different analysis, but it too was based on female employment. It envisioned female liberation arising out of socialist revolution; if women were wage workers, revolution would emancipate them as well as their proletarian brethren. Only then would women be capable of solidarity (as members of the proletariat, not as women) and only then, owing to their economic independence, could women throw off the slavery of domesticity.

Although the bourgeois and the socialist theories varied, they both foresaw extensive change occurring in the private as well as the public sphere owing simply to female employment. Both ignored the actual role of women in the home, their burden of domestic responsibility under the headship of their husbands. The bourgeois all-female associations expected marriage to become a partnership, given women's new self-confidence and independence, even though upon marriage women left employment to retreat into a domestic world. Socialist feminists believed the private sphere would disappear once married women were gainfully employed and household tasks were mechanized, because economic dependence (the material base) had caused women's oppression in the home.

At the same time that bourgeois feminists predicted that improvements in women's status would emerge from their employment role, they insisted that the primary obligation of married women was to the home. Within the bourgeois all-female associations, therefore, a contradiction emerged between leadership claims that marriage and motherhood comprised woman's "natural" and highest vocation and its demand for female clerks to develop a "professional consciousness" and to organize. Clerks' associations endeavored to help members become more assertive and independent, while at the same time, organizational leaders praised "feminine" traits of deference and dependence. They emphasized that women were a distinct employment grouping, but at the same time demanded that male clerks, employers, and government officials grant women equal employment rights.

Women in the socialist Central Alliance encountered a different contradiction, that between union insistence on female equality in employment and the toleration of or connivance at female subordination in the organization and at home. Theory held that female employment would end women's domestic oppression. Yet the union's call for equal pay for equal work and its insistence that women struggle shoulder to shoulder with union men did not bring them equality within the organization.

Feminist analyses accepted by leaders in both the bourgeois and the socialist clerks' organizations led them to expect that female emancipation would result once women were fully integrated into the labor force and had achieved equality in clerking. Leaders did not focus on employment issues at the cost of feminist activism, but rather saw those issues as central to women's emancipation. Arising out of particular historical circumstances that divided women's lives into two distinct parts – the public and the private – it was the analysis itself that was limited, not the dedication of leaders to feminism.

A second set of difficulties arose from the proletarianization of clerking in Germany between 1890 and 1914, coupled with the emergence of a dual labor market in the field. Women's pay was less than men's, and women had fewer opportunities to enroll in apprenticeship programs or to attend state-supported commercial schools. Nor did women advance to middle-level or senior positions; on the contrary, they usually held routine jobs, such as retail selling or stenotyping, that had earlier not existed as separate positions when clerking had been a higher status, all-male field. Moreover, the women who became clerks tended to be drawn in ever greater numbers from blue-collar families, making the job-holders proletarian as well as the jobs. These structural changes meant that women were not only a distinct employment category on account of their role in the home, but also owing to their position as secondary workers in clerking, so that women were differentiated on the basis of class as well as gender.

The bourgeois all-female clerks' associations dealt with proletarianization and secondary status by following the lead of male clerks' associations and seeking to fix clerking firmly within the middle estate. Using the strategy of professionalization, they attempted to close ranks against the proletariat, excluding working-class girls unless they modified their behavior and attitudes to approach those of "better circles." They hoped thereby to create a responsible profession with few routine positions, with improved pay and working conditions, and with women fully integrated at all levels.

This was bound to fail. The blue-collar craft fields and middle-class professions that successfully limited or prevented deskilling were able to set training and educational requirements and to control entry to their occupations. Clerking however had expanded in the late nineteenth century precisely because the number and variety of routine white-collar tasks had increased. Employers were satisfied if their employees had merely basic educational skills, and they were not willing to become bound by the sort of apprentice and educational levels demanded by clerks' organizations. If employers were prepared to accept any degree of professionalization, it was for their male employees, whom they expected to have advanced secondary schooling, and who received apprenticeships, better pay and working conditions, and career mobility, even advancing into the service class as managers. Women in clerking were limited to the secondary labor market, and neither employers and government officials

nor their male colleagues were interested in their professionalization.

It suited the strategy of professionalization to have leaders emphasize clerks' membership in the "middle estate." But theories of white-
collar work also arose out of a concrete historical situation, just as
feminist analyzes had, for clerking had once been a middle-class occupation, and in the period during which this was ceasing to be true,
other factors prevented recognition of this. First, feminization masked
proletarianization, for the increasing presence of female clerks was
perceived by many men as the cause of job segmentation.[2] In addition,
the polarization of Wilhelmine Germany affected clerks' associations, for
accepting a proletarian identity would have allied clerks with socialism.

A cleft ran throughout German society before World War I. A majority of German citizens accepted capitalism, felt comfortable working
within the authoritarian German constitutional system, and feared
and was suspicious of socialism. However, a sizeable minority, largely
working class, rejected a society content to relegate them to a marginal
position with few rewards and turned to the socialist and Free Union
movements.

A division arose therefore in the "white-collar movement," which
also contributed to the difficulties besetting organizations of women
clerks. Some defined themselves as part of the middle estate and
pinned their hopes on professionalization and legislative reform,
shunning any direct attack on employers. The socialist Central
Alliance, on the contrary, insisted that proletarianization was the fate
of all clerks, male as well as female, and sought solidarity between
white-collar and blue-collar workers. It therefore pressed for reform
legislation but relied as well upon union tactics directed against
employers. However, the union found itself isolated and unable to
win many clerks to its ranks. Its allegiance to socialism and Free Unionism made many women clerks suspicious. The bourgeois all-female
associations, on the other hand, intent on preventing proletarianization, were left no alternative but to fight their uphill battle for professional status. It is clear today that lower-level white-collar workers
have lost that battle in the industrialized world: they are just workers
of another sort.

Class and gender both affected the strategies and decisions of
leaders in the female clerks' associations. They had continually to
decide the extent to which they would press to improve the situation
of women in the field or to which they would, rather, work for the
profession as a whole – which might well mean granting new advantages to males in clerking. This posed a real dilemma for female clerks'
organizations, for they could only improve the position of their women
constituents if males acquiesced or, in some cases (such as insurance),

if legislative reform pertaining to all clerks was enacted. No satisfactory solution existed to this problem. The Confederation attempted most consistently to place the needs of women before those of the profession, but the more insistent it was, the more it became marginal, as is illustrated by its "women's demands" for white-collar insurance. The Berlin Commercial Alliance minimized its feminism and sought allies among male clerks' groups, but then found that it could achieve little that male clerks or business interests did not themselves desire, while being largely unable to bargain for reforms favorable to women. Although educational policy was central to Commercial Alliance strategy, no Imperial or state laws were passed requiring female attendance at commercial continuation schools.

Wedged uncomfortably between the demands of class and those of gender, clerks' associations with female members moved before World War I to make perceived class interests paramount. The consequences after the war were enormous. Members flocked to the Central Alliance and to other white-collar unions affiliated with the victorious SPD, but the group did not develop programs for its female members. The Confederation and the Berlin Commercial Alliance merged – and then joined the DHV in a volkish white-collar organization.[3]

The study of Germany's women clerks indicates that the pattern of their lives was one of contradictions and tensions. Before World War I, feminists and association leaders failed to address the complexity of women's lives and failed at the same time to develop strategies or policies that succeeded in improving the lot of their constituents. They defined themselves by gender and by class; they sought fulfillment in the public and the private sphere; they found it impossible to be both "woman" and "worker."

*Notes*

---

**1 Clerks and clerking**

1 Rolf Engelsing, "Die wirtschaftliche und soziale Differenzierung der deutschen kaufmännischen Angestellten im In- und Ausland, 1690–1900," in Rolf Engelsing, ed., *Zur Sozialgeschichte deutscher Mittel- und Unterschichten* (Göttingen, 1973), p. 81; Gewerkschaftsbund der Angestellten, *Epochen der Angestellten-Bewegung, 1774–1930* (Berlin, 1930), p. 60; Hans Paul Bahrdt, *Industriebürokratie* (Stuttgart, 1958), p. 41; and Werner Deich, *Der Angestellte im Roman: Zur Sozialgeschichte des Handlungsgehilfen um 1900* (Cologne, 1974), p. 35. I am using "clerk" as a general translation for the terms *Handlungsgehilfe, Handlungskommis*, and *kaufmännischer Angestellte*. It is synonymous with "commercial assistant" and "commercial employee."

2 Engelsing, "Differenzierung," p. 55.

3 David Lockwood, *The Blackcoated Worker: A Study in Class Consciousness* (London, 1958); Harry Braverman, *Labor and Monopoly Capital: The Degradation of Work in the Twentieth Century* (New York, 1974); and Gregory Anderson, *Victorian Clerks* (Manchester, 1976).

4 Engelsing, "Differenzierung," p. 90; Günter Hartfiel, *Angestellte und Angestelltengewerkschaften in Deutschland* (Berlin, 1961), pp. 84–86; and Braverman, *Labor*, pp. 293–312.

5 Bahrdt, *Industriebürokratie*, p. 44; and Jürgen Kocka, *Unternehmensverwaltung und Angestelltenschaft am Beispiel Siemens, 1847–1914*, Schriftenreihe des Arbeitskreises für moderne Sozialgeschichte 11 (Stuttgart, 1969), p. 309.

6 Bahrdt, *Industriebürokratie*, pp. 45–47; Hartfiel, *Angestellte*, p. 44.

7 Werner Sombart, "Die Entwicklungstendenzen im modernen Kleinhandel," *SVS* 88 (1899): 142ff; Käthe Lux, *Studien über die Entwicklung der Warenhäuser in Deutschland* (Jena, 1910); Kaufhof A.G., *75 Jahre Kaufhof: Die Kaufhof Illustrierte*, Jubiläums-Sonderheft 31 (Cologne, n.d. [1954?]).

8 Zentralverband der Handlungsgehilfen und Gehilfinnen, *Bericht des*

134

*Vorstandes und Ausschusses über die 7. Geschäftsperiode 1908–09 nebst Protokoll der 7. Generalversammlung, 16.-17. Mai 1910* (Hamburg, 1910), p. 16.

9 Friedrich K. Kern, *Zur sozialen Lage der Verkäuferinnen* (Heidelberg, 1910), p. 28.

10 Nicholas Abercrombie and John Urry, *Capital, Labour and the Middle Classes* (London, 1983); Margery W. Davies, *Woman's Place is at the Typewriter: Office Work and Office Workers, 1870–1930* (Philadelphia, 1982); Paul Thompson, *The Nature of Work: An Introduction to Debates on the Labour Process* (London, 1983); and Braverman, *Labor*.

11 *ZWH* 11 (1906): 52.

12 *MWA* 9 (1904): 72.

13 *KB* 9 (1910): 20.

14 Kocka, *Unternehmensverwaltung*, p. 482 and pp. 504–5.

15 *HZ* 16 (1912): 93.

16 *HZ* 15 (1911): 139.

17 Käthe Mende, *Münchener jugendliche Ladnerinnen: zu Hause und im Beruf* (Stuttgart, 1912), p. xxii.

18 *HZ* 16 (1912): 6.

19 The most complete figures are in *Statistik des deutschen Reichs*, 211, pp. 132*–34* and pp. 156*–57* [sic].

20 Hartfiel, *Angestellte*, p. 35.

21 R. D. Barron and G. M. Norris, "Sexual Divisions and the Dual Labour Market," in Diana L. Barker and Sheila Allen, eds., *Dependence and Exploitation in Work and Marriage* (London, 1976), pp. 47–53.

22 Hans-Ulrich Howe, *Die berufstätige Frau als Verkaufsangestellte* (Lübeck, 1930), p. 5.

23 *Stat. d. dt. Reichs*, 202, p. 108; and 211, p. 193, pp. 132*–34* and pp. 156*–57* [sic]. The figures vary without explanation in different volumes and on different pages.

24 *Stat. d. dt. Reichs*, 203, pp. 258–61; and Gertrud Bäumer, *Die Frau in Volkswirtschaft und Staatsleben der Gegenwart* (Stuttgart, 1914), p. 122.

25 Reichsamt des Innern, *Die wirtschaftliche Lage der Privatangestellten. Denkschrift über die im Oktober 1903 angestellten Erhebungen* (Berlin, 1907), p. 35.

26 *Stat. d. dt. Reichs*, 211, p. 193 and pp. 132*ff [sic]; and 202, p. 108; Manfred Dittrich, *Die Entstehung der Angestelltenschaft in Deutschland* (Berlin, 1939), p. 66; and Ida Kisker, *Die Frauenarbeit in den Kontoren einer Grossstadt: eine Studie über die Leipziger Kontoristinnen, ASS* Ergänzungsheft III (Tübingen, 1911), p. 12.

27 Kisker, *Frauenarbeit*, p. 15; Dr. Behrend, *Enquete über weibliche Handlungsangestellte Magdeburgs* (Magdeburg, n.d. [c. 1906]), pp. 6–7 and p. 21, in AHKD, Abt. 20, #195–1, RWWA.

28 *Stat. d. dt. Reichs*, 202; 203, pp. 258–61.

29 Käthe Lövinson, "Arbeitsleistung der Frauen im Bankbetrieb," *JfF* 3 (1927): 63–64 and 86–88.

30 *Stat. d. dt. Reichs*, 203, pp. 258–61; and 211, pp. 132*–34* and pp. 156*–57* [sic]; Behrend, *Enquete*, pp. 4, 6, 7; and Theodore Blum, "Die Wirkung

des Fortbildungszwanges für weibliche Handelsangestellte," *Deutsche Handelsschul-Lehrer-Zeitung* 6 (1909), in BB I, B166, Hamb.St.A.

31  Hedwig Vonschott, *Frauenbildung-Frauenberufe* (Freiburg i. B., 1933), p. 153; Ilse Müller-Östreich, "Die Arbeitsbedingungen für die Angestellten in Zweiggeschäften, II," *S. Praxis* 23 (1913), col. 183; Adele Beerensson, "Filialleiterinnen," *Frau* 21 (1913/14): 287–92.

32  Hans Horbat, *Die wirtschaftliche Lage des deutschen Angestellten* (Berlin, 1926), p. 26; Josef Silbermann, "Die Lage der deutschen Handelsgehilfen und ihre gesetzliche Reform," *AGS* 9 (1896): 372ff.

33  Silbermann, "Gesetzliche Reform," p. 375.

34  Josef Silbermann, *Praktische Lehre und theoretische Fachbildung der weiblichen Handlungsgehilfen* (Berlin, 1907), p. 6.

35  Agnes Herrmann, quoted in Verband der weiblichen Angestellten, *75 Jahre Verband der weiblichen Angestellten, 1889–1964* (Hannover, 1964), p. 11. All translations from the German are mine, unless otherwise noted.

36  Mende, *Ladnerinnen*, p. xxxix and pp. xl–xli; Gewerkschaftsbund der Angestellten, *Epochen*, pp. 66–69; Silbermann, "Gesetzliche Reform," p. 372; and Ursula Nienhaus, *Berufsstand weiblich: die ersten weiblichen Angestellten* (Berlin, 1982), pp. 150–62.

37  A. Kasten and Hans Heinrich, *Die kommende Angestelltengeneration* (Berlin, 1933), p. 52; Erna Reimann, *Die Frau als kaufmännische Angestellte im Handelsgewerbe* (Jena, 1915), p. 50; Josef Silbermann, "Die Arbeitszeit der kaufmännischen Angestellten in den Engros- und Fabrikgeschäften Berlins," *AGS* 16 (1901): 739–40.

38  Agnes Herrmann, "Aus der Werdezeit," in Kaufmännischer Verband für weibliche Angestellte, *25 Jahre Berufsorganisation: 1889–1914* (Berlin, n.d.), p. 2. Clerks' journals occasionally reported cases of extreme overtime.

39  *Ibid.*, p. 2; Silbermann, "Arbeitszeit," pp. 721ff.

40  Paul Adler, *Die Lage der Handlungsgehilfen* (Stuttgart, 1900), pp. 76–77.

41  Kocka, *Unternehmensverwaltung*, p. 497; Engelsing, "Differenzierung," pp. 73–80 and pp. 102–4. Gerd Hohorst, Jürgen Kocka, and Gerhard A. Ritter, *Sozialgeschichtliches Arbeitsbuch: Materialien zur Statistik des Kaiserreichs, 1870–1914* (Munich, 1975), p. 96, argues that real salaries increased between 1896 and 1912 for clerks, but do not use direct salary data to support their conclusion.

42  Reichsamt des Innern, *Lage*, p. 14. See also Alice Salomon, *Die Ursachen der ungleichen Entlohnung von Männer- und Frauenarbeit*, Staats- und sozialwissenschaftliche Forschungen 122 (Leipzig, 1906).

43  Ashok V. Desai, *Real Wages in Germany, 1871–1913* (Oxford, 1968), p. 21.

44  Dr. Heinrich Herkner, "Probleme der Arbeiterpsychologie unter besonderer Rücksichtsnahme auf Methode und Ergebnisse der Vereinserhebungen," report at convention of Verein für Sozialpolitik, 10.8.1911, in "Verhandlungen," *SVS* 138 (1912): 126.

45  "Die Erhebung über die wirtschaftliche Lage der deutschen Handlungsgehilfen," *Reichs-Arbeitsblatt* 8 (1910): 664; Josef Silbermann, "Zur Entlohnung der Frauenarbeit," *JGVV* 23 (1899): 1,408, 1,413, and 1,424; Silbermann, *Praktische Lehre*, pp. 10–11.

46 Salomon, *Entlohnung*, p. 83.
47 Silbermann, *Praktische Lehre*, pp. 10–11.
48 For the following discussion, general statistical material is taken from *Stat. d. dt. Reichs*, 211, pp. 186–87, 237, 317. In addition, the sources listed below draw on contemporary polls. They vary in their results primarily because they group fathers' occupations in different ways. See "Die wirtschaftliche Lage der deutschen Handlungsgehilfen," *S. Praxis* 19 (1910): col. 1,212; Gertrud Bäumer, *Frau in Volkswirtschaft und Staatsleben*, p. 123; Olga Essig, "Das Ergebnis unserer Umfrage," *HG* 5 (1909): 157; Marie Baum, *Drei Klassen von Lohnarbeiterinnen in Industrie und Handel der Stadt Karlsruhe* (Karlsruhe, 1906), p. 135; Valentin Sittel, *Die Frauenarbeit im Handelsgewerbe* (Leipzig, 1911), pp. 34–35; Friedrich K. Kern, *Zur sozialen Lage der Verkäuferinnen* (Heidelberg, 1910), p. 10; Erna Reimann, *Frau als Angestellte*, pp. 25, 27; "Soziale Herkunft der Kontoristinnen," *AfF* 1 (1913): 76; Kisker, *Frauenarbeit*, p. 56; Mende, *Ladnerinnen*, p. 10; and Silbermann, "Entlohnung," p. 1,413. For a contemporary analysis, see Ursula Nienhaus, *Berufsstand*, pp. 38–41; and Ursula Nienhaus, "Von Töchtern und Schwestern: Zur vergessenen Geschichte der weiblichen Angestellten im deutschen Kaiserreich," in Jürgen Kocka, ed., *Angestellte im europäischen Vergleich: Die Herausbildung angestellter Mittelschichten seit dem späten 19. Jahrhundert* (Göttingen, 1981), pp. 313–14.

## 2 Women clerks at home and work

1 Johanna Waescher, *Wegbereiter der deutschen Frau. 18 Lebensbilder aus der Frühzeit der deutschen Frauenbewegung* (Cassel, 1931); Rosa Mayreder, "Die Dame," *Die Zukunft* 36 (1901): 496–504; Lady Blennerhassett, "German Girlhood," *The English Illustrated Magazine* (1889/90): 634.
2 Waescher, *Wegbereiter*, p. 33.
3 Gunhild Kübler, *Die soziale Aufsteigerin: Wandlungen einer Geschlechtsspezifischen Rollenzuschreibung im deutschen Roman, 1870–1900* (Bonn, 1982); Werner Deich, *Der Angestellte im Roman: Zur Sozialgeschichte des Handlungsgehilfen um 1900* (Cologne, 1974), p. 162; see also the press clippings in Hamb.St.A.
4 Gertrud Bäumer, *Die Frau in Volkswirtschaft und Staatsleben der Gegenwart* (Stuttgart, 1914), pp. 3–5; Karl Schrader, "Weibliche Erziehung," *Die Nation* 6 (1889): 628ff and 643ff, reprinted in Margrit Twellmann, *Die deutsche Frauenbewegung: Ihre Anfänge und erste Entwicklung*, vol. 2, *Quellen*, *1843–1889* (Meisenheim am Glan, 1972), pp. 277–84; "Gutachtliche Äusserung des Armen-Collegium," 14.6.1900, BBI B164, Hamb.St.A.; Anka Mann, "Eine Hamburger Handelsschule," *Hamburger Hausfrau*, 20.1.07, PP S6741, Hamb.St.A.; Lily Braun, "Weiblichkeit?" *Die Zukunft* 41(1902): 413–19; Frieda von Bülow, "Schwachsinn des Weibes," *Die Zukunft* 37 (1901): 13–19; Käthe Schirmacher, "Die Konkurrenz der Frau," *HN* 19.3.08, PP 5808, vol. 2, Hamb.St.A.
5 Käthe Mende, *Münchener jugendliche Ladnerinnen: zu Hause und im Beruf* (Stuttgart, 1912); Adolf Günther, "Zur Frage der Lebenshaltung des Mittelstandes," *JGVV* 37 (1913): 1,788–89.
6 Marriott Pyne, "Woman's Position in Germany," *McBride's Magazine* 24

(1879): 309; Edwin W. Bowen, "The German Woman of Today and Yesterday," *The Sewanee Review* 7 (1899): 23.

7  Willy Cohn, *Verkäuferinnen, Gedanken und Vorschläge eines Praktikers* (Berlin, 1911), p. 7; Mende, *Ladnerinnen*, pp. 106–7.

8  Ashok V. Desai, *Real Wages in Germany, 1871–1913* (Oxford, 1968), p. 21; Kaiserliches Statistisches Amt, Abt. für Arbeiterstatistik, *Erhebung von Wirtschaftsrechnungen minderbemittelter Familien im Deutschen Reich*. 2. Sonderheft zum *Reichsarbeitsblatt* (Berlin, 1909), p. 5; Mende, *Ladnerinnen*, pp. 25–27, 31, 39–40. See also Joan W. Scott and Louise A. Tilly, "Women's Work and the Family in Nineteenth-Century Europe," *Comparative Studies in Society and History* 17 (1975): 58–59.

9  Susanne Suhr, *Die weiblichen Angestellten: Arbeits- und Lebensverhältnisse* (Berlin, 1930), p. 42.

10  Bäumer, *Frau in Volkswirtschaft*, pp. 121–22; Mende, *Ladnerinnen*, pp. 32–33; Marie Baum, *Drei Klassen von Lohnarbeiterinnen in Industrie und Handel der Stadt Karlsruhe* (Karlsruhe, 1906), pp. 179–80; *Stat. d. dt. Reichs*, 211, p. 214.

11  Mende, *Ladnerinnen*, pp. 29, 49, 170.

12  *Ibid.*, pp. 25–27; Waescher, *Wegbereiter, passim*; Günther, "Lebenshaltung des Mittelstandes," pp. 1,793–94; "Die Erhebung über die wirtschaftliche Lage der deutschen Handlungsgehilfen," *Reichs-Arbeitsblatt* 8 (1910): 664; Statistisches Amt, *Minderbemittelter Familien*, pp. 6–7.

13  Günther, "Lebenshaltung des Mittelstandes," pp. 1,788–89; Else Kesten-Conrad, "Zur Dienstbotenfrage. Erhebungen der Arbeiterinnenschutzkommission des Bundes Deutscher Frauenvereine," *ASS* 31 (1910): 528.

14  Sibylle Meyer, "Die mühsame Arbeit des demonstrativen Müssiggangs. Über die häuslichen Pflichten der Beamtenfrauen im Kaiserreich," in Karin Hausen, ed., *Frauen suchen ihre Geschichte*. Beck'sche Schwarze Reihe 276 (Munich, 1983), pp. 172–94; Blennerhassett, "Girlhood," p. 636; Marriott Pyne, "Woman's Position in Germany," *McBride's Magazine* 24 (1879): 309–11.

15  Zentralverband der Handlungsgehilfen und Gehilfinnen Deutschlands, *Bericht des Vorstandes und Ausschusses über die 7. Geschäftsperiode 1908–09 nebst Protokoll der 7. Generalversammlung, 16.–17.5.1910 in Hamburg* (Hamburg, 1910), p. 31.

16  Ida Kisker, *Die Frauenarbeit in den Kontoren einer Grossstadt: eine Studie über die Leipziger Kontoristinnen*. *ASS* Ergänzungsheft III (Tübingen, 1911), pp. 101, 105.

17  *Ibid.*, p. 59; Mende, *Ladnerinnen*, p. 99–100.

18  Baum, *Lohnarbeiterinnen*, p. 219; Suhr, *Weiblichen Angestellten*, p. 42.

19  Gertrud Bäumer, "Frauenfrage und Mittelstandspolitik," *Frau* 15 (1907/8): 456; Hulda Maurenbrecher, *Das Allzuweibliche: Ein Buch von neuer Erziehung und Lebensgestaltung* (Munich, 1912), pp. 63–65.

20  Kisker, *Frauenarbeit*, pp. 60, 101.

21  Josef Silbermann, "Die Ausgaben der Handlungsgehilfinnen für den Lebensunterhalt," *AfF* 2 (1914): 106.

22  A Commercial Alliance poll of 1907 showed 19.1 percent of all

saleswomen and 11.0 percent of all office women had worked over ten years. Josef Silbermann, "Kaufmännische Angestellte," *AfF* 1 (1913): 236.

23  Mende, *Ladnerinnen*, p. 52.
24  *Ibid.*, p. 81; Baum, *Lohnarbeiterinnen*, p. 167; Silbermann, "Ausgaben . . . Lebensunterhalt," p. 106. This pattern held too in Scotland; see Lynn Jamieson, "Limited Resources and Limiting Conventions: Working-Class Mothers and Daughters in Urban Scotland c. 1890–1940," in Jane Lewis, ed., *Labour and Love: Women's Experience of Home and Family, 1850–1940* (Oxford, 1986), pp. 49–69.
25  Mende, *Ladnerinnen*, p. 81.
26  "Angestellte," *AfF* 1 (1913): 73.
27  Mende, *Ladnerinnen*, pp. 55–77.
28  Günther, "Lebenshaltung des Mittelstandes," pp. 1800–1.
29  "Erhebung . . . wirtschaftliche Lage," p. 663.
30  Josef Silbermann, "Die Lebenshaltung der weiblichen Angestellten," *JdF* 5 (1929): 106; Mende, *Ladnerinnen*, p. 41; Frieda Glass, "Die weiblichen Handels- und Büroangestellten," in Frieda Glass and Dorothea Kische, *Die wirtschaftliche und soziale Verhältnisse der berufstätigen Frauen: Erhebung 1928/9* (Berlin, 1930), p. 62; Suhr, *Weiblichen Angestellten*, pp. 38–39.
31  "Erhebung . . . wirtschaftliche Lage," p. 662.
32  For this and the following, see Laura Krause, "Die weiblichen Angestellten," *S. Praxis* 8 (1898/99): cols. 1,376–77; Tilla Dillmann, "Wie teile ich mein jährliches Einkommen am besten ein?" *HG* 5 (1909): 107; Agnes Bluhm, "Zur Lage der Handlungsgehilfinnen," *Sozialpolitisches Centralblatt* 2 (1892/93): 311; Kisker, *Frauenarbeit*, pp. 94ff; Statistisches Amt, *Minderbemittelter Familien*, pp. 6–7; Silbermann, "Ausgaben," pp. 89ff; Silbermann, "Lebenshaltung," pp. 66ff; Suhr, *Weiblichen Angestellten*, pp. 41ff.
33  Suhr, *Weiblichen Angestellten*, p. 42.
34  "Wie ich wohne," *ZWH* 16 (1911): 164.
35  "Das Wohnheim der alleinstehenden Frau," *HG* 10 (1914): 42–43; "Die Gründung von Mädchenheimen für Handlungsgehilfinnen," *ZWH* 14 (1909): 86–87; Clara Mleinek, "Mädchenheime," *ZWH* 14 (1909): 103.
36  Mleinek, "Mädchenheime"; Kisker, *Frauenarbeit*, p. 108.
37  Meta Gadesmann, "Ein Altersheim für Handlungsgehilfinnen," *ZWH* 14 (1909): 134.
38  "An die Grossstädterinnen," II and III, *MWA* 6 (1902): 611; "Ein verkannter und unterschätzter Beruf," *ZWH* 18 (1913): 66.
39  "Unterschätzter Beruf," p. 67.
40  *HG* 4 (1908): 92.
41  Baum, *Lohnarbeiterinnen*, pp. 220–22; Mende, *Ladnerinnen*, pp. 216–19; Silbermann, "Lebenshaltung," p. 105. See also reports of activities of clerks' organizations in *HG, ZWH*, etc.
42  Deich, *Angestellte im Roman*, pp. 162, 163, 166; see the first-person accounts in Marie Hörbrandt, *Die weiblichen Handels- und Bureau-Angestellten* (Berlin, 1930).
43  "Ein deutscher Bund zur Bekämpfung der Frauenemanzipation," *HG* 8 (1912): 76–77.

44  For example, Richard Döring, *Die Frauenarbeit im Handelsgewerbe*, DHV vol. 44 (Hamburg, 1909), p. 26; "Dem Verderben entgegen?" *ZWH* 13 (1908): 132; "Kann die weibliche Arbeitskraft einen Vergleich mit der männlichen aushalten?" *HG* 8 (1912): 76–77; Franz Schneider, "Der Deutschnationale Handlungsgehilfen-Verband und die Frauenarbeit im Handelsgewerbe, ii," *ZWH* 10 (1905): 108; Georg Hiller, *Die Frauenbewegung*. 16. Schrift des VDH (Leipzig, 1907), p. 17.

45  Georg Hiller, *Die Lage der Handlungsgehilfen* (Leipzig, 1890), p. 12.

46  "Zur Lage der Angestellten: Schauergeschichten über Warenhausangestellte," *HZ* 18 (1914): 37; *HG* 5 (1909): 192. For a parallel with female servants, see Karin Walser, "Frauenarbeit und Weiblichkeits – bilder – Phantasien über Dienstmädchen um 1900," in Ruth-Ellen B. Joeres and Annette Kuhn, eds., *Frauen in der Geschichte VI. Frauenbilder und Frauenwirklichkeit. Interdisziplinäre Studien zur Frauengeschichte in Deutschland im 18. und 19. Jahrhundert*. Geschichtsdidaktik 26 (Düsseldorf, 1985), pp. 237–66.

47  For this and the following legal discussion, see H. Rosin, "Ehefrau und Mutter," *ASS* 28 (1909): 774–82; Edward B. Tylor, "The Woman Movement in Germany," *Nineteenth Century* 40 (1896): 99–100; and excerpts from the Code in "Das Bürgerliche Gesetzbuch (1900)," in Heinz Niggemann, ed., *Frauenemancipation und Sozialdemokratie*. Die Frau in der Gesellschaft. Frühe Texte, Gisela Brinker-Gabler, ed. (Frankfurt a. M., 1981), pp. 283–84.

48  Peter Lundgreen, "Industrialization and the Educational Formation of Manpower in Germany," *JSH* 9 (1975): 74.

49  Helene Lange, *Lebenserinnerungen* (Berlin, 1925); Waescher, *Wegbereiter*; James C. Albisetti, "Frauen und die akademischen Berufe im Kaiserlichen Deutschland," trans. Gerhard Seidel, in Joeres and Kuhn, eds., *Frauen in der Geschichte VI*, pp. 286–303.

50  Richard J. Evans, *The Feminist Movement in Germany, 1894–1933* (London, 1976), p. 10.

## 3  An ambivalent estate

1  Käthe Mende, *Münchener jugendliche Ladnerinnen: zu Hause und im Beruf* (Stuttgart, 1912), p. lvi.

2  Kaufmännischer Verband für weibliche Angestellte, *Der kaufmännische Verband für weibliche Angestellte: Ein Rückblick auf seine Tätigkeit aus Anlass seines 15 jährigen Bestehens* (Berlin, 1904), p. 18. It was the Civil Code, for instance, that covered the termination of employment.

3  Günter Hartfiel, *Angestellte und Angestelltengewerkschaften in Deutschland* (Berlin, 1961), p. 68. For Bismarck's social legislation, see Florian Tennstedt, "Sozialgeschichte der Sozialversicherung," in Maria Blohmke *et al.*, eds., *Handbuch der Sozialmedizin*, vol. 3 (Stuttgart, 1975), pp. 385–96; Detlev Zöllner, "Germany," in Peter A. Köhler, Hans F. Zacher, and Martin Partington, eds., *The Evolution of Social Insurance, 1881–1981: Studies of Germany, France, Great Britain, Austria and Switzerland* (London, 1982), pp. 12–33; and Jürgen Kocka, "Class Formation, Interest Articulation, and Public Policy: The Origins of the German White-Collar Class in the Late

Nineteenth and Early Twentieth Centuries," in Suzanne Berger, ed., *Organizing Interests in Western Europe: Pluralism, Corporatism, and the Transformation of Politics* (Cambridge, 1982), pp. 73–75.

4 Herman Lebovics, *Social Conservatism and the Middle Classes in Germany, 1914–1933* (Princeton, 1969); Lebovics, "'Agrarians' versus 'Industrializers': Social Conservative Resistance to Industrialism and Capitalism in Late Nineteenth-Century Germany," *IRSH* 12 (1967): 32–65; Walter Struve, *Elites against Democracy: Leadership Ideals in Bourgeois Political Thought in Germany, 1890–1933* (Princeton, 1973); Dieter Lindenlaub, *Richtungskämpfe im Verein für Sozialpolitik: Wissenschaft und Sozialpolitik im Kaiserreich, vornehmlich vom Beginn des "neuen Kurses" bis zum Ausbruch des ersten Weltkrieges (1890–1914)*, 2 vols., Vierteljahresschrift für Sozial- und Wirtschaftsgeschichte, 52 and 53 (Wiesbaden, 1967); Kenneth D. Barkin, *The Controversy over German Industrialization: 1890–1902* (Chicago, 1970).

5 Lebovics, "'Industrializers,'" p. 47.

6 Ursula Ratz, *Sozialreform und Arbeiterschaft: Die "Gesellschaft für Soziale Reform" und die sozialdemokratische Arbeiterbewegung von der Jahrhundertwende bis zum Ausbruch des Ersten Weltkrieges* (Berlin, 1980). For a brief account in English, see Gerald D. Feldman, *Army, Industry, and Labor in Germany, 1914–1918* (Princeton, 1966), pp. 22–26.

7 Siegfried Aufhäuser, *Eine unromantische Betrachtung zum Geschichtsbild der Angestelltenbewegung* (Berlin, 1960), pp. 8ff; Erich Gierke, ed., *Zur Geschichte der Angestellten-Gewerkschaften*, Schriftenreihe der "Freiheit," Heft 1 (Berlin, 1949), pp. 4ff; Gewerkschaftsbund der Angestellten, *Epochen der Angestellten-Bewegung, 1774–1930* (Berlin, 1930), pp. 22ff; and Leo Müffelmann, *Die moderne Mittelstandsbewegung* (Leipzig, 1913), pp. 88ff.

8 About 8–12 percent of the membership of the two largest parity groups was composed of non-clerks. *Statistisches Jahrbuch für das Deutsche Reich*, 28 (1907), pp. 324–25.

9 Quoted in Gewerkschaftsbund, *Epochen*, p. 105.

10 George Sayers Bain, David Coates, and Valerie Ellis, *Social Stratification and Trade Unionism: A Critique* (London, 1973), pp. 107–8, conclude that, especially at a national level, there is little relationship between social stratification and the characters of blue-collar or white-collar unions or professional associations.

11 In addition to other sources, see Iris Hamel, *Völkischer Verband und nationale Gewerkschaft: Der Deutschnationale Handlungsgehilfen-Verband, 1893–1933* (Frankfurt, 1967).

12 The statutes are cited in Walter Lambach, "DHV," in Gierke, ed., *Geschichte*, p. 24.

13 "Die Erhebung über die wirtschaftliche Lage der deutschen Handlungsgehilfen," *Reichs-Arbeitsblatt* 8 (1910): 664.

## 4 Contending strategies for women

1 The German term *"bürgerlich"* connotes cultivation and respectability as well as class rule.

2 Cited in Margrit Twellmann, *Die deutsche Frauenbewegung: Ihre Anfänge und erste Entwicklung*, vol. 2, *Quellen, 1843–1889* (Meisenheim am Glan, 1972), pp. 137–40.
3 Minna Cauer, "Kaiserin Friedrich," in Twellmann, *Quellen*, pp. 289–90. The original executive board had twenty male and five female members. Jenny Hirsch, *Geschichte . . . Lette-Vereins* (Berlin, 1891), excerpted in Twellman, *Quellen*, pp. 142–44. See also *ibid.*, p. 463; and Lette-Verein, *100 Jahre Lette-Verein, 100 Jahre Entwicklung von Frauenberufen: Eine Chronik* (Berlin, 1968), p. 29.
4 Frauenbildungsverein Braunschweig, 1869 statutes of their school, cited in Twellmann, *Quellen*, p. 458. The group was a member organization of the ADF.
5 Helene Lange and Gertrud Bäumer, eds., *Handbuch der Frauenbewegung* (Berlin, 1901), p. 59.
6 Statutes cited in Twellmann, *Quellen*, p. 136. For the work of the ADF, see Johanna Waescher, *Wegbereiter der deutschen Frau. 18 Lebensbilder aus der Frühzeit der deutschen Frauenbewegung* (Cassel, 1913); Gisela Losseff-Tillmanns, "Frauenemanzipation und Gewerkschaften (1800–1975)." Ph.D. diss. (Bochum, 1975), pp. 77–78, pp. 95–98 and pp. 165–73; and Twellmann, *Quellen*, pp. 136–37 and p. 149. For a general study of the period, see Herrad-Ulrike Bussemer, *Frauenemanzipation und Bildungsbürgertum. Sozialgeschichte der Frauenbewegung in der Reichsgründungszeit*. Series Ergebnisse der Frauenforschung 7 (Weinheim, 1985).
7 Quoted in Losseff-Tillmanns, "Frauenemanzipation," p. 21.
8 Hugh Wiley Puckett, *Germany's Women Go Forward* (New York, 1930), p. 140; and Hedwig Maass, *Von Frauenarbeit zu Frauenfabrikarbeit* (Heidelberg, 1938), p. 112.
9 Richard J. Evans, *The Feminist Movement in Germany, 1894–1933* (London, 1976), pp. 29–30.
10 The terms "radical" and "moderate" feminism were coined by contemporaries to describe their positions. I am using them in that way and not as categories of my analysis.
11 For an example, see Birgit Sauer, "Den Zusammenhang zwischen der Frauenfrage und der sozialen Frage begreifen. Die 'Frauen- und Mädchengruppe für soziale Hilfsarbeit' (1893–1908)," in Christiane Eifert and Susanne Rouette, eds., *Unter allen Umständen. Frauengeschichte(n) in Berlin* (Berlin, 1986), pp. 80–98.
12 Elsa Lüders, *Minna Cauer, Leben und Werk* (Gotha, 1925), p. 51, which excerpted Cauer's unpublished autobiography. For other accounts of the founding of Frauenwohl, see Elsa Lüders, *Der "linke Flügel": Ein Blatt aus der Geschichte der deutschen Frauenbewegung* (Berlin, n.d.), pp. 16ff; and Minna Cauer, *25 Jahre Verein Frauenwohl Gross-Berlin* (Berlin, 1913), pp. 6ff.
13 Quoted by Lüders, *Flügel*, p. 16.
14 Cauer, *Frauenwohl*, p. 8.
15 *GA*, 2.10.1900, PP S8004, Hamb.St.A. Evans, *Feminist Movement*, details the history of the BDF. See also his "Liberalism and Society: The Feminist Movement and Social Change," in Evans, ed., *Society and Politics in*

*Wilhelmine Germany* (London, 1976), pp. 186–207 and Barbara Greven-Aschoff, *Die bürgerliche Frauenbewegung in Deutschland, 1894–1933.* Kritische Studien zur Geschichtswissenschaft 46 (Göttingen, 1981).
16 Cauer writing in *Frauenbewegung*, 1.1.1896, quoted in Lüders, *Cauer*, p. 93.
17 *BV*, 13.7.1896, PP 5466, vol. 1, Hamb.St.A.
18 Cauer, *Frauenwohl*, p. 9.
19 The clearest discussion is Gertrud Bäumer, "Was bedeutet in der deutschen Frauenbewegung 'jüngere' und 'ältere' Richtung?" *Frau* 12 (1904/5): 321–28. Among contemporary writings, see Greven-Aschoff, *Bürgerliche Frauenbewegung*, pp. 62–69; Irene Stoehr, "'Organisierte Mütterlichkeit.' Zur Politik der deutschen Frauenbewegung um 1900," in Karin Hausen, ed., *Frauen suchen ihre Geschichte.* Beck'sche Schwarze Reihe 276 (Munich, 1983), pp. 221–49; Elisabeth Meyer-Renschhausen, "Zur Geschichte der Gefühle. Das Reden von 'Scham' und 'Ehre' innerhalb der Frauenbewegung um die Jahrhundertwende," in Christiane Eifert and Susanne Rouette, eds., *Unter allen Umständen. Frauengeschichte(n) in Berlin* (Berlin, 1986), pp. 99–122; and Theresa Wobbe, "Die Frau als Zoon politikon – Überlegungen zur historischen Rekonstruktion der Politik der deutschen bürgerlichen Frauenbewegung um 1900," in Jutta Dalhoff, Uschi Frey, and Ingrid Scholl, eds., *Frauenmacht in der Geschichte. Beiträge des Historikerinnentreffens 1985 zur Frauengeschichtsforschung.* Geschichtsdidaktik vol. 41 (Düsseldorf, 1986), pp. 326–37.
20 Helene Lange, "Moderne Streitfragen in der Frauenbewegung," *Frau* 13 (1905/6): 70.
21 Helene Lange, "Die Hand von der Politik!" *Frau* 11 (1903/4): 356ff. Note how Lange connects women's rights and employment.
22 Cited in Evans, *Feminist Movement*, p. 76; his translation.
23 Frieda Radel, *Warum fordern wir das Frauenstimmrecht* (1910), cited in Evans, *Feminist Movement*, p. 76; his translation.
24 Minna Cauer, "Die Frauenfrage in den Mittelklassen," *HC*, 11.10.1896, PP 5466, vol. 1, Hamb.St.A.
25 Bund Deutscher Frauenvereine, *Internationaler Frauenkongress, 1904, Officieller Originalbericht* (n.p., n.d.), pp. 1–5, pp. 12–14, and pp. 25–29. The German term *Frauenbildung* connotes a wider sense of education than simply schooling, to include all those elements which mold the character and cultivate the mind.
26 Gisela Losseff-Tillmanns, "Einleitung," in Losseff-Tillmans, ed., *Frau und Gewerkschaft* (Frankfurt a. M., 1982), pp. 23–24.
27 Programmatic statement expressed at an 1866 Lassallean party convention, quoted in *ibid*, p. 24.
28 Losseff-Tillmanns, "Frauenemanzipation," p. 102.
29 Losseff-Tillmanns, "Einleitung," pp. 17–18. The Association for the Representation of the Interests of Working Women, founded in 1885 in Berlin by Emma Ihrer and Gertrud Guillaume-Schack, was disbanded within a year as a "political" organization. Lange and Bäumer, eds., *Handbuch*, pp. 79–80; and "Emma Ihrer," *Correspondenzblatt* (1911), reprinted in Losseff-Tillmanns, ed., *Frau*, p. 261.

30 Jean Quataert, *Reluctant Feminists in German Social Democracy, 1885–1917* (Princeton, 1979), p. 14 and pp. 140–44.

31 Quoted in Werner Thönnessen, *The Emancipation of Women: The Rise and Decline of the Women's Movement in German Social Democracy, 1863–1933,* trans. Joris de Bres (Bristol, 1973), p. 47.

32 *Ibid.*, p. 49 and pp. 52–54.

33 Losseff-Tillmanns, "Einleitung," pp. 22–38; Losseff-Tillmanns, "Frauenemancipation," pp. 186–284; Quataert, *Reluctant Feminists,* pp. 53–76 and pp. 160–89; and Gerhard A. Ritter, *Arbeiterbewegung, Parteien, und Parlamentarismus: Aufsätze zur deutschen Sozial- und Verfassungsgeschichte des 19. und 20. Jahrhunderts,* Kritische Studien zur Geschichtswissenschaft 23 (Göttingen, 1976), pp. 84–94.

34 Losseff-Tillmanns, "Einleitung," p. 33.

35 For analyses of Marx's position on women, see Roisin McDonough and Rachel Harrison, "Patriarchy and Relations of Production," in Annette Kuhn and Ann-Marie Wolpe, eds., *Feminism and Materialism: Women and Modes of Production* (London, 1978), pp. 27–32; and Zillah Eisenstein, "Developing a Theory of Capitalist Patriarchy and Socialist Feminism," in Zillah Eisenstein, ed., *Capitalist Patriarchy and the Case for Socialist Feminism* (New York, 1979), pp. 6–16.

36 August Bebel, *Woman under Socialism* (New York, 1971), p. 9; italics in original.

37 Clara Zetkin, *Die Arbeiterinnen- und Frauenfrage der Gegenwart* (1889), excerpted in Gisela Brinker-Gabler, ed., *Frauenarbeit und Beruf* (Frankfurt a. M., 1979), pp. 139–45; italics in original.

38 For discussions of socialist theory, see Karen Honeycutt, "Socialism and Feminism in Imperial Germany," *Signs* 5 (1979): 30–41; and Marielouise Janssen-Jurreit, *Sexism: The Male Monopoly on History and Thought,* trans. by Verne Moberg (New York, 1982), pp. 114–24.

39 The orthodox theory did not go unchallenged. See Quataert, *Reluctant Feminists,* pp. 69–70 and pp. 76–132, for a thorough discussion of the challenges, especially that mounted by Lily Braun, who came to socialism from the bourgeois women's movement. Braun seems to have had some implicit understanding of what contemporary feminist usage identifies as patriarchy, but she was forced to the sidelines of socialist feminism and was not even mentioned in *Gleichheit* after 1901. See Lily Braun, "Reform der Hauswirtschaft," excerpts of *Frauenarbeit und Hauswirtschaft* (Berlin, 1901) in Brinker-Gabler, ed., *Frauenarbeit,* pp. 275–84; and Lily Braun, "Vorschläge zur Agitation," *Gleichheit* (1897), reprinted in Losseff-Tillmanns, ed., *Frau,* pp. 151–53.

40 Zetkin, *Arbeiterinnen- und Frauenfrage,* pp. 139–45; italics in original.

41 Clara Zetkin, "Schwierigkeiten der gewerkschaftlichen Organisierung der Arbeiterinnen," *Gleichheit* (1898/1901), reprinted in Brinker-Gabler, ed., *Frauenarbeit,* pp. 149–54; Ida Altmann, "Die Arbeiterin in der Gewerkschaftsbewegung," *Correspondenzblatt* (1905), reprinted in *ibid,* pp. 147–49; Emma Ihrer, "Die proletarische Frau und die Berufstätigkeit," *Sozialistische Monatshefte* (1905), reprinted in *ibid.,* pp. 296–305; and "Wie sollen sich die Arbeiterinnen organisieren?" *Gleichheit* (1896), reprinted

in Losseff-Tillmanns, ed., *Frau*, pp. 56–58.

42  Else Lüders, "Die Arbeiterin in der Gewerkschaftsbewegung," *Correspondenzblatt* (1905), excerpted in Losseff-Tillmanns, ed., *Frau*, pp. 143–46. Her suggestions came during the period when radical bourgeois feminists were attempting to reach proletarian women and to ally with socialist feminists.

43  Altmann, "Arbeiterin," p. 147.

44  Lily Braun, "Vorschläge," pp. 151–53; and Clara Zetkin, "Kritische Bemerkungen zu Genossin Brauns Vorschlag," *Gleichheit* (1897), excerpted in Losseff-Tillmanns, ed., *Frau*, pp. 154–56.

45  *BV*, 9.10.1899, PP 5466, vol. 1, Hamb.St.A. reports the convention. For accounts of attempts to organize working-class women, which on the whole failed, see *BV*, 27.1.1897; *Echo*, 22.3.1900; *Berlin Vorwärts*, 31.3.1900; *BV*, 3.1.1901; *HC*, 16.3.1902; *HN*, 27.3.1903; and *BT*, 25.3.1905; all in PP 5466, vol. 1, Hamb.St.A. See also Janssen-Jurreit, *Sexism*, pp. 124–26 and Herrad-Ulrike Bussemer, "Bürgerliche und proletarische Frauenbewegung (1865–1914)," in Annette Kuhn and Gerhard Schneider, eds., *Frauen in der Geschichte I. Frauenrechte und die gesellschaftliche Arbeit der Frauen im Wandel. Fachwissenschaftliche und fachdidaktische Studien zur Geschichte der Frauen. Geschichtsdidaktik* vol. 6 (Düsseldorf, 1984), pp. 34–55.

46  Lüders, *Cauer*, quoting Cauer's diary from 13.8.1896, p. 95.

47  Lüders, *Flügel*, p. 58; and BDF, *Frauenkongress*, pp. 58ff.

48  Alice Salomon writing in *BT*, 17.6.1905, PP 5466, vol. 1, Hamb.St.A.

49  Cited in *Echo*, 26.9.1896, PP 5466, vol. 1, Hamb.St.A.

50  "M.N.," "Sprechsaal: Zur Frauenbewegung," *Echo*, 3.12.1896, PP 5808, vol. 1, Hamb.St.A.

51  BDF, *Frauenkongress*, p. 59.

52  Gertrud Bäumer, "Über das Ideal einer einheitlichen deutschen Frauenbewegung," *Frau* 12 (1904/5): 549ff.

## 5  Bourgeois feminism and female clerks

1  Kaufmännischer Verband für weibliche Angestellte, *Ein Rückblick auf seine Tätigkeit aus Anlass seines 15 jährigen Bestehens* (Berlin, 1904), p. 3.

2  Little is known about the actual beginning of this association. Cauer's papers and any documents of the association in this period are lost, and most narratives were written by Agnes Herrmann, who appears to have disliked Cauer. In an article she wrote in 1903, for instance – for the leading feminist periodical of the time – Herrmann recounted the group's history without once mentioning Cauer! Agnes Herrmann, "Entwicklung und Organisation der weiblichen Handlungsgehilfen," *Frau* 10 (1902/3): 328. For Cauer's role, see Else Lüders, *Minna Cauer, Leben und Werk* (Gotha, 1925), pp. 70–71; and Minna Cauer, *25 Jahre Verein Frauenwohl Gross-Berlin* (Berlin, 1913), p. 25. See also Ursula Nienhaus, *Berufsstand Weiblich: Die ersten weiblichen Angestellten* (Berlin, 1982), pp. 52–59.

3 Kaufmännischer Verband für weibliche Angestellte, *Taschenbuch für die Mitglieder des kaufmännischen Verbandes für weibliche Angestellte* (Berlin, 1905), p. 15, PP S6741, Hamb.St.A.

4 Nienhaus, *Berufsstand*, p. 56, gives complete membership data from 1890 to 1904.

5 "Vorträge über die Organisation von Handlungsgehilfinnen," *MWA* 1 (1896): 54; Kaufmännischer Verband, *Taschenbuch*, p. 10; and *MWA* 5 (1901): 481.

6 *HG* 10 (1914): 5; Ida Kisker, *Die Frauenarbeit in den Kontoren einer Grossstadt: eine Studie über die Leipziger Kontoristinnen, ASS* Ergänzungsheft III (Tübingen, 1911), p. 152.

7 *FB*, 9.10.1902, PP 5466, vol. 1, Hamb.St.A.

8 Letter from Waescher to *MWA* 6 (1902): 586.

9 *MKV* 6 (1910): 238.

10 *Bayerisches Vaterland*, 13.12.1892, PDM 4498, St.A.Mu. See also the handwritten mimeo of the organization's statutes from 1893, p. 1; and letter to police, 25.4.1904, *ibid.*

11 See for example the account of von Roy's participation in founding a group in Memel, *MWA* 8 (1904): 22.

12 Letter Heymann to Senate, 12.2.1903, PP S8004; and *FB*, 29.12.1897, PP 5808, Hamb.St.A.

13 *MWA* 1 (1896): 37; and police files, 5.12.1897; *FB*, 17.1.1898; *HN*, 18.2.1898; and passim, PP S6741, Hamb.St.A.

14 "Industria": Verein zur Förderung der im Handel und Gewerbe tätigen weiblichen Angestellten zu Hamburg, *Satzungen* (Hamburg, 1898), p. 5, PP S6741, Hamb.St.A.; see also PP S6741 *passim* for 1897/98, Hamb.St.A.

15 Emil Ritter, *Die katholisch-soziale Bewegung Deutschlands im 19. Jahrhundert und der Volksverein* (Cologne, 1954), pp. 135–36.

16 Ronald J. Ross, *The Beleaguered Tower: The Dilemma of Political Catholicism in Wilhelmine Germany* (South Bend, Indiana, 1976), pp. 79ff.

17 *Ibid.*, pp. 33ff; and Ritter, *Katholisch-soziale Bewegung*, pp. 174–75.

18 Ritter, *Katholisch-soziale Bewegung*, p. 345.

19 *KB* 2 (1903): 8.

20 Dr. Trimborn, "Die Aufgaben der charitative Frauenvereinigungen," talk reported in *Germania* (1904?), clipping in NL Herold, #127, BA; *KB* 1 and 2 (1902/3) *passim*.

21 *KB* 2 (1903): 34; and *KB* 4 (1905): 24.

22 For examples of activities, see *KB* 3 (1904): 72; *KB* 4 (1905): 31; *KB* 2 (1903): 8 and 20; *KB* 2 (1903): 8; and Kisker, *Frauenarbeit*, p. 143.

23 Indeed, in 1904 the Offenbach chapter presented a lecture insisting on the need for members to support the Catholic Women's Federation. *KB* 3 (1904): 72.

24 "Berechtigte Forderungen der Frauenbewegung," *KB* 2 (1903): 21; see also "Männliches oder weibliches Personal?" *KB* 3 (1904): 46; "Wie viele kaufmännische Gehilfinnen werden heiraten?" *ibid.*, p. 17; and *KB* 2 (1903): 25.

25 "Berechtigte Forderungen," p. 22; also *KB* 2 (1903): 23; and *KB* 3 (1904): 24.

26  By 1900 the BDF had established a commission for "the social position of female commercial assistants." Report on the fourth convention of the BDF, *GA*, 2.10.1900, PP S8004, Hamb.St.A.

27  They justified their action by citing an 1894 statement from the Imperial Ministry of Health about the dangers of standing for too long. Josef Silbermann, "Allgemeine Sozialpolitik," in Kaufmännischer Verband für weibliche Angestellte, *25 Jahre Berufsorganisation: 1889–1914: Zugleich Verwaltungsbericht für das Jahr 1913* (Berlin, n.d.), p. 79; and *BV*, 25.4.1896 and 27.1.1897, PP 5466, vol. 1, Hamb.St.A.

28  ADF first year report, cited in *HC*, 2.10.1897, PP 5808, vol. 1, Hamb.St.A. At this time, Lida Gustava Heymann was active in the ADF. See also PP 5808, vol. 1 *passim* for 1897, Hamb.St.A. The campaign received good coverage in the local press.

29  Silbermann, "Sozialpolitik," p. 80; report of BDF convention, Wiesbaden, *FB*, 9.10.1902, PP 5466, vol. 1, Hamb.St.A.

30  *MWA* 2 (1897): 121.

31  *NHZ*, 28.2.1905, PP 5466, vol. 2, Hamb.St.A.; and Alice Salomon, "Käuferinnen-Vereine und Consumentenmoral," speech to 1901 ADF convention, reported in *HN*, 5.11.1901, PP 5808, vol. 1, Hamb.St.A.; "Aufruf," *MWA* 2 (1897): 98 and 105; "Pflichten! Ein Mahnwort an *alle* Angestellte!" *MWA* 3 (1898): 209. *MWA* 8 (1903): 96, asks members to remember that women from "various women's organizations," "our sisters," are also working for early closing.

32  Richard J. Evans, *The Feminist Movement in Germany, 1894–1933* (London, 1976), pp. 53ff. Elisabeth Meyer-Renschhausen, "Zur Geschichte der Gefühle. Das Reden von 'Scham' und 'Ehre' innerhalb der Frauenbewegung um die Jahrhundertwende," in Christiane Eifert and Susanne Rouette, eds., *Unter allen Umständen. Frauengeschichte(n) in Berlin* (Berlin, 1986), pp. 99–122. For a selection of documents, see Marielouise Janssen-Jurreit, ed., *Frauen und Sexualmoral*. Series Die Frau in der Gesellschaft: Frühe Texte, G. Brinker-Gabler, ed. (Frankfurt a. M., 1986).

33  Letter to editor from Bieber-Böhm, *BV*, 7.12.1897, PP 5466, vol. 1, Hamb.St.A.

34  Agnes Herrmann, "Arbeiterschutz und Gewerbeinspektion. Sittlichkeits-Schutz für weibliche Angestellte in kaufmännischen Geschäften," *S.Praxis* 5 (1895/96), col. 931–32.

35  *BV*, 23.9.1896, PP 5466, vol. 1, Hamb.St.A.

36  *MWA* 7 (1902): 627.

37  For instance, "Rechtsprechung," *MWA* 2 (1897): 109; Dr. Korn, "Etwas über Beleidigungen," *ibid.*, pp. 67–68.

38  "Das kleine Journal," source unknown, police file, 11.12.1897, and *BV*, 7.12.1897, PP 5466, vol. 1, Hamb.St.A.

39  For reports of the case and its consequences, see *Berliner Nationale Zeitung*, 31.12.1897, and *passim* for December 1897 and January 1898, PP 5466, vol. 1, Hamb.St.A. Helene Lange and Gertrud Bäumer, *Handbuch der Frauenbewegung*, (Berlin, 1901), p. 185, also mention the case, as does Meyer–Renschhausen, "Geschichte der Gefühle," pp. 99–102.

40  *Echo*, 13.1.1898, PP 5466, vol. 1, Hamb.St.A.

41 *Weser Zeitung* (Bremen), 10.1.1898; *Berliner Nationale Zeitung*, 31.12.1897; both in PP 5466, vol. 1, Hamb.St.A.; and Lange and Bäumer, *Handbuch*, p. 185.

42 Lange and Bäumer, *Handbuch*, pp. 185–86; Dec. 1897–Jan. 1898 *passim*, PP 5466, vol. 1; and *FB*, 8.10.1898, PP S6741; both in Hamb.St.A.

43 See for instance "Zeitungsenten," *MWA* 7 (1902): 627; or "Die Frau im Beruf," *MWA* 8 (1903): 12.

44 For instance, *KB* 3 (1904): 8 and 68; *KB* 3 (1904): 11.

45 Minna Cauer was one of the first. See Lüders, *Cauer*, p. 70.

46 *MWA* 7 (1902): 641; and *MWA* 8 (1903): 11 and 19.

47 Else Zodtke-Heyde, "Das Wahlrecht der berufstätigen Frauen in sozialen Organen," *AfF* 1 (1913): 116–17; "Kaufmannsgericht," *MWA* 8 (1903): 19; *MWA* 9 (1904): 9, 19, 23, and 27; *Echo*, 30.3.1903 and 15.2.1904; and *FB*, 20.4.1903; both in PP S6741, Hamb.St.A.

48 *KB* 2 (1903): 23.

49 "Protokoll des 4. Jahres-Hauptversammlung des Deutschen Verbandes kaufmännischer Vereine, 6.6.1904," AHKD, Abt. 20, #90–2, RWWA. The BDF petitioned the Reichstag in support of female voting rights on the courts. Twelfth report of the executive board, cited in *HC*, 19.7.1903, PP 5466, vol. 2, Hamb.St.A.

50 Silbermann, "Sozialpolitik," pp. 82–83.

51 Reported in BDF, *Frauenkongress*, pp. 28–29.

52 Cited in "Kaufmannsgericht," p. 55. See also Johanna Waescher and Eva von Roy, *Denkschrift der Verbündeten kaufmännischen Vereine für weibliche Angestellte* (Frankfurt a. M., 1912), p. 6. Eva von Roy and Agnes Herrmann both spoke at the meeting.

53 "Mitarbeit der Handlungsgehilfinnen bei der Besetzung der Kaufmannsgerichte," *MWA* 9 (1904): 92; *KB* 4 (1905): 33.

54 Kaufmännischer Verband, *Taschenbuch*, p. 3; and Nienhaus, *Berufsstand*, pp. 56 and 59–60, for figures.

55 George Sayers Bain, *The Growth of White-Collar Unionism* (Oxford, 1970), p. 86; and Roger Lumley, *White-Collar Unionism in Britain: A Survey of the Present Position* (London, 1973), pp. 51–53.

56 In 1900, Industria gained 318 new members, but lost 177 old members; *Echo*, 23.2.1901, PP S6741, Hamb.St.A. In 1902, it gained 325 new members, but lost 266 old; *FB*, 24.3.1903, *ibid*. In 1904, the Association for Female Office Workers gained 337 new members, but lost 159; *HKZ*, 4.2.1905, PP 9095, *ibid*.

57 "Vereins- und Versammlungsrecht," *ZWH* 12 (1907): 179. Bain, *Growth . . . Unionism*, p. 87 and pp. 140–41, and Lumley, *White-Collar Unionism*, pp. 56–59, found that negative attitudes on the part of employers were a factor hindering white-collar unionism. For obstacles in the 1920s, see Ute Frevert, "Emanzipation und Berufstätigkeit. Das Beispiel der weiblichen Angestellten und ihrer Organisationen in der Weimarer Republik," Staatsexamination (Bielefeld, 1977), p. 117.

58 "Vereins- und Versammlungsrecht," p. 178; and PP S6741 *passim*, Hamb.St.A. In 1903, Heymann complained to the police about their behavior, which included attending a meeting of the executive board and

dissolving it. Letters to police from Heymann: 22.3.1903, PP S6741 and 22.4.1903, PP S8004, Hamb.St.A. See also Munich police in PDM, St.A.Mu.

59  A number of these are discussed in Kisker, *Frauenarbeit*, pp. 153–55.

60  For instance, "Das kaufmännische Bildungswesen," *MWA* 6 (1901): 563; "Was wir von den Männern lernen können!" *MKV* 5 (1909): 172; and Gertrud Bäumer, "Frauenfrage und Mittelstandspolitik," *Frau* 15 (1907/8): 456.

61  Police files and organization statements reveal that most board members were unmarried and usually over twenty-five. Since the same women often had long careers within the chapters, by World War I many older, single professional women dominated clerks' associations. The only exception I have found in the higher ranks is Paula Intlekofer-Liepmannssohn of the Berlin Alliance, who began organizational work with her sister when they were both single and remained active after marriage. Other exceptions were married feminists such as Laura Krause and Johanna Waescher, who had never been clerks.

62  "Die 'alte Jungfer,'" *MWA* 8 (1903): 70. See also *MWA* 9 (1904): 28; *KB* 3 (1904): 50.

63  Franziska Altmann, "Eine Mahnung und eine Bitte an die Kolleginnen," *MWA* 8 (1903): 1.

64  Agnes Herrmann, "Zur Beherzigung," *MWA* 5 (1900): 361; *MKV* 8 (1912): 81; and *NHZ*, 9.6.1898; *HC*, 28.4.1900; *HN*, 26.5.1902; all in PP S6741, Hamb.St.A.

65  Industria had about 10 percent of its members enrolled in evening courses in 1901; stenography and bookkeeping were the most popular, followed by typing. Annual report, 1901, *HN*, 26.5.1902, Hamb.St.A. See also "Kölner Frauen-Fortbildungsverein," April 1901, AHKD, Abt. 20, #92–5, RWWA.

66  "Offener Brief," *ZWH* 13 (1908): 38.

67  PP S6741 *passim*, Hamb.St.A.; and *ZWH*, *MKV*, and *KB passim*. Lectures or cultural events, on the other hand, were not as well attended, which upset leaders. See *MKV* 4 (1908): 93; *HG* 10 (1914): 7; or *KB* 5 (1906): 53. The Catholic Alliance convention in 1907 agreed that the organization had to offer entertainments to attract members. *KB* 6 (1907): 53.

68  Herrmann, "Beherzigung," p. 361; Gertrud Israel, "Was bietet der Verein?" *ZWH* 10 (1905): 85; *HG* 10 (1914): 7; and Kisker, *Frauenarbeit*, pp. 154–55. Catholic leaders stated that members would not read the journal or contribute time to it. Report of the second annual convention, *KB* 3 (1904): 34.

69  The journals regularly reported such group activities. See also Nienhaus, *Berufsstand*, pp. 141–50, for a detailed discussion.

70  *KB* 2 (1903): 34.

71  Organization journals reported in their local events columns which members would be on hand to welcome newcomers at weekly socials. *ZWH* 12 (1907), Sonderbeilage . . . Brandenburg und Wiesbaden, September; and *MKV* 8 (1912): 104.

72  *HG* 10 (1914): 7.

73 Kisker, *Frauenarbeit*, p. 154.
74 Martha Zietz, "Frauenrechte und Pflichte," lecture reported by police, 23.10.1903, PP S6741, Hamb.St.A.

## 6 Professionalization or feminism

1 See PP 5466, vol. 1 *passim*, Hamb.St.A.; "Weshalb sollte jede Hamburgerin Mitglied eines Frauenvereins werden?" *NHZ*, 30.4.1910, PP 5808, vol. 2, Hamb.St.A.; and Alice Salomon, *Die Ursachen der ungleichen Entlohnung von Männer- und Frauenarbeit*, (Leipzig, 1906), pp. 5ff. For examples of the arguments in clerks' associations, see Julius Meyer, "Die Frauenarbeit im Handelsgewerbe," *MWA* 1 (1896): 1–3; [Agnes Herrmann], *Fortbildungsschulzwang für weibliche Handlungsgehilfen und Lehrlinge* (Berlin, 1903), pp. 4–7; and Agnes Herrmann, "Entwicklung und Organisation der weiblichen Handlungsgehilfen," *Frau* 10 (1902/3): 326–27.
2 Kaufmännischer Verband für weibliche Angestellte, *Ein Rückblick auf seine Tätigkeit aus Anlass seines 15 jährigen Bestehens* (Berlin, 1904), p. 6 and p. 9; "Protokoll des 14. Jahres-Hauptversammlung des deutschen Verbandes kaufmännischer Vereine, 6.6.1904," AHKD, Abt. 20, #90–2, RWWA; and Franz Schneider, "Der Deutschnationale Handlungsgehilfen-Verband und die Frauenarbeit im Handelsgewerbe, ii," *ZWH* 10 (1905): 108.
3 Hamburg Industria's commercial day school tested girls in arithmetic and German. *FB*, 21.8.1899, PP S6741, Hamb.St.A.
4 *FB*, 9.5.1898; *FB*, 24.3.1903; and *GA*, 4.4.1903; all in PP S6741, Hamb.St.A.; and Margarete Schweichler, "Stellennachweis," in Kaufmännischer Verband für weibliche Angestellte, *25 Jahre Berufsorganisation: 1889–1914: Zugleich Verwaltungsbericht für das Jahr 1913* (Berlin, n.d.), p. 18.
5 *NHZ*, 9.6.1898, PP S6741, Hamb.St.A.; and Schweichler, "Stellennachweis," p. 21.
6 *HC*, 14.10.1900, PP 5808, vol. 1; and *FB*, 30.9.1900, PP 5466; both in Hamb.St.A. See also Verein Frauenwohl, *Jahresbericht des Vereins "Frauenwohl" in Königsberg i. Pr.* (Königsberg, 1889 *et seq.*); see 1903, p. 5; 1905, p. 7; and 1906, p. 6.
7 Hamburg ADF ran a school to teach domestic service. PP 5808, vols. 1 and 2, *FB*, 3.11.1903 and *passim*, Hamb.St.A.
8 Meta Gadesmann, "Berufsberatung," in Kaufmännischer Verband, *25 Jahre Berufsorganisation*, pp. 61–63.
9 *KB* 2 (1903): 27; and PP S6741 *passim*, Hamb.St.A.
10 *MWA* 8 (1903): 77.
11 Kaufmännischer Verband, *Rückblick*, p. 11.
12 "Protokoll," *KB* 3 (1904): 64.
13 Kaufmännischer Verband für weibliche Angestellte, *Taschenbuch für die Mitglieder des kaufmännischen Verbandes für weibliche Angestellte* (Berlin, 1905), p. 3, PP S6741, Hamb.St.A.
14 Herrmann, "Entwicklung," p. 327.
15 *NHZ*, 9.6.1898, PP S6741, Hamb.St.A.

16 Jürgen Kocka has a pertinent discussion of the process by which various salaried employees came to consider themselves part of a unified white-collar labor force based upon estate. See "Class Formation, Interest Articulation, and Public Policy: The Origins of the German White-Collar Class in the Late Nineteenth and Early Twentieth Centuries," in Suzanne Berger, *Organizing Interests in Western Europe: Pluralism, Corporatism, and the Transformation of Politics* (Cambridge, 1982), pp. 65–78. He underemphasizes the role of clerks in this, especially women, and the degree to which the older concept of a "commercial estate" was still accepted.

17 Silbermann, "Äussere und Innere Entwicklung," in Kaufmännischer Verband, *25 Jahre Berufsorganisation*, pp. 8 and 11; and leaflet of the Kaufmännischer Verband für weibliche Angestellte, 30.4.1905, PP S6741, Hamb.St.A.

18 Else Lüders, *Minna Cauer, Leben und Werk* (Gotha, 1925), p. 135. Lüders was a board member at the time.

19 Heymann referred later in her life to the "strong hatred of 'women's lib'" on the part of the Berlin executive board. Lida Gustava Heymann, with Anita Augspurg, *Erlebtes – Erschautes: Deutsche Frauen kämpfen für Freiheit, Recht und Frieden, 1850–1940*, ed. Margrit Twellmann (Meisenheim am Glan, 1972), p. 47. Ursula Nienhaus, who has had access to documents in private hands, states that Herrmann felt personal animosity toward Cauer as well. Personal communication, March 1982.

20 Minna Cauer, *25 Jahre Verein Frauenwohl Gross-Berlin* (Berlin, 1913), p. 18.

21 *HC*, 5.10.1900, PP 5466, vol. 1, Hamb.St.A.

22 Franziska Altmann, "Eine Mahnung und eine Bitte an die Kolleginnen," *MWA* 8 (1903): 2.

23 Letter to editor by "Durch," *FB*, 20.2.1905, PP S8004, Hamb.St.A. See also "Stand der deutschen Frauenbewegung," *MWA* 7 (1902): 602.

24 Letter from Martha B., *FB*, 13.1.1898, PP S6741, Hamb.St.A.

25 "Berichte aus den Ortsgruppen," *ZWH* 12 (1907): 168.

26 Paulina Franck, "Warum?" *ZWH* 11 (1906): 35–36.

27 Cited in Lüders, *Cauer*, p. 170.

28 Franz Schneider, "Hinein in die Öffentlichkeit," *ZWH* 10 (1905): 24; "Von den Gegnern," *ZWH* 11 (1906): 71.

29 See Josef Silbermann [J. Sabin], "Zwölf Jahre deutscher Parteikämpfe, 1881–1892," *Deutsche Schriften für nationales Leben*, Reihe 2, Heft 5 (1892).

30 "Unsere Hauptversammlung," *ZWH* 12 (1907): 82.

31 Letter to police, 22.7.1905, and police report, 6.2.1907, PP S6741, Hamb.St.A.

32 Silbermann, "Äussere und Innere," pp. 6 and 17.

33 *Ibid.*, pp. 8–9; and Johanna Waescher and Eva von Roy, *Denkschrift der Verbündeten kaufmännischen Vereine für weibliche Angestellte, 1901–1911* (Frankfurt a. M., 1912), pp. 5ff.

34 "Eine Zusammenkunft der Schwestervereine," *MWA* 6 (1901): 521; and "Die 2. Konferenz der Verbündeten kaufmännischen Vereine für weibliche Angestellte," *MWA* 7 (1902): 617–18. Surprisingly, the single collective action taken by the Confederation in the period was relatively

radical, calling a public meeting in Berlin in 1904 to demonstrate against female exclusion from voting rights on the commercial courts, which testifies to the strong feminism of many Confederation leaders.

35  "Verbündete, 1901–1911," p. 90; "Erwiderung," *ZWH* 11 (1906): 5; "Was unser Verband im Jahre 1905 getan und erreicht hat," *ZWH* 11 (1906): 34 and 36; and Friederike Broell, "Ein Wort zur Klarlegung," *ibid.*, p. 4.

36  "Unsere Versammlung in Erfurt," *ZWH* 11 (1906): 66.

37  *ZWH* 11 (1906): 107.

38  "Erfurt," p. 66.

39  Quoted in Lüders, *Cauer*, p. 135. Lüders, who was also a delegate to the convention, said that the leadership tried to maintain good relations with Cauer. *Ibid.*, p. 136.

40  "Erfurt", p. 67.

41  *Ibid.*

42  *Ibid.*, p. 68. What was new was the elaboration of a set of concrete proposals for reform. For a contrasting view suggesting that the new Alliance position was the equivalent of unionism, see Ursula Nienhaus, "Von Töchtern und Schwestern: Zur vergessenen Geschichte der weiblichen Angestellten im deutschen Kaiserreich," in Jürgen Kocka, ed., *Angestellte im europäischen Vergleich: Die Herausbildung angestellter Mittelschichten seit dem späten 19. Jahrhundert* (Göttingen, 1981), p. 323.

43  "Hoffnungen und Wünsche," *ZWH* 12 (1907): 1.

44  "Zur Abwehr," *ZWH* 11 (1906): 152. See also "Der rechte Weg," *ZWH* 11 (1906): 115, 117; and "Aus anderen Vereinen," *ZWH* 15 (1910): 117.

45  "Rechte Weg," p. 115.

46  Broell, "Klarlegung," pp. 3–4; Verbandsleitung Kassel, "Zur Richtigstellung," *ZWH* 11 (1906): 5–6; and Elisabeth von Mumm, "Eine 'Berichtigung,'" *ibid.*, p. 6.

47  Waescher and von Roy, *Denkschrift*, p. 18; *Kontoristinnen Zeitung*, 4.11.1907, PP 9095, Hamb.St.A.; and *ZWH* 13 (1908): 120.

48  Waescher and von Roy, *Denkschrift*, p. 35; *MKV* 4 (1908): 93.

49  Waescher and von Roy, *Denkschrift*, pp. 36–37.

50  Rosa Urbach, "Der Wert der Organisation," in Verbündete Kaufmännische Vereine für weibliche Angestellte, *Jahrbuch für Handlungsgehilfinnen* (Cassel, 1913), p. 37.

51  Cited in Johanna Waescher, "Warum sind die Verbündeten kaufmännischen Vereine dem Bund deutscher Frauenvereine beigetreten?" *MKV* 4 (1908): 25–26. See also Richard J. Evans, *The Feminist Movement in Germany, 1894–1933* (London, 1976), pp. 146–47.

52  Waescher, "Beigetreten," pp. 25–26.

53  A public competition actually occurred between the Berlin Commercial Alliance and its rivals. See "Der rechte Weg," *ZWH* 11 (1906): 117; "Zur Abwehr," *ibid.*, p. 138; and "Aus anderen Vereinen," *ZWH* 12 (1907): 53. For accounts of confrontations between the organizations, see *ZWH* 11 (1906): 155, 167, and 171.

54  Adele Beerensson, "Aus der Frauenbewegung. Die Generalversammlung des Bundes deutscher Frauenvereine," *ZWH* 13 (1908): 178.

55  "Hannover," *ZWH* 15 (1910): 83; also Gertrud Israel, "Verbandsarbeit und

Frauenbewegung," in Kaufmännischer Verband, *25 Jahre Berufsorganisation*, p. 70. The Berlin Clerks' Aid Association had briefly joined the BDF, but quit in 1898. Ursula Nienhaus, *Berufsstand weiblich: Die ersten weiblichen Angestellten* (Berlin, 1982), p. 57.

56 Evans, *Feminist Movement*; Amy Hackett, "Feminism and Liberalism in Wilhelmine Germany, 1890–1918," in Berenice A. Carroll, ed., *Liberating Women's History* (Urbana, 1976), pp. 127–37.

57 Josef Silbermann [J.S.], "Beruf und Frauenbewegung," *ZWH* 15 (1910): 145–48. This is probably a written version of the lecture Silbermann had earlier given in a number of cities.

58 Israel, "Verbandsarbeit und Frauenbewegung," pp. 72–73.

59 Gertrud Israel, "Was bedeutet die Organisation für unser berufliches und persönliches Leben?" *Frau* 19 (1911/12): 418–21. For the Congress, see Bund Deutscher Frauenvereine, ed., *Deutscher Frauenkongress, Berlin, 27. Februar-2. März 1912: Sämtliche Vorträge* (Leipzig, 1912). See also Gertrud Israel, "Die Ausstellung 'Die Frau in Haus und Beruf' und der Deutsche Frauenkongress," *ZWH* 17 (1912): 18–19 and 51–52.

## 7 The socialist Central Alliance

1 The account of the early years of socialist clerks' unions comes from Zentralverband der Handlungsgehilfen und Gehilfinnen Deutschlands, "Einleitung," *Protokoll der 4. Generalversammlung v. 22.–23.5.1904 in Magdeburg und Bericht 1902/3* (Hamburg, 1904), pp. 3–11; "Aus fünfundzwanzigjähriger Geschichte," *HZ* 14 (1910): 67–69; Konrad Stehr, *Der Zentralverband der Angestellten: Sein Werdegang, seine Gestalt und sein Charakter* (Berlin, 1926), pp. 9–32; and Otto Urban, "Zentralverband der Angestellten," in Erich Gierke, ed., *Zur Geschichte der Angestellten-Gewerkschaften*, Schriftenreihe der "Freiheit," Heft 1 (Berlin, 1949), pp. 57–58.

2 "Was wir wollen!" *Der Handlungs-Gehilfe*, #1 (1885):1; facsimile in "Geschichte," p. 67.

3 *Berlin Vorwärts*, 4.6.1897, in PP V676, vol. 1, Hamb.St.A. The Free Union movement as a whole had engaged in the same controversy. See Klaus Schönhoven, "Localism – Craft Union – Industrial Union: Organizational Patterns in German Trade Unionism," and Dirk H. Müller, "Syndicalism and Localism in the German Trade-Union Movement," both in Wolfgang J. Mommsen and Hans-Gerhard Husung, eds., *The Development of Trade Unionism in Great Britain and Germany, 1880–1914* (London, 1985), pp. 219–49; and Gerhard A. Ritter, *Arbeiterbewegung, Parteien, und Parlamentarismus: Aufsätze zur deutschen Sozial- und Verfassungsgeschichte des 19. und 20. Jahrhunderts* (Göttingen, 1986), p. 80.

4 Vorstand des Zentralverbandes der Handlungsgehilfen und Gehilfinnen Deutschlands, "Was wir wollen!" *HB* 1 (1897): 1; facsimile in "Geschichte," p. 69. See also Paul Lange, "Handlungsgehilfenbewegung und Sozialpolitik," in Zentralverband der Handlungsgehilfen und Gehilfinnen Deutschlands, *Protokoll der 6. Generalversammlung in München, 8.–9.6.1908* (Hamburg, 1908), pp. 64–68.

5 PP V676 *passim*, Hamb.St.A.; and *HZ passim*.

6  "Streiks und Lohnbewegungen," Zentralverband, *Protokoll 1904*, pp. 20–23. See also the *Protokolle* of later years.

7  "Arbeitsverhältnisse in Konsumvereine," in Zentralverband der Handlungsgehilfen und Gehilfinnen Deutschlands, *Bericht des Vorstandes und Ausschusses über die 5te Geschäftsperiode 1904–05 nebst Protokoll der 5te Generalversammlung, 4.–5.6.1906 in Chemnitz* (Hamburg, 1906), p. 22.

8  Stehr, *Zentralverband*, p. 22; "Geschichte," p. 68; and Zentralverband, *Protokoll 1904*, p. 4. For a negative evaluation of women in the Central Alliance, see Ursula Nienhaus, *Berufsstand weiblich: die ersten weiblichen Angestellten* (Berlin, 1982), pp. 68–71.

9  "Einleitung," Zentralverband, *Protokoll 1904*, p. 5; Zentralverband der Handlungsgehilfen und Gehilfinnen Deutschlands, *Bericht des Vorstandes und Ausschusses über die 6. Geschäftsperiode 1906–07* (Hamburg, 1908), p. 5.

10  "Forderungen," reprinted in Zentralverband, *Protokoll 1904*, p. 32. No convention minutes were printed before 1904; the first reference to women was in 1906, when there were five female delegates out of thirty-five. See Julian Borchart, "Lehrzeit und Frauenarbeit im Handelsgewerbe," Zentralverband, *Protokoll 1906*, pp. 63–64.

11  Stehr, *Zentralverband*, p. 12. Among speeches, see Frida Storch in Stettin, *HZ* 13 (1909): 191; or Regina Friedländer in Dresden, *HZ* 14 (1910) 167; for plant meetings, see *HZ* 14 (1910): 23 concerning Berlin, and *HZ* 15 (1911): 146 for Frankfurt, Hamburg, Mainz, and Munich. See also "Lohnbewegungen," in Zentralverband der Handlungsgehilfen und Gehilfinnen Deutschlands, *Bericht des Vorstandes und Ausschusses über die 7. Geschäftsperiode 1908–09 nebst Protokoll der 7. Generalversammlung, 16.–17.5.1910* (Hamburg, 1910), pp. 16–17; and "Lohnbewegungen," Zentralverband der Handlungsgehilfen und Gehilfinnen Deutschlands, *Geschäftsbericht für das Jahr 1910/1911 nebst Protokoll der 8. Generalversammlung, 5.–7. Mai 1912, Berlin* (Berlin, 1912), pp. 10–11.

12  August Bebel, "Die Frauen und die Gewerkschaften," *HZ* 14 (1910): 19; "Lohnfragen und Frauenarbeit," *HZ* 15 (1911): 51–52.

13  In the cases when local office holders were reported in the journal, one or two positions out of eight to fifteen available seem to have gone to women. See *HZ passim*.

14  Krauss married the head of the Berlin local and continued her agitation as Regina Friedländer. Stehr, *Zentralverband*, p. 32; Zentralverband, *Geschäftsperiode 1906–07*, p. 5; and *HZ* 18 (1914): 41.

15  Kollege Landgraf and Kollege Urban, discussion of Lange, "Handlungsgehilfenbewegung," in Zentralverband, *Protokoll 1908*, pp. 68–71.

16  "Beziehungen zu anderen Organisationen," in Zentralverband, *Protokoll 1906*, p. 24.

17  *HZ* 16 (1912): 87.

18  *Ibid.*, p. 38.

19  *HZ* 14 (1910): 109.

20  For examples, see "Jetzt ist es Zeit zur Tat!" *Ibid.*, p. 143; or "Die Bankerotterklärung," *HZ* 18 (1914): 82.

21 "Die Unterdrückung des Volkes in Preussen," *HZ* 14 (1910): 26–27. See also "Menschenrechte," *HZ* 16 (1912): 1–2.

22 Zentralverband, *Protokoll 1908*, p. 83.

23 Zentralverband, *Protokoll 1912*, p. 81.

24 Max Josephsohn, "Rückblick auf die Entwicklung, 1892–1907," *Echo*, 9.1.1907, PP V676, vol. 2, Hamb.St.A.

25 Police report, 8.7.1897 and *FB*, 10.7.1897, both in PP V676, vol. 1, Hamb.St.A.

26 For department stores, see police report, 5.8.1898; and *FB*, 10.8.1898, PP V676, vol. 1, Hamb.St.A. In 1903, Josephsohn reported that most members were from cooperatives. *Echo*, 11.6.1903, PP V676, vol. 1, Hamb.St.A.

27 *HB*, 15.2.1902 and *Echo*, 9.10.1902, in PP V676, vol. 1, Hamb.St.A.

28 Police report, 3.10.1902, PP V676, vol. 1, Hamb.St.A. Unfortunately, few records of plant meetings are held in police files. See letter from the organization to police, 4.5.1908, PP V676, vol. 2, Hamb.St.A. The 1909 yearly report for Hamburg stated that thirteen were held in that year. *Echo*, 9.2.1910, *ibid.*

29 *Echo*, 2.10.1908; *Echo*, 6.11.1909; and 1909 annual report in *Echo*, 9.2.1910; all in PP V676, vol. 2, Hamb.St.A. Although the Central Alliance won improvements, stores later reneged. *Echo*, 13.9.1911, *ibid.*

30 Luise Zietz, "Die Erwerbstätigkeit der Frau einst und jetzt," report in *Echo*, 11.9.1901, PP V676, vol. 1, Hamb.St.A.; Regina Krauss, "Welcher Organisation haben sich die weiblichen Handlungsgehilfinnen anzuschliessen?" report by police, 25.10.1906, and Regina Friedländer, "Was bedrückt die Angestellten der Waren- und Kaufhäuser, und wie ist ihre Lage zu verbessern?" report in *Echo*, 22.9.1912, both in PP V676, vol. 2, Hamb.St.A.

31 See, for example, Frl. M. Chapira, cited in *FB*, 11.1.1898, and Max Josephsohn in *Echo*, 15.7.1900 and *FB*, 28.11.1900, both in PP V676, vol. 1, Hamb.St.A.; and Zentralverband der Handlungsgehilfen und Gehilfinnen, Ortsgruppe Hamburg, *An die Handlungsgehilfen und Gehilfinnen!*, pamphlet (Hamburg, n.d. [c. 1907]), PP V676, vol. 2, Hamb.St.A.

32 Zentralverband der Handlungsgehilfen und Gehilfinnen Deutschlands, Ortsgruppe Hamburg, "An die Handlungsgehilfinnen! Eine ernstes Wort in ernster Zeit!" (n.d. [1909]), pp. 1–3. Italics in original.

33 See PP V676, vols. 1 and 2 *passim*, Hamb.St.A. Records are incomplete, making it likely that women held other positions as well.

34 Report in *Echo*, 8.2.1911, PP V676, vol. 2, Hamb.St.A.

35 Report in *Echo*, 11.10.1911, PP V676, vol. 2, Hamb.St.A. A woman was elected. No similar scepticism was ever expressed about male candidates.

36 Reported in *Echo*, 4.10.1908 and 12.11.1908, PP V676, vol. 2, Hamb.St.A.

## 8 Jobs or marriage

1 "Können alleinstehende Damen zur Ausstellung nach Paris reisen?" *MWA* 6 (1901): 55; "Wenn jemand eine Reise tut!" *MWA* 9 (1904): 64–65.

2 "Londoner Brief," *ZWH* 11 (1906): 116; "Aus anderen Ländern," *ibid.*, p. 152.
3 Josef Silbermann [J.S.], "Beruf und Frauenbewegung," *ZWH* 15 (1910): 146.
4 "Berechtigte Forderungen der Frauenbewegung," *KB* 2 (1903): 21.
5 Kaufmännischer Verband für weibliche Angestellte, Ortsgruppe Hamburg, "Kolleginnen, habt ihr schon darüber nachgedacht?" (c. 1905), PP S6741, Hamb.St.A.
6 *ZWH* 11 (1906): 56; and *ZWH* 15 (1910), Sonderbeilage Brandenburg und Anhalt, April; respectively.
7 "How can I improve my position?" asked a Confederation speaker. *MKV* 4 (1908): 13. Also "Nimm und Lies!" *KB* 2 (1903): 26.
8 "Was wir von den Männern lernen können!" *MKV* 5 (1909): 172.
9 "Welcher Charaktereigenschaften bedarf der Mensch zur Begründung des Lebensglucks?" *KB* 7 (1908): 5; and "Gewissenhaft!" *KB* 6 (1907): 35.
10 Verbündete kaufmännische Vereine für weibliche Angestellte, *Jahrbuch für Handlungsgehilfinnen* (Cassel, 1913); Kaufmännischer Verband für weibliche Angestellte, *Taschenbuch des kaufmännischen Verbandes für weibliche Angestellte* (Berlin, 1905), in PP S6741, Hamb.St.A. For examples of tips, see Emma Laser, "Wie kleide ich mich bei der Vorstellung?" *ZWH* 16 (1911): 163; and "Wohlgerücke," *KB* 9 (1910): 5.
11 "An die Grossstädterinnen," *MWA* 7 (1902): 610.
12 "Kolleginnen . . . nachgedacht?"
13 [Gumpoldt], "Entfremdet," pp. 2–3. See also Johanna Waescher in *MKV* 4 (1908): 81.
14 *MKV* 4 (1908): 93.
15 Rosa Urbach, "Der Wert der Organisation," in Verbündete, *Jahrbuch*, p. 33.
16 Else Kesting, "Ein Gespräch in der Eisenbahn," *ZWH* 11 (1906): 101–2; a similar didactic story is in Franziska Altmann, "Eine Mahnung und eine Bitte an die Kolleginnen," *MWA* 8 (1903): 1.
17 *ZWH* 13 (1908), Sonderbeilage Brandenburg, Mai.
18 Courses were offered, for example, in Cassel, *MKV* 10 (1914): 31; Heidelberg, *ZWH* 11 (1906): 24; and Berlin, "Ortsgruppe Berlin: Diskussionabende," *MWA* 9 (1904): 99.
19 Kaufmännischer Verband für weibliche Angestellte, *25 Jahre Berufsorganisation: 1889–1914: Zugleich Verwaltungsbericht für das Jahr 1913* (Berlin, n.d.), p. 38; *ZWH* 13 (1908), Sonderbeilage Brandenburg, April.
20 Dr. A. Höfle, "Soziale Kurse," *KB* 10 (1911): 2–4.
21 Paula Degenhardt, "Die soziale Schulung der Handlungsgehilfinnen," *ZWH* 17 (1912): 115 and Sonderbeilage Berlin, November.
22 "Beispiele und ihre Lehren. Zuschrift einer Kollegin," *ZWH* 18 (1913): 130.
23 "Kann die weibliche Arbeitskraft einen Vergleich mit der männlichen aushalten?" *MKV* 8 (1912): 77.
24 Kaufmännischer Verband für weibliche Angestellte, *Ein Rückblick auf seine Tätigkeit aus Anlass seines 15. jährigen Bestehens* (Berlin, 1904), p. 28.
25 Urbach, "Wert der Organisation," p. 36. See also "Wo Pflichten – da

Rechte!" *ZWH* 14 (1909): 116.

26 For instance, Bona Pfeifer, "Was darf man vom Beruf erwarten?" *MWA* 8 (1903): 200–1; the discussion in the Erfurt Commercial Alliance chapter, "Ehe und Beruf," reported in *ZWH* 11 (1906): 41; Paula Intlekofer, "Gegner der Frauenarbeit im Handelsgewerbe," *ZWH* 12 (1907): 129–30; Josef Silbermann, "Beruf und Frauenbewegung," *ZWH* 15 (1910): 146–47; and "Kann die weibliche Arbeitskraft . . ." p. 77.

27 "Aus trauter Dämmerstunde," *HG* 10 (1914): 30–31.

28 "Berechtigte Forderungen der Frauenbewegung," *KB* 2 (1903): 21–22.

29 Meta Gadesmann, *Die Frau als kaufmännische Angestellte* (Berlin, 1910/11), p. 47. The single exception to this was a lecture given to the Berlin Aid Association in 1901 entitled "Married Women as Clerks," which detailed their legal rights. *MWA* 6 (1901): 494.

30 "Für Kolleginnen, die sich verheiraten wollen," *ZWH* 10 (1905), Sonderbeilage Berlin, März.

31 Agnes Herrmann, "Die Mädchenfortbildungsschule," *Ein Volk – Eine Schule*, cited in "Ehekurse," *ZWH* 13 (1908): 87.

32 Agnes Herrmann [H.], "An alle Handlungsgehilfinnen, die im Begriff sind zu heiraten," *ZWH* 12 (1907), Sonderbeilage Brandenburg, Oktober.

33 For examples, [Gumpoldt], "Entfremdet," p. 2; Intlekofer, "Gegner der Frauenarbeit," pp. 129–30; Silbermann, "Beruf und Frauenbewegung," p. 145; and "Die deutschnationalen Handlungsgehilfen und die Frauenarbeit," *MKV* 7 (1911): 105.

34 "Überzählige Frauen," *MWA* 8 (1903): 96.

35 Eva von Roy, "Frauenerwerb und -berufe," in Bund Deutscher Frauenvereine, *Internationaler Frauenkongress. 1904. Officieller Originalbericht* (n.p., n.d.), p. 29. See also Agnes Herrmann, "Frauenbildung eine Kulturfrage," *ZWH* 15 (1910): 17–19.

36 Margarete Pick, "Der Wert der Verkäuferin," *ZWH* 11 (1906): 150.

37 "Zur Frauenfrage," *KB* 9 (1910): 31.

38 S. Neubauer, *Lehrplan für Verkäuferinnenklassen der Mädchenpflichtfortbildungsschule* (Berlin, 1912), pp. 9–11.

39 "Berufs- und soziale Bildung der Handlungsgehilfin," *KB* 9 (1910): 45.

40 "Kleinigkeiten," *ZWH: Ausgabe für Mitgleider unter 18 Jahren* 2 (1911): 49.

## 9 Improved commercial training

1 The argument, or elements of it, appeared continually in the organizational press and was discussed in members' meetings. For major articles and speeches, see Julius Meyer, "Die Frauenarbeit im Handelsgewerbe," *MWA* 1 (1896): 2–3; Agnes Herrmann, "Entwicklung und Organisation der weiblichen Handlungsgehilfen," *Frau* 10 (1902/3): 326–28; [Agnes Herrmann], *Fortbildungsschulzwang für weibliche Handlungsgehilfen und Lehrlinge* (Berlin, 1903); Elisabeth von Mumm, "Die Pflichtfortbildungsschule des weiblichen Geschlechts in hygenischer Beziehung," lecture to the Generalversammlung des niederrheinischen Vereins für öffentliche Gesundheitspflege, Cologne, 31.10.1906; Josef

Silbermann, *Praktische Lehre und theoretische Fachbildung des weiblichen Handlungsgehilfen* (Berlin, 1907); Josef Silbermann, "Das weibliche kaufmännische Bildungswesen," *Volkswirtschaftliche Zeitfragen* 35, Heft 273 (Berlin, 1913); Rosa Kempf, "Die Organisation der Fortbildungsschule für Mädchen," *S. Praxis* 19 (1909/10), col. 1,158; Johanna Waescher, "Die obligatorischen kaufmännischen Fortbildungsschulen für weibliche Angestellte," *VVKU* 45 (1911): 12ff; "Salärierung des weiblichen Arbeitskraft," *KB* 4 (1905): 29.

2 Paul Lange, *Die Angestellten im wirtschaftlichen Kampf*, Zentralverband der Handlungsgehilfen und Gehilfinnen Deutschlands, Schrift 23 (Hamburg, 1911); Zentralverband der Handlungsgehilfen und Gehilfinnen Deutschlands, *Geschäftsbericht für die Jahre 1910/1911 nebst Protokoll der 8. Generalversammlung, 5.–7. Mai 1912, Berlin* (Berlin, 1912), pp. 66–67.

3 Julian Borchardt, "Lehrzeit und Frauenarbeit im Handelsgewerbe," in Zentralverband der Handlungsgehilfen und Gehilfinnen Deutschlands, *Bericht des Vorstandes und Ausschusses über die 5te Geschäftsperiode 1904–1905 nebst Protokoll der 5te Generalversammlung, 4.–5.6.1906 in Chemnitz* (Hamburg, 1906), p. 65; also the lectures to the Hamburg local: Julian Borchardt, "Bildung und Arbeiterbewegung," police report, 7.2.1901, PP V676, vol. 1, Hamb.St.A.; Harro Köhncke, "Erziehung und Sozialismus," report in *Echo*, 14.6.1907, PP V676, vol. 2, Hamb.St.A.; and "Arbeiterbildung," talk at Hamburg local, report in *Echo*, 10.8.1912, PP V676, vol. 2, Hamb.St.A.

4 See Silbermann, *Praktische Lehre*; Eva von Roy, "Die Notwendigkeit einer kaufmännischen Lehre für weibliche Handelsangestellte," *MWA* 6 (1901): 561; Sophie Bachmann, "Sollen die angehenden Handlungsgehilfinnen Lehrlingsstellen annehmen?" *MWA* 7 (1902): 569–71; and Agnes Herrmann and M. Henckel, "Zur Lehrlingsfrage," *MWA* 7 (1902): 577–78.

5 Dr. Brandt, "Die privaten kaufmännischen Unterrichtsanstalten," in Verein des kaufmännischen Unterrichtswesens in Rheinland und Westfalen, "Bericht über die Hauptversammlung," 20.7.1902, AHKD, Abt. 20, #90–3, RWWA; Hildegard Sachs, *Die Massnahmen zur Bekämpfung unlauterer privater Unterrichtsunternehmungen*, Auftrag des Kartells der Auskunftstellen für Frauenberufe (Berlin, 1914); and Anna Köhler, *Über das private Handelsschulwesen in Deutschland* (Berlin, 1906). For an example, see 1906 leaflet from "Naumann's Handels-Lehranstalt," AHKD, Abt. 20, #91–2, RWWA.

6 Agnes Herrmann, "Bildungswesen," in Kaufmännischer Verband für weibliche Angestellte, *25 Jahre Berufsorganisation: 1889–1914: Zugleich Verwaltungsbericht für das Jahr 1913* (Berlin, n.d.), p. 54.

7 Kaufmännischer Verband für weibliche Angestellte, "Eingabe an das preussische Abgeordnetenhaus," cited in "Die 'kaufmännischen Pressen,'" *ZWH* 12 (1907): 17; Köhler, *Handelschulwesen*; and Minna Cauer, "Die Frau im Beruf und ihr Standesbewusstsein," speech to Industria, report in *Echo*, 30.3.1903, PP S6741, Hamb.St.A.

8 Kaufmännischer Verband, "Eingabe Abgeordnetenhaus," pp. 17–18; Herrmann, "Bildungswesen," p. 54; and Sachs, *Massnahmen zur Bekämpfung*, p. 20.

9  Willy Cohn, *Verkäuferinnenschulen, Gedanken und Vorschläge eines Praktikers* (Berlin, 1911), p. 9.

10  Cited in "Förderung der kaufmännischen Unterrichtsanstalten für weibliche Angestellte," *MWA* 6 (1901): 513. See also Käthe Gaebel, *Die Bekämpfung der unlauteren und unzulänglichen privaten Fachschulen unter besonderer Berücksichtigung von Handel und Gewerbe*, Heft 5, Flugschriften zur Berufsberatung (Berlin, 1922), p. 7; and Sachs, *Massnahmen zur Bekämpfung*, pp. 18–19.

11  See the report of the Central German Chambers of Commerce convention in "Frauenbewegung: Berufliches: Zur Frage der weiblichen Angestellten," *Frau* 14 (1907/8): 695; Prof. Scheffen, "Denkschrift betr. Ausgestaltung des kaufmännischen Unterrichtswesens in Duisburg," 7.2.1910, AHKD, Abt. 20, #190–7, RWWA; and "Anstellungsvertrag #226, Handelskammer Duisburg to city government, 30.1.1911, AHKD, Abt. 20, #195–2, RWWA; and Sachs, *Massnahmen zur Bekämpfung*, p. 19.

12  "Bildungswesen," *ZWH* 12 (1907): 69; "Ein kleiner Schritt vorwärts," *ZWH* 13 (1908): 54; and Sachs, *Massnahmen zur Bekämpfung*, pp. 24–26, 30, 36.

13  "Kleiner Schritt," p. 54.

14  For Hamburg, see PP S6741, Hamb.St.A.; also Silbermann, *Praktische Lehre*; and Rosa Kempf, *Berufswahl und Berufsbildung* (Berlin, 1912).

15  [Herrmann], *Fortbildungsschulzwang*, p. 4 and pp. 65–66; "Allerhand Irrtümer," *ZWH* 14 (1909): 5. For state laws, see "Berufsbildung: Fach-Fortbildungsschule," *AfF* 1, 1 (1913): 83.

16  L. Tronnier, "Verzeichnis der in Deutschland bestehenden kaufmännischen Unterrichtsanstalten," *VVKU* 47 (1912): 6. See also Jürgen Kocka, *Unternehmensverwaltung und Angestelltenschaft am Beispiel Siemens, 1847–1914* (Stuttgart, 1969), p. 472; Peter Lundgreen, "Industrialization and the Educational Formation of Manpower in Germany," *JSH* 9 (1975): 64ff.

17  Herrmann, "Bildungswesen," p. 54; and Johanna Waescher and Eva von Roy, *Denkschrift der Verbündeten kaufmännischen Vereine für weibliche Angestellte, 1901–1911* (Frankfurt a. M., 1912), p. 13.

18  *Ibid.*; "Eingabe des kaufmännischen und gewerblichen Vereins der weiblichen Angestellten an den Magistrat der Stadt Königsberg," cited in "Fortbildungsschulwesen," *MWA* 6 (1901): 503; "Eingabe an den Magistrat zu Berlin," reprinted in "Fortbildungsschulzwang," *MWA* 9 (1904): 35; "Erziehung und Bildung: Ausbildung der weiblichen kaufmännischen Angestellten," *S. Praxis* 16 (1906/7), col. 1,148; "Die Konferenz der Verbündeten," *MKV* 4 (1908): 42; "Betrifft obligatorische Fortbildungsschulen!" *MKV* 5 (1909): 105; "Der Kampf um und für die Fortbildungsschule in Preussen," *ZWH* 16 (1911): 65–66; "Brennende Fragen für Handelsgehilfinnen," *KB* 8 (1909): 67–68.

19  For the BDF, see *BT*, 7.10.1906, in PP 5466, vol. 2, Hamb.St.A.; and Gertrud Bäumer, "Frauenfrage und Mittelstandspolitik," *Frau* 15 (1908/9): 456–57. For East German Women's Day, see *KB* 2 (1903): 50. For the ADF, *HC*, 10.10.1907; and *HN*, 17.10.1909, both in PP 5808, vol. 2, Hamb.St.A. For Women's Education – Women's University Studies, see "Aus anderen

Vereinen," *ZWH* 14 (1909): 118. For Women's Weal, Hamburg, *NHZ*, 25.10.1905, PP 5466, vol. 2, Hamb.St.A. For Berlin, see "Magistrat zu Berlin," p. 35.

20  "Bildungswesen," *ZWH* 12 (1907): 69.

21  Herrmann, "Bildungswesen," p. 56; and "Kampf um Fortbildungsschule," pp. 65–66. The Confederation claimed that it too had sponsored the meeting; see "Preussisches Fortbildungsgesetz," p. 55.

22  "Brennende Fragen," pp. 67–68.

23  "Förderung der kaufmännischen Unterrichtsanstalten für weibliche Angestellte," *MWA* 6 (1901): 513; Waescher and von Roy, *Denkschrift*, p. 13; and Herrmann, "Bildungswesen," p. 55. There was stiff opposition from many male members. See the Weimar meeting, 1901, in AHKD, Abt. 20, #90–1, RWWA.

24  For example, the Alliance of German Department Store Owners in 1905, "Immer weiter! Vorwärts!" *KB* 4 (1905): 22; also Sitzungsprotokoll der Handelskammer Duisburg, 12.2.1907, AHKD, Abt. 20, #195–2, RWWA. For chambers of commerce, see HKBf, K 3, #391, and HKB, K 2, #127, SWWA. For the German Alliance for Commercial Education, *KB* 6 (1907): 51.

25  For example, see "Fortbildungsschule für Mädchen," *Monatsschrift für Handel, Industrie, und Schifffahrt* (May, 1900), in AHKD, Abt. 20, #92–5; Verein für Handlungs-Commis von 1858, "An den Hohen Bundesrat, Berlin, obligatorischen Fortbildungsunterricht betreffend," 23.12.1907, AHKD, Abt. 20, #91–2; and Die Direktion der kaufmännischen Schulen Duisburg, 10.11.1909, AHKD, Abt. 20, #195–2; all in RWWA; and Richard Döring, *Die Frauenarbeit im Handelsgewerbe* (Hamburg, 1909), p. 38.

26  Cited by [Herrmann], *Fortbildungsschulzwang*, p. 7.

27  For 1903 see *KB* 2 (1903): 34; for 1906, Agnes Herrmann, "Die Einwände gegen den Fortbildungsschulzwang für weibliche Handlungsgehilfen und Lehrlinge," *ZWH* 11 (1906): 83; for 1907 and 1912, see Tronnier, "Verzeichnis," pp. 6–7.

28  "Frauenarbeit und Fortbildungsschulpflicht," *HZ* 14 (1910): 3; Borchardt, "Lehrzeit," pp. 63–65; Paul Lange, "Die praktische und theoretische Ausbildung der Handlungsgehilfen," *HZ* 14 (1910): 89–91; "Wo bleibt die Pflichtfortbildungsschule in Berlin?" *HZ* 16 (1912): 159; and "Fortbildungsschule für weibliche kaufmännische Angestellte in Barmen," *HZ* 18 (1914): 44–45.

29  Josephine Levy-Rathenau, "Wie bildet die Grossstadt die weibliche Jugend für Handel und Gewerbe aus?" in Eliza Ichenhäuser, ed., *Was die Frau von Berlin wissen muss: ein praktisches Frauenbuch für Einheimische und Fremde* (Berlin, n.d. [c. 1912]), pp. 208–10.

30  Königsberg talk, *MWA* 6 (1901): 481. See also Gertrud Meyer, "Zur Lage der Verkäuferinnen," *HG* 9 (1913): 86.

31  Waescher and von Roy, *Denkschrift*, pp. 15–16.

32  Herrmann, "Bildungswesen," p. 54. See also Johanna Waescher, "Zur Lage der Verkäuferinnen," *HG* 9 (1913): 62–63.

33  For early efforts, see Herrmann, "Bildungswesen," p. 56; von Roy in Königsberg, 1901, *MWA* 6 (1901): 481; Josef Silbermann at a congress of

the German Alliance for Commercial Education in 1903, "Kurse für Verkäuferinnen," *ZWH* 14 (1909): 52–53.

34 Agnes Herrmann, "Widerlegung von Einwänden gegen den Fortbildungsschulzwang für weibliche Handlungsgehilfen und Lehrlinge," *VVKU* 45 (1911): 10–12; "Höhere Töchter als Verkäuferinnen," *ZWH* 16 (1911): 145–46; "Ein verkannter und unterschätzter Beruf," *ZWH* 18 (1913): 66–67; and "Schulen für Verkäuferinnen," *ZWH* 16 (1911): 99.

35 See von Roy's talk, *MWA* 6 (1901): 481; "Die Kunst des Verkaufens und die Verkäuferin," *MKV* 7 (1911): 41–43; Waescher, "Obligatorische Fortbildungsschulen," pp. 12ff.

36 Elisabeth von Mumm, "Teilung der kaufmännischen Vorbildung für Verkäuferinnen und Kontoristinnen?" *MKV* 4 (1908): 58. See also the letter in her support, C. Schauenhammer, "Teilung der kaufmännischen Vorbildung für Verkäuferinnen und Kontoristinnen," *MKV* 4 (1908): 78.

37 Cited in A. Kasten, *Die Fortbildungsschule für Verkäuferinnen*, Denkschrift des Verbands deutscher Detailgeschäfte der Textilbranche (Hamburg, 1914), pp. 10–11.

38 "Unsere Hauptversammlung," *HG* 9 (1913): 74.

39 Cohn, *Verkäuferinnenschulen*, pp. 29–34 and p. 42. See also "Soziale Umschau," *MKV* 7 (1911): 4; *KB* 4 (1905): 30; Kasten, *Fortbildungsschule*, p. 8; and letter from Dr. Rasch to Bochum Chamber of Commerce, March 1912, HKB, K 2, #413, SWWA.

40 Josef Aufseesser, "Aufgaben und Mittel zur Förderung unseres Verkaufspersonals, insbesondere der Verkäuferinnen," lecture at convention of the Verband deutscher Detailgeschäfte der Textilbranche, Hamburg, held in Berlin, 13.2.1912, in HKB, K 2, #127, SWWA. See also Beschlussantrag des Kleinhandelsausschusses der Handelskammer Bochum, n.d. [1912], HKB, K 2, #413, SWWA; letter from the Verband deutscher Detailgeschäfte der Textilbranche, circulated among "die amtliche Handelsvertretungen des Reichs," 28.2.1910, AHKD, Abt. 20, #195–1, RWWA, a form letter in support of special sales courses and asking chambers of commerce for support; Kasten, *Fortbildungsschulen*, p. 8; and Cohn, *Verkäuferinnenschulen*, p. 44.

41 Verein zur Förderung des kaufmännischen Fortbildungsschulwesens in Rheinland und Westfalen, "Bericht über die 10. Hauptversammlung," 27.10.1907, and "Bericht über die 14. Hauptversammlung," 12.11.1911; both in AHKD, Abt. 20, #190–4, RWWA; von Mumm, "Teilung," p. 57; and Kasten, *Fortbildungsschulen*, pp. 8–13.

42 For example, S. Neubauer, *Lehrplan für Verkäuferinnenklassen der Mädchenpflichtfortbildungsschule*, Schriften des kaufmännischen Verbands für weibliche Angestellte 9 (Berlin, 1912).

43 Cohn, *Verkäuferinnenschulen*, pp. 22–23 and p. 25.

44 Elly von Rössing, "Zur Frage der Verkäuferinnenschulen," *ZGKU* 16, Sonderdruck #7–#9 (n.d.); and Elly von Rössing, "Verkäuferinnenschulen," *HG* 9 (1913): 110–11. See also Johanna Witzell, "Die branchenkundige Verkäuferin," *MKV* 4 (1908): 76–77; and Johanna Waescher [J.W.], "Zur Lage der Verkäuferinnen," *HG* 9 (1913): 62–63.

45 For example, "Gutachtliche Äusserung des Armen-Collegiums über die Errichtung von Fortbildungsschulen für Mädchen," 14.6.1900, BB I, B164, Hamb.St.A.
46 For talks at Women's Weal chapters, see *Echo*, 9.12.1904 and *NHZ*, 25.10.1905, PP 5466, vol. 2, Hamb.St.A. Agnes Herrmann attacked the "right wing of the women's movement" for supporting home economics within vocational education in a speech in Hamburg in 1908. Report in *FB*, 22.1.1908, PP S6741, Hamb.St.A.
47 Agnes Herrmann stated that the DHV was behind the proposal, an exaggeration. "Bildungswesen," p. 57.
48 Agnes Herrmann, "Die Mädchenfortbildungsschule," in *Ein Volk – Eine Schule*, cited in "Ehekurse," *ZWH* 13 (1908): 87.
49 Herrmann, "Einwände," pp. 82–83.
50 At a speech to Women's Education – Women's University Studies, which endorsed it. "Aus anderen Vereinen," *ZWH* 14 (1909): 118.
51 Von Mumm, *Pflichtfortbildungsschule . . . hygenisch*, pp. 1–3.
52 *KB* 9 (1910): 9. For its earlier enthusiasm, see "Es lebe der Kochtopf!" *KB* 6 (1907): 20.
53 "Einrichtung und Lehrpläne kaufmännischer Fortbildungsschulen und kaufmännischer Fachklassen an gewerblichen Fortbildungsschulen," 1.7.1911, cited in Kasten, *Fortbildungsschulen*, p. 13.
54 "Wissenschaftliche Berufsbildung gefährdet!" *ZWH* 17 (1912): 9.
55 Agnes Herrmann, "Hauswirtschaftlicher Unterricht in kaufmännischen Fortbildungsschulen," *ZWH* 17 (1912): 102; "Zur Frage des Haushaltungsunterricht in der kaufmännischen Pflicht-fortbildungsschule," *MKV* 8 (1912): 101.
56 "Unsere Hauptversammlung," *HG* 9 (1913): 74.
57 *AfF* 3, #2 (1915): 120, and "Aus der Frauenbewegung: Fortbildungsschule und Haushaltungsunterricht," *HG* 10 (1914): 27.
58 The Alliance alone had sent a letter in 1912. "An die verehrlichen Handelskammern, Vorsteher der Kaufmannschaft und Ältesten der Kaufmannschaft," September 1912, HKB, K 2, #413, SWWA. In 1914 the Alliance joined with the Confederation, the Central Alliance for the Interests of Female Workers, the Alliance for the Craft and Skilled Education of Woman, the Alliance of German Skilled Women Workers, Women's Education – Women's University Studies, and the Rhineland-Westphalen Women's Alliance. Letter, n.d. [c. January, 1914], *ibid.* and letter, n.d. [c. January 1914], HKBf, K 3, #391, SWWA.
59 Verein zur Förderung des kaufmännischen Fortbildungsschulwesens in Rheinland und Westfalen, "Bericht über die 16. Hauptversammlung," 25.5.1913, AHKD, Abt. 20, #190–4, RWWA. The speaker also referred to the decline of the family.

## 10  White-collar insurance

1 Jürgen Kocka, *White-Collar Workers in America, 1890–1940. A Social-Political History in International Perspective* (London, 1980), pp. 252–55; Jürgen Kocka, "Capitalism and Bureaucracy in German Industrialization before

1914," *EHR* 34 (1981): 453–68 and "Class Formation, Interest Articulation, and Public Policy: The Origins of the German White-Collar Class in the Late Nineteenth and Early Twentieth Centuries," in Suzanne Berger, ed., *Organizing Interests in Western Europe: Pluralism, Corporatism, and the Transformation of Politics* (Cambridge, 1982), pp. 72–75. See also Günter Hartfiel, *Angestellte und Angestelltengewerkschaften in Deutschland* (Berlin, 1961), pp. 134–36; Gewerkschaftsbund der Angestellten, *Epochen der Angestellten-Bewegung, 1774–1930* (Berlin, 1930), p. 89; Siegfried Aufhäuser, *Weltkrieg und Angestelltenbewegung*, Sozialwissenschaftliche Bibliothek 6 (Berlin, 1918), pp. 13–14; and *25 Jahre Angestelltenversicherung, 1913–1937* (Berlin, 1937), pp. 4–13.

2 For criticisms of the state program, see Johanna Waescher, "Die staatliche Pensionsversicherung der Privatbeamten," *Frau* 14 (1906/7): 714.

3 *Ibid.*, p. 714; and Waescher and Eva von Roy, *Denkschrift der Verbündeten kaufmännischen Vereine für weibliche Angestellte, 1901–1911* (Frankfurt a.M., 1912), pp. 18–19.

4 The Commercial Alliance was aware of and complained about the tactic. See "Unsere Hauptversammlung," *ZWH* 12 (1907): 82; and its 1908 annual report in *HN*, 14.5.1909, PP S6741, Hamb.St.A. For the Confederation, see Auguste Bruhn's report, in *HKZ*, 4.11.1907, PP 9095, Hamb.St.A.

5 Waescher and von Roy, *Denkschrift*, p. 18.

6 The questionnaire had data on economic situation, marital status, and insurance needs. See Waescher, "Pensionsversicherung," pp. 714–15. For the results, see Reichsamt des Innern, *Die wirtschaftliche Lage der Privatangestellten. Denkschrift über die im Oktober 1903 angestellten Erhebungen* (Berlin, 1907). Only about 3 percent of the respondents were women, indicative of the male predominance of the Committee. Single men were also underrepresented in the survey (compared with 1907 census data).

7 Waescher, "Pensionsversicherung," pp. 716–18.

8 Until 1909 the Free Alliance remained in the Main Pension Committee. "Zur Frage der Pensionsversicherung," *ZWH* 12 (1907): 177–78.

9 "Zur Reichsversicherungsordnung," *HZ* 14 (1910): 73; "Das Versicherungsgesetz für Angestellte," *HZ* 15 (1911): 194; "Bericht des Vorstandes für das Jahr 1911," *HZ* 16 (1912): 51–52; "Feinde des Fortschritts," *ibid.*, p. 162; all in PP V676, vol. 2, Hamb.St.A. See also "Sozialpolitische Angelegenheiten," in Zentralverband der Handlungsgehilfen Deutschlands, *Geschäftsbericht für die Jahre 1910/1911 nebst Protokoll der 8. Generalversammlung, 5.–7. Mai 1912, Berlin* (Berlin, 1912), p. 6. For events in Hamburg, see "Was wird der Handlungsgehilfenschaft durch den Entwurf der neuen Reichsversicherungsordnung geboten?" report in *Echo*, 4.9.1909, PP V676, vol. 2, and *passim*, Hamb.St.A.

10 "Die Geblendeten," *HZ* 15 (1911): 89.

11 "Vierter Konferenz der Verbündeten kaufmännischen Vereine für weibliche Angestellte," *MWA* 9 (1904): 56; and Waescher and von Roy, *Denkschrift*, p. 20. The Alliance was at the time still a member of the Confederation (see Chapter 6). Elise Ogurky, "Staatliche Pensionsversicherung der Privatangestellten," *MWA* 8 (1903): 97.

12 Waescher and von Roy, *Denkschrift*, p. 20; and Waescher,

"Pensionsversicherung," pp. 718–19.

13 Cited in Waescher, "Pensionsversicherung," p. 719. Although I have found no copy of the original points circulated by the Confederation, the BDF query was undoubtedly drawn from it and shows great similarity to von Roy's particular concerns. Women's Education – Women's University Studies and the General German Female Teachers' Association discussed the Confederation questions at their 1907 annual conventions; *ibid.*, p. 719. So too did the North German Women's Association, at the behest of the Hamburg Association of Female Office Workers (soon to join the Confederation) and the female clerks' association in Flensburg. *HKZ*, 4.10.1907 and 4.11.1907, PP 9095, Hamb.St.A.

14 Waescher, "Pensionsversicherung," p. 719; and Eva von Roy, "Witwenversorgung oder Ehefrauenversicherung?" *MKV* 4 (1908): 85–88.

15 Von Roy, "Ehefrauenversicherung?" p. 86. The terms were *Versicherungspflichtige* or *Versorgungsbedürftige*.

16 *Ibid.*

17 *Ibid.*, pp. 86–87.

18 *Ibid.*, p. 87. See also Waescher, "Pensionsversicherung," p. 719, for similar arguments.

19 At meetings of the Central German Alliance for Pension Insurance and other similar groups, Confederation members demanded that the organizations reject government suggestions that insurance premiums be paid back to women when they married, for that would have meant that wives were not to be insured. "Der Hauptausschuss für die staatliche Pensions- und Hinterbliebenen-Versicherung der Privatangestellten," *MKV* 4 (1908): 76.

20 Waescher and von Roy, *Denkschrift*, pp. 20–21.

21 "Der Hauptausschuss," p. 76.

22 "Zur Frage," p. 178; and Waescher and von Roy, *Denkschrift*, p. 21.

23 "Hoffnungen und Wünsche," *ZWH* 12 (1907): 2, claimed that whether to expand existing disability insurance "is not a question of principle." Also "Unsere Hauptversammlung," *ibid.*, p. 82. Only "Zur Frage der Pensionsversicherung," *ibid.*, pp. 177–78, at the end of the year, discussed the issue. However, Silbermann later claimed that the executive board of the Berlin Commercial Alliance had carefully considered the position of women in the insurance program in meetings throughout 1907. "Ehefrauen- oder Witwenversicherung," *ZWH* 14 (1909): 164. See also "Weiteres zur Frage der Pensionsversicherung," *ZWH* 13 (1908): 17–18; and 1908 annual report in *HN*, 14.5.1909, PP S6741, Hamb.St.A.

24 The Berlin Commercial Alliance joined the progressive Free Pension Alliance in 1907 but also maintained its membership in the Main Committee. Early in 1908 the Commercial Alliance joined the Free Alliance faction to send a petition to the Ministry of the Interior calling for the expansion of existing insurance. "Weiteres zur Frage," p. 17. By mid-year the group had come to reject expansion. It then favored a separate fund and left the Free Alliance. "Pensionsversicherung auf gesetzliche Grundlage," *ZWH* 13 (1908): 113.

25 "Weiteres zur Frage," p. 18. The Confederation also rejected the idea

of lower female fees. See von Roy, "Ehefrauenversicherung?" p. 87.

26 "Weiteres zur Frage," p. 18.

27 *Ibid.*, pp. 17–20.

28 The difficulty of deciding who qualified as a dependent was also overwhelming. Waescher, "Pensionsversicherung," p. 720.

29 The Main Pension Committee contended that the number of women members did not warrant their inclusion; and in any case, it remarked, women were divided into two camps, so that a single representative would serve no purpose. Waescher and von Roy, *Denkschrift*, p. 22.

30 Women would have a shorter waiting period before eligibility for provisions; would receive burial funds if they did not use the pension; and would be paid back half of their fees were they to marry. "Neues zur staatlichen Pensionsversicherung der Privatangestellten," *ZWH* 14 (1909): 17.

31 *25 Jahre Angestelltenversicherung*, p. 6.

32 The all-female clerks' journals maintained a discreet silence about the scandal, but the left daily press and the Central Alliance published all the details: Schack had advertised for a traveling companion for his wife, but the teenager who responded found that she was expected to engage in a sexual threesome with the couple. *HZ* 13 (1909): *passim*.

33 Although the Commercial Alliance was larger than the Confederation, it was smaller than the grouping that supported the women's demands, comprised of the Confederation, the teachers, and the nurses. The latter should have first been represented.

34 The Confederation created a press committee of von Roy, Waescher, and Rosa Urbach of Breslau. Waescher and von Roy, *Denkschrift*, p. 22; "Unsere Hauptversammlung," *MKV* 5 (1909): 157. For the Berlin Commercial Alliance, [Clara Mleinek], "Ehefrauenversicherung oder Witwenversorgung?" *ZWH* 14 (1909): 129–31; and "Ehefrauen- oder Witwenversicherung," *ibid.*, p. 164.

35 [Mleinek], "Ehefrauenversicherung," p. 131.

36 Eva von Roy, "Ehefrauen-Versicherung oder Witwenversorgung?" *MKV* 5 (1909): 179–80.

37 Waescher and von Roy, *Denkschrift*, pp. 62–63.

38 [Johanna Waescher and Eva von Roy], "Verbündete Kaufmännische Vereine für weibliche Angestellte, 1901–1911," *MKV* 7 (1911): 116.

39 Clara Mleinek later explained that "in the last hour we abandoned all particularistic wishes . . . in order to speed the passage of the law." Clara Mleinek, "Versicherungswesen," in Kaufmännischer Verband für weibliche Angestellte, *25 Jahre Berufsorganisation: 1889–1914: Zugleich Verwaltungsbericht für das Jahr 1913* (Berlin, n.d.), p. 76.

40 [Waescher and von Roy], "Verbündete, 1901–1911," p. 116; and "Unsere Tagung in Dresden," *MKV* 7 (1911): 78. See also "Unsere ausserordentliche Hauptversammlung in Leipzig," *MKV* 8 (1912): 85.

41 [Waescher and von Roy], "Verbündete, 1901–1911," p. 116; and Mleinek, "Versicherungswesen," pp. 76–77.

42 "Die wichtigste Bestimmungen aus dem Versicherungsgesetz für Angestellte," in Verbündete Kaufmännische Vereine für weibliche

Angestellte, *Jahrbuch für Handlungsgehilfinnen* (Cassel, 1913), pp. 72–75; and "Was bringt uns die Angestelltenversicherung?" *MKV* 8 (1912): 110.

43  All state insurance programs had various administrative boards responsible for policy-making, hiring staff, etc. Employers and employees were represented. Women had voting rights on health insurance boards, but not on any of the others (such as disability insurance) until the white-collar pension insurance program. For details, see Florian Tennstedt, "Sozialgeschichte der Sozialversicherung," in Maria Blohmke *et al.*, eds., *Handbuch der Medizin*, vol. 3 (Stuttgart, 1975), pp. 385–96; and Detlev Zöllner, "Germany," in Peter A. Köhler, Hans F. Zacher, and Martin Partington, eds., *The Evolution of Social Insurance, 1881–1981: Studies of Germany, France, Great Britain, Austria and Switzerland* (London, 1982), pp. 12–33. In the new white-collar insurance, women were only excluded from boards making legal judgments. *Ibid.* and Else Zodtke-Heyde, "Das Wahlrecht der berufstätigen Frauen in sozialen Organen," *AfF* 1 (1913): 107–8.

44  A 1906 Hamburg study by the Association for Women's Suffrage showed that the vote for OKK delegates was light for both men and women, with the exceptions of male Free Union members and female clerks. "Unberechtigte Vorwürfe," *ZWH* 12 (1907): 5.

45  [Margarete Schweichler], "Die Handlungsgehilfinnen und die Wahlen zu den Ortskrankenkassen," *ZWH* 16 (1911): 38.

46  Waescher and von Roy, *Denkschrift*, p. 29; Laura Krause, "Die Ortskrankenkassen und die Frau," *MKV* 4 (1908): 27; and Franziska Altmann, "Die Ortskrankenkasse und die Frauen," *MKV* 4 (1908): 35.

47  Leipzig, for instance, worked on a joint slate with other female professional groups. *HG* 10 (1914): 30.

48  *FB*, 15.2.1906, PP S6741, Hamb.St.A.; "Die Beteiligung der Frauen bei den Krankenkassenwahlen," *ZWH* 13 (1908): 5; *ibid.*, p. 41; and [Schweichler], "Wahlen Ortskrankenkassen," p. 39.

49  "Die Frauenwahlen zur Angestellten-Versicherung," *HG* 8 (1912): 134.

50  "Frauenwahlen," p. 134; and Mleinek, "Versicherungswesen," pp. 76–77.

51  A 1914 article stressed the need for a unified slate of "national forces." "Achtung! Wahl der Beisitzer bei den Versicherungsämtern!" *KB* 13 (1914): 13.

52  "Krankenkassenwahlen," *ZWH* 17 (1912): 134–35; and Clara Mleinek, "Unsere Frühlingsbezirkstage," *ZWH* 16 (1911): 82.

53  In Hamburg, for instance, there was a unified women's slate including both the Commercial Alliance chapter (Industria) and the Confederation local (Association of Female Office Workers). See *HG* 8 (1912): 139. In Krefeld the Confederation, the Commercial Alliance, and the Catholic Alliance chapters all joined to run a women's slate. *MKV* 8 (1912): 116.

54  "Frauenwahlen," pp. 134–35; "Die Angriffe der freien Vereinigung auf unseren Verband," *ZWH* 17 (1912): 164–65; and Mleinek, "Versicherungswesen," pp. 77–78.

55  Otto Urban, "Das Wahlrecht der weiblichen Angestellten in der Versicherungsordnung, im Versicherungsgesetz für Angestellte und bei den Kaufmannsgerichten," in Zentralverband, *Geschäftsbericht 1910/1911*,

p. 68; and "Das Frauenwahlrecht im Versicherungsgesetz für
Angestellte," *HZ* 15 (1911): 194–95.

56 "Angriffe," p. 164; "Feinde des Fortschritts," *HZ* 16 (1912): 162; and
Zodtke-Heyde, "Wahlrecht," p. 108. For Confederation claims that
members were "rudely" approached by the Free Alliance, see *HG* 8 (1912):
138. For Hamburg see "Die neue Versicherung, der Hauptausschuss und
die enttäuschten Privatangestellten." Leaflet, 24.9.1912 and report in
*Echo*, 26.9.1912, PP V676, vol. 2, Hamb.St.A.; also *Echo*, 22.9.1912; *NHZ*,
n.d. [fall, 1912]; and *Echo*, 17.11.1912; all in *ibid.*

57 "Frauenwahlen," p. 134; and "Angriffe," p. 165.

58 Cited in *HG* 8 (1912): 117.

59 Zodtke-Heyde, "Wahlrecht," p. 108.


**Conclusion**

1 Gertrud Israel, "Grosse Aufgaben – und wie wir sie erleben," *ZWH* 17
(1912): 114.

2 This point was first made by Margery W. Davies. See *Woman's Place is
at the Typewriter: Office Work and Office Workers, 1870–1930* (Philadelphia,
1982).

3 The best source for female white-collar organizations in Germany in the
1920s is Ute Frevert, "Emanzipation und Berufstätigkeit. Das Beispiel der
weiblichen Angestellten und Ihrer Organisationen in der Weimarer
Republik," Staatsexamination (Bielefeld, 1977). See also A. Kasten and
Heinrich Hans, *Die kommende Angestellten-Generation* (Berlin, 1933); Afa-
Bund Vorstand, *Die Angestellten Bewegung, 1925–1928: Geschichts- und
Handbuch der Wirtschafts-, Sozial- und der Gewerkschaftspolitik* (Berlin, 1928);
and Erich Gierke, ed., *Zur Geschichte der Angestellten-Gewerkschaften*,
Schriftenreihe der "Freiheit," Heft 1 (Berlin, 1949).

## PRIMARY SOURCES

*Archives*

Hamburg Staatsarchiv:

| | |
|---|---|
| PP S6741 | Kaufmännischer und gewerblicher Hilfsverein für weibliche Angestellte; Verein für Förderung der im Handel und Gewerbe tätigen weiblichen Angestellten zu Hamburg; Hamburger Zweigverein des kaufmännischen Verbandes für weibliche Angestellte, Berlin |
| PP 9095 | Verein für Kontoristinnen |
| PP V580 | Verein für Handlungsgehilfinnen von Hamburg-Altona |
| PP V676 | Zentralverband der Handlungsgehilfen und Gehilfinnen Deutschlands – Hauptvorstand und Bezirk Hamburg. 3 vols. |
| PP S8004 | Lida Gustava Heymann |
| PP 14 139 | Anita Augspurg |
| PP 5466 | Verein Frauenwohl. 3 vols. |
| PP 5808 | Allgemeiner Deutscher Frauenverein, Hamburg Ortsgruppe. 2 vols. |
| PP V618 | Zentralausschuss Hamburg-Altona Detaillisten-Vereine, 1895–1905 |
| PP V858 | Verein zur Bekämpfung der Frauenarbeit im Handelsgewerbe |
| BB I, B164 | Errichtung eine Fortbildungsschule für weibliche Handelsbeflissene (1900–1902) |
| BB I, B166 | Verwaltung des Gewerbeschulwesens: Ausbildung junger Mädchen für den Handelsstand (1908–1910) |
| BB I, B167 | Frage der Ausbildung junger Mädchen für den Handelsstand (1912–1913) |
| BB I, B177 | Fortbildungsschule für weibliche Handelsbeflissene (1902–1906) |

BB I, B178   Fortbildungsschule für weibliche Handelsbeflissene (1906–1908)


Stiftung westfälisches Wirtschaftsarchiv, Dortmund:

K 1, #28      Stenographisches Prüfungsamt, Akten der Industrie-und Handelskammer zu Dortmund
K 2, #127     Errichtung einer Verkäuferinnen-schule 1912–1914, Handelskammer Bochum
K 2, #228     Sonntagsruhe 1906–1914, Handelskammer Bochum
K 2, #295     Vertretung vor Gewerbe- und Kaufmannsgerichten 1913–1915, Handelskammer Bochum
K 2, #371     Errichtung einer kaufmännischen Schule für Mädchen in Bochum 1902–1914, Handelskammer Bochum
K 2, #379     Kaufmännische Schiedsgerichte 1901–1913, Handelskammer Bochum
K 2, #413     Fortbildungsschulpflicht für weibliche kaufmännische Angestellte 1911–1914, Handelskammer Bochum
K 2, #971     Kaufmännisches Unterrichtswesen (Allge.) 1897–1901, Handelskammer Bochum.
K 2, #1,030   Kaufmännische Schiedsgerichte 1897–1902, Handelskammer Bochum
K 2, #1,071   Achtuhrladenschluss 1904–1912, Handelskammer Bochum
K 3, #391     Gesetz über die Errichtung und den Besuch von Pflichtfortbildungsschulen, Handelskammer zu Bielefeld
K 3, #400     Versicherung der Privatangestellten, Handelskammer zu Bielefeld


Rheinisch-westfälisches Wirtschafts-Archiv, Cologne:

Abteilung 20 Akten der Handelskammer Duisburg


Archiv des deutschen Gewerkschaftsbundes, Düsseldorf:

Zentralverband der Handlungsgehilfen und Gehilfinnen Deutschlands,
    *Protokoll der 4. Generalversammlung von 22.–23.5.1904 in Magdeburg und
    Bericht 1902 / 03* (Hamburg, 1904)
    *Bericht des Vorstandes und Ausschusses über die 5te Geschäftsperiode 1904–1905
    nebst Protokoll der 5te Generalversammlung, 4.–5.6.1906 in Chemnitz*
    (Hamburg, 1906)
    *Bericht des Vorstandes und Ausschusses über die 6. Geschäftsperiode 1906–07*
    (Hamburg, 1908)
    *Protokoll der 6. Generalversammlung, München, 8.–9. 6.1908* (Hamburg, 1908)
    *Bericht des Vorstandes und Ausschusses über die 7. Geschäftsperiode 1908–09
    nebst Protokoll der 7. Generalversammlung, 16.–17. 5.1910, Hamburg*
    (Hamburg, 1910)

*Geschäftsbericht für die Jahre 1910 / 1911 nebst Protokoll der 8.*
  *Generalversammlung, 5.–7. Mai 1912, Berlin* (Berlin, 1912)
Zentralverband der Handlungsgehilfen Deutschlands, *Geschäftsbericht für das*
  *Jahr 1912* (Berlin, 1913)
  *Protokoll der 9. Generalversammlung, 19.–21.5.1914, Hannover* (Berlin, 1914)
  *Geschäftsbericht für das Jahr 1913* (Berlin, 1914)
Kaufmännischer Verband für weibliche Angestellte, *25 Jahre*
  *Berufsorganisation: 1889–1914: Zugleich Verwaltungsbericht für das Jahr 1913*
  (Berlin, n.d.)


Bundesarchiv, Coblenz:

*Nachlass* Herold
*Nachlass* Camilla Jellinek
*Nachlass* Marie-Elisabeth Lüders
*Nachlass* Rottenburg


Staatsarchiv, Munich:

PDM 4498    Kaufmännischer Verein für weibliche Angestellte
PDM 592     Deutscher Frauen-Verein Reform
PDM 954     Sonntagsfeier
PDM 955     Sonntagsruhe im Handelsgewerbe


*Statistical yearbooks*

*Reichsarbeitsblatt* (Berlin, 1893 *et seq.*)
*Statistik des Deutschen Reichs* (Berlin, 1872 *et seq.*)
*Statistisches Jahrbuch für das Deutsche Reich* (Berlin, 1880 *et seq.*)


*Periodicals*

*Archiv für Frauenarbeit*, 1913 *et seq.*
*Die Frau: Monatsschrift für das gesamte Frauenleben unserer Zeit*, 1893 / 94 *et seq.*
*Die Handlungsgehilfen-Zeitung*, 1908–12 available
*Die Handlungsgehilfin*, 1912 *et seq.*
*Jahrbuch für Handlungs-Gehilfinnen*, 1913 and 1914 available
*Jugend-Rundschau der Zeitschrift für weibliche Handlungsgehilfen*, 1910
*Korrespondenzblatt für den Verband katholischer kaufmännischer Gehilfinnen*
  *Deutschlands*, 1903 *et seq.*
*Mitteilungen der kaufmännischen Vereine weiblicher Angestellten*, 1908–12
  available
*Mitteilungen für weibliche Angestellte*, 1896 *et seq.*
*Schriften der Gesellschaft für Soziale Reform*, 1897 *et seq.*
*Sozialpolitisches Centralblatt*, 1892 *et seq.*
*Soziale Praxis. Zentralblatt für Sozialpolitik*, 1894 *et seq.*

*Zeitschrift für weibliche Handlungsgehilfen*, 1905 *et seq.*
*Zeitschrift für weibliche Handlungsgehilfen: Ausgabe für Mitglieder unter 18 Jahren*, 1911 *et seq.*

## Published sources

Adler, Paul, *Die Lage der Handlungsgehilfen*, Münchener Volkswirtschaftliche Studien 39, Lujo Brentano and Walther Lotz, eds. Stuttgart: J. G. Cotta'sche Buchhandlung, 1900

Bäumer, Gertrud, *Die Frau in Volkswirtschaft und Staatsleben der Gegenwart*. Stuttgart: Deutsche Verlags-anstalt, 1914

Baum, Marie, *Drei Klassen von Lohnarbeiterinnen in Industrie und Handel der Stadt Karlsruhe*. Grossherzogliche Ministerium des Innern; Grossherzogliche Badische Fabrikinspektion. Karlsruhe: Verlag G. Braunschen Hofbuchdruckerei, 1906

Bebel, August, *Woman under Socialism*. Trans. from the 33rd edn by Daniel de Leon. Reprinted from the 1904 American edn of New York Labor News Press. Studies in the Life of Women. New York: Schocken Books, 1971

Braun, Lily, "Der Kampf um Arbeit in der bürgerlichen Frauenwelt," *Archiv für soziale Gesetzgebung und Statistik* 16 (1901): 305–12

Brinker-Gabler, Gisela, ed. *Frauenarbeit und Beruf*. Series Die Frau in der Gesellschaft: Frühe Texte, G. Brinker-Gabler, ed. Frankfurt-on-Main: Fischer Taschenbuch Verlag, 1979

Bund Deutscher Frauenvereine, ed., *Deutscher Frauenkongress, Berlin, 27. Feb.–2. März 1912. Sämtliche Vorträge*. Leipzig: Verlag B. G. Teubner, 1912

*Internationaler Frauenkongress. 1904. Officieller Originalbericht.* N.p., n.d.

Cauer, Minna, *25 Jahre Verein Frauenwohl Gross-Berlin*. Berlin: n.p., 1913

Claasen, Walter, "Die soziale Berufsgliederung des deutschen Volkes nach Nahrungsquellen und Familien," *Staats- und sozialwissenschaftliche Forschungen* 23 (1905): 278–309.

Döring, Richard, *Die Frauenarbeit im Handelsgewerbe*. DHV vol. 44. Hamburg: Verlag des DHV, 1909

Gadesmann, Meta, *Die Frau als kaufmännische Angestellte*. Schriften des Kaufmännischen Verbandes für weibliche Angestellte 8. Berlin: Verlag des Verbandes, 1910/11

[Herrmann, Agnes], *Fortbildungsschulzwang für weibliche Handlungsgehilfen und Lehrlinge*. Schriften des Kaufmännischen Verbandes für weibliche Angestellte 3. Berlin: Verlag des Verbandes, 1903

Hermann, Agnes, *Der Stand des kaufmännischen Unterrichtswesens für weibliche Angestellte*, Veröffentlichungen des Deutschen Verbandes für das kaufmännische Unterrichtswesen 34 (1905)

Heymann, Lida Gustava, with Anita Augspurg, *Erlebtes – Erschautes: Deutsche Frauen kämpfen für Freiheit, Recht und Frieden, 1850–1940*. Margrit Twellmann, ed. Meisenheim-on-Glan: Verlag Anton Hain, 1972

Hohorst, Gerd, Jürgen Kocka, and Gerhard A. Ritter, *Sozialgeschichtliches Arbeitsbuch: Materialien zur Statistik des Kaiserreichs, 1870–1914*. Munich: Verlag C. H. Beck, 1975

Kaiserliches Statistisches Amt, Abt. für Arbeiterstatistik, *Erhebung von Wirtschaftsrechnungen minderbemittelter Familien im Deutschen Reich*. 2. Sonderheft zum *Reichsarbeitsblatt*. Berlin: Carl Heymanns Verlag, 1909

Kempf, Rosa, *Berufswahl und Berufsbildung*. Schriften des Kaufmännischen Verbandes für weibliche Angestellte 10. Berlin: Verlag des Verbandes, 1912

Kern, Friedrich Karl, *Zur sozialen Lage der Verkäuferinnen*, Ph.D. Diss. Heidelberg, 1910

Kisker, Ida, *Die Frauenarbeit in den Kontoren einer Grossstadt: eine Studie über die Leipziger Kontoristinnen*. Archiv für Sozialwissenschaft und Sozialpolitik, Ergänzungsheft III. Tübingen: Verlag J. C. B. Mohr, 1911

Köhler, Anna, *Über das private Handelsschulwesen in Deutschland*. Schriften des Kaufmännischen Verbandes für weibliche Angestellte 5. Berlin: Verlag des Verbandes, 1906

Lange, Helene, and Gertrud Bäumer, *Handbuch der Frauenbewegung*. Berlin: W. Möser Buchhandlung, 1901 *et seq.*

Lange, Paul, *Angestellte und Arbeiter im Wirtschaftsleben*. Berlin: Handlungsgehilfen-Verlag, 1912

Losseff-Tillmanns, Gisela, ed. *Frau und Gewerkschaft*. Series Die Frau in der Gesellschaft: Frühe Texte, Gisela Brinker-Gabler, ed. Frankfurt-on-Main: Fischer Taschenbuch Verlag, 1982

Lüders, Else, *Der "linke Flügel": Ein Blatt aus der Geschichte der deutschen Frauenbewegung*. Berlin: Verlag W. and S. Löwenthal, n.d.

*Minna Cauer, Leben and Werk*. Gotha: Verlag Fr. Andreas Perthes, 1925

Mende, Käthe, *Münchener jugendliche Ladnerinnen: zu Hause und im Beruf*. Münchener Volkswirtschaftliche Studien, Lujo Brentano and Walther Lotz, eds. Stuttgart: J. G. Cotta'sche Buchhandlung, 1912

Mleinek, Clara, *Die Arbeitszeit in den Kontoren*. Schriften des Kaufmännischen Verbandes für weibliche Angestellte 7. Berlin: Verlag des Verbandes, 1907

Potthoff, Heinz, *Die soziale Frage der Handlungsgehilfinnen*. Gautsch bei Leipzig: Felix Dietrich, 1910

Reichsamt des Innern, *Die wirtschaftliche Lage der Privatangestellten*. Denkschrift über die im Oktober 1903 angestellten Erhebungen. Berlin: Heymanns Verlag, 1907

Reimann, Erna, *Die Frau als kaufmännische Angestellte im Handelsgewerbe*, Ph.D. Diss. Jena, 1915

Salomon, Alice, *Die Ursachen der ungleichen Entlohnung von Männer- und Frauenarbeit*. Staats- und sozialwissenschaftliche Forschungen 122. Leipzig: Duncker und Humblot, 1906

Silbermann, Josef, *Die Angestellten als Stand*. Berlin: Verlag des Verbandes der weiblichen Handels- und Büroangestellten, 1932

"Die Arbeitszeit der kaufmännischen Angestellten in den Engros- und Fabrikgeschäften Berlins," *Archiv für soziale Gesetzgebung und Statistik* 16 (1901): 719–42

*Drei Vorträge: Kulturfragen*. Berlin: Verlag des Verbandes der weiblichen Handels- und Büroangestellten, 1924

"Die Lage der deutschen Handelsgehilfen und ihre gesetzliche Reform," *Archiv für Gesetzgebung and Statistik* 9 (1896): 341–86

*Die Privatbeamten und die Versicherungsgesetzgebung.* Schriften der Gesellschaft für Soziale Reform 25. Jena: Gustav Fischer Verlag, 1908

*Das weibliche kaufmännische Bildungswesen.* Volkswirtschaftliche Zeitfragen, no. 273, vol. 35, Heft 1. Berlin: Verlag Leonhard Simion, 1913

"Zur Entlohnung der Frauenarbeit," *Jahrbuch für Gesetzgebung, Verwaltung und Volkswirtschaft im Deutschen Reich* 23 (1899): 1,405–31

[J. Sabin], *Zwölf Jahre Deutscher Parteikämpfe, 1881–1892.* Deutsche Schriften für Nationales Leben, Reihe 2, Heft 5. N.p., 1892

Sittel, Valentin, *Die Frauenarbeit im Handelsgewerbe.* Leipzig: Johannes Wörners Verlag, 1911

Verein Frauenwohl, *Jahresbericht des Vereins "Frauenwohl" in Königsberg i. Pr.* Königsberg: Hartungsche Buchdruck, 1892 *et seq.*

von Rössing, Elly, *Zur Frage der Verkäuferinnenschulen.* Sonderdruck der Zeitschrift für das gesammte kaufmännische Unterrichtswesen 16, nos. 7–9. N.p., n.d.

Waescher, Johanna and Eva von Roy, *Denkschrift der Verbündeten kaufmännischen Vereine für weibliche Angestellte, 1901–1911.* Frankfurt-on-Main: Selbstverlag, 1912


SECONDARY SOURCES

*Women and white-collar work*

Davies, Margery Wynne, *Woman's Place is at the Typewriter: Office Work and Office Workers, 1870–1930.* Class and Culture Series, Bruce Laurie and Milton Cantor, eds. Philadelphia: Temple University Press, 1982

Frevert, Ute, "Emanzipation und Berufstätigkeit. Das Beispiel der weiblichen Angestellten und Ihrer Organisationen in der Weimarer Republik." Universität Bielefeld Staatsexamination, 1977

Hörbrand, Maria, *Die weibliche Handels- und Bureau-Angestellte.* Berlin: Hermann Pätel Verlag, 1926

Howe, Hans Ulrich, *Die berufstätige Frau als Verkaufsangestellte.* Lübeck: n.p., 1930

Nienhaus, Ursula, *Berufsstand weiblich: Die ersten weiblichen Angestellten.* Berlin: Transit Verlag, 1982

Suhr, Susanne, *Die weiblichen Angestellten: Arbeits- und Lebensverhältnisse.* Berlin: Verlag Zentralverband der Angestellten, 1930

Verband der weiblichen Angestellten, *75 Jahre Verband der weiblichen Angestellten, 1889–1964: Festschrift zum 75 jährigen Jubiläum.* Hannover: n.p., 1964


*White-collar workers*

Abercrombie, Nicholas, and John Urry, *Capital, Labour and the Middle Classes.* Controversies in Sociology 15, T. B. Bottomore and M. J. Mulkay, eds. London: Allen and Unwin, 1983

Afa-Bund Vorstand, *Die Angestellten Bewegung, 1925 bis 1928: Geschichts- und Handbuch der Wirtschafts-, Sozial- und der Gewerkschaftspolitik.* Berlin: Freier Volksverlag, 1928

Anderson, Gregory, *Victorian Clerks.* Manchester University Press, 1976

Aufhäuser, Siegfried, *Eine unromantische Betrachtung zum Geschichtsbild der Angestelltenbewegung.* Berlin: Deutsche Angestellten Gewerkschaft, 1960

Bain, George Sayers, *The Growth of White-Collar Unionism.* Oxford: Clarendon Press, 1970

Bain, George Sayers, David Coates, and Valerie Ellis, *Social Stratification and Trade Unionism: A Critique.* Warwick Studies in Industrial Relations. London: Heinemann, 1973

Braverman, Harry, *Labor and Monopoly Capital: The Degradation of Work in the Twentieth Century.* New York: Monthly Review Press, 1974

Coyner, Sandra J., "Class Patterns of Family Income and Expenditure During the Weimar Republic: German White-Collar Employees as Harbingers of Modern Society," Rutgers University Ph.D. Diss. 1975

Deich, Werner, *Der Angestellte im Roman: Zur Sozialgeschichte des Handlungsgehilfen um 1900.* Cologne: Grote'sche Verlagsbuchhandlung, 1974

Engelsing, Rolf, "Die wirtschaftliche und soziale Differenzierung der deutschen kaufmännischen Angestellten im In- und Ausland, 1690–1900," in Rolf Engelsing, *Zur Sozialgeschichte deutscher Mittel- und Unterschichten.* Göttingen: Vandenhoeck und Ruprecht, 1973

*25 Jahre Angestelltenversicherung, 1913–1937.* Berlin: Otto Elsner, 1937

Gewerkschaftsbund der Angestellten, *Epochen der Angestellten-Bewegung, 1774–1930.* Berlin: Verlag des Gewerkschaftsbundes, 1930.

Gierke, Erich, ed., *Zur Geschichte der Angestellten-Gewerkschaften.* Schriftenreihe der "Freiheit," Heft 1. Berlin: A. G. der Angestellten-Gewerkschaften, 1949

Hamel, Iris, *Völkischer Verband und nationale Gewerkschaft: Der Deutschnationale Handlungsgehilfen-Verband, 1893–1933.* Frankfurt-on-Main: Europäische Verlagsanstalt, 1967

Hartfiel, Günter, *Angestellte und Angestelltengewerkschaften in Deutschland.* Berlin: Duncker und Humblot, 1961

Horbat, Hans, *Die wirtschaftliche Lage des deutschen Angestellten.* Schriftenreihe des Gewerkschaftsbundes der Angestellten 29; 2nd edn. N.p., 1926

Kocka, Jürgen, "Class Formation, Interest Articulation, and Public Policy: The Origins of the German White-Collar Class in the Late Nineteenth and Early Twentieth Centuries," in Suzanne Berger, ed., *Organizing Interests in Western Europe: Pluralism, Corporatism, and the Transformation of Politics.* Cambridge University Press, 1982

*Unternehmensverwaltung und Angestelltenschaft am Beispiel Siemens, 1847–1914. Zum Verhältnis von Kapitalismus und Bürokratie in der deutschen Industrialisierung.* Schriftenreihe des Arbeitskreises für moderne Sozialgeschichte 11. Stuttgart: Ernst Klett Verlag, 1969

Lederer, Emil, and Jakob Marschak, "Der neue Mittelstand," *Grundriss der Sozialökonomie* IX / I (1926): 120–41.
Lockwood, David, *The Blackcoated Worker: A Study in Class Consciousness.* London: Allen and Unwin, 1958
Lumley, Roger, *White-Collar Unionism in Britain: A Survey of the Present Position.* London: Methuen, 1973
Stehr, Konrad, *Der Zentralverband der Angestellten: Sein Werdegang, seine Gestalt und sein Charakter.* Berlin: Hausdruckerei des Zentralverbands, 1926
Sturmthal, Adolf, ed., *White-Collar Trade Unions: Contemporary Developments in Industrialized Societies.* Urbana: University of Illinois Press, 1967

*Women's history and feminist theory*

Barker, Diana L., and Sheila Allen, eds., *Dependence and Exploitation in Work and Marriage.* London: Longman Group Limited, 1976
Crompton, Rosemary, and Michael Mann, *Gender and Stratification.* Cambridge: Polity Press, 1986
Eisenstein, Zillah, ed., *Capitalist Patriarchy and the Case for Socialist Feminism.* New York: Monthly Review Press, 1979
Evans, Richard J., *The Feminist Movement in Germany, 1894–1933.* Sage Studies in Twentieth Century History 6. London: Sage Publications, 1976
  "Liberalism and Society: The Feminist Movement and Social Change," in Richard Evans, ed., *Society and Politics in Wilhelmine Germany.* New York: Barnes and Noble Books, 1978, pp. 186–207
  *Sozialdemokratie und Frauemanzipation im deutschen Kaiserreich.* Internationale Bibliothek 119. Berlin: Verlag Dietz, 1979
Feminist Review, ed., *Waged Work: A Reader.* London: Virago, 1986
Geyer, Anna, *Frauenerwerbsarbeit in Deutschland.* Jena: n.p., 1924
Glass, Frieda, and Dorothea Kische, *Die wirtschaftlichen und sozialen Verhältnisse der berufstätigen Frauen: Erhebung 1928/9.* Arbeitsgemeinschaft Deutscher Frauenberufsverbände. Berlin: Carl Heymanns, 1930
Hackett, Amy, "Feminism and Liberalism in Wilhelmine Germany, 1890–1918," in Berenice A. Carroll, ed., *Liberating Women's History.* Urbana: University of Illinois Press, 1976, pp. 127–37
Hausen, Karin, ed., *Frauen suchen ihre Geschichte: Historische Studien zum 19. and 20. Jahrhundert.* Beck'sche Schwarze Reihe 276. Munich: Beck, 1983
Holton, Sandra S., *Feminism and Democracy: Women's Suffrage and Reform Politics in Britain, 1900–1918.* Cambridge University Press, 1986
Honeycutt, Karen, "Socialism and Feminism in Imperial Germany," *Signs* 5 (1979): 30–41
Juchacz, Marie, *Sie lebten für eine bessere Welt.* Berlin: Verlag J. H. W. Dietz, 1955
Kessler-Harris, Alice, *Out to Work: A History of Wage-Earning Women in the United States.* Oxford University Press, 1982
Kuhn, Annette, and AnnMarie Wolpe, eds., *Feminism and Materialism: Women and Modes of Production.* London: Routledge and Kegan Paul, 1978
Losseff-Tillmanns, Gisela, "Frauenemanzipation und Gewerkschaften (1800–1975)," Ruhr-University Bochum, Ph.D. Diss., 1975

Meyer-Renschhausen, Elisabeth, "Zur Geschichte der Gefühle. Das Reden von 'Scham' und 'Ehre' innerhalb der Frauenbewegung um die Jahrhundertwende," in Christiane Eifert and Susanne Rouette, eds., *Unter allen Umständen. Frauengeschichte(n) in Berlin.* Berlin: Rotation Verlag, 1986, pp. 99–122.

Pleck, Elizabeth H., "Two Worlds in One: Work and Family," *Journal of Social History* 10 (1976/77): 178–95

Quataert, Jean H., *Reluctant Feminists in German Social Democracy, 1885–1917.* Princeton University Press, 1979

Scott, Joan W., and Louise A. Tilly, "Women's Work and the Family in Nineteenth-Century Europe," *Comparative Studies in Society and History* 17 (1975): 36–59

Sperling, Hans, *Die ökonomischen Gründe für die Minderbezahlung der weiblichen Arbeitskraft.* Berlin: Carl Heymanns Verlag, 1930

*Die Tätigkeit des Allgemeinen Deutschen Frauenvereins, Ortsgruppe Hamburg: 1896–1921.* Hamburg: Druck Paul Meyer, 1921

Thönnessen, Werner, *The Emancipation of Women: The Rise and Decline of the Women's Movement in German Social Democracy, 1863–1933.* Trans. by Joris de Bres. Bristol: Pluto Press, 1973

Twellmann, Margrit, *Die Deutsche Frauenbewegung: Ihre Anfänge und erste Entwicklung.* Vol. 2: *Quellen: 1843–1889.* Meisenheim-on-Glan: Verlag Anton Hain, 1972

Waescher, Johanna, *Wegbereiter der deutschen Frau. 18 Lebensbilder aus der Frühzeit der deutschen Frauenbewegung.* Kassel: A. G. für Druck und Verlag, 1931

*German history*

Barkin, Kenneth D., *The Controversy over German Industrialization: 1890–1902.* University of Chicago Press, 1970

Craig, Gordon A., *Germany – 1866–1945.* New York: Oxford University Press, 1978

Gellately, Robert, *The Politics of Economic Despair: Shopkeepers and German Politics, 1890–1914.* Sage Studies in Twentieth Century History 1. Beverly Hills: Sage Publications, 1974

Lebovics, Herman, *Social Conservatism and the Middle Classes in Germany, 1914–1933.* Princeton University Press, 1969

"'Agrarians' versus 'Industrializers': Social Conservative Resistance to Industrialism and Capitalism in Late Nineteenth-Century Germany," *International Review of Social History* 12 (1967): 32–65

Mielke, Siegfried, *Der Hansa-Bund für Gewerbe, Handel und Industrie, 1909–1914. Der gescheiterte Versuch einer antifeudalen Sammlungspolitik.* Kritische Studien zur Geschichtswissenschaft 17. Göttingen: Vandenhoeck und Ruprecht, 1976

Mommsen, Wolfgang J., and Hans-Gerhard Husung, *The Development of Trade Unionism in Great Britain and Germany, 1880–1914.* German Historical Institute. London: Allen and Unwin, 1985

Ritter, Emil, *Die Katholisch-Soziale Bewegung Deutschlands im 19. Jahrhundert und der Volksverein.* Cologne: Verlag J. P. Bachem, 1954

Ritter, Gerhard A., *Arbeiterbewegung, Parteien und Parlamentarismus: Aufsätze zur deutschen Sozial- und Verfassungsgeschichte des 19. und 20. Jahrhunderts.* Kritische Studien zur Geschichtswissenschaft 23. Göttingen: Vandenhoeck und Ruprecht, 1976

Ross, Ronald J., *The Beleaguered Tower: The Dilemma of Political Catholicism in Wilhelmine Germany.* South Bend: University of Notre Dame Press, 1976

Schönhoven, Klaus, "Selbsthilfe als Form von Solidarität: Das gewerkschaftliche Unterstützungswesen im Deutschen Kaiserreich bis 1914," *Archiv für Sozialgeschichte* 20 (1980): 147–93

Stegmann, Dirk, *Die Erben Bismarcks: Parteien und Verbände in der Spätphase des Wilhelminischen Deutschlands: Sammlungspolitik, 1897–1918.* Cologne: Kieperheuer und Witsch, 1970

Struve, Walter, *Elites against Democracy: Leadership Ideals in Bourgeois Political Thought in Germany, 1890–1933.* Princeton University Press, 1973

Zeender, John K., *The German Center Party, 1890–1906.* Transactions of the American Philosophical Society, New Series, vol. 66, part 1. Philadelphia: American Philosophical Society, 1976